Journal of the Society of

Christian

Ethics

VOLUME 35, NUMBER 2 • FALL/WINTER 2015

D1279864

Contents

Preface

Somewhere between a rigid legalism and a lax antinomianism, the law has its place, if not its virtues, in Christian ethics. In Judaism, the law, or *halakah*, refers generally to the *Torah*, both written and oral, and in Islam, *Shari'ah* is derived from the *Qur'an* and the *Sunnah*. For each of these Abrahamic faiths, perennial and provocative questions arise concerning the interrelationship between law and ethics, between jurisprudence and morality. The theme of the 2015 Annual Meeting of the Society of Christian Ethics (SCE), which was held in Chicago, Illinois, was "Law and Christian Ethics." SCE president M. Cathleen Kaveny, who is the Darald and Juliet Libby Professor at Boston College, with appointments in both the department of theology and the law school, selected this thematic emphasis, inviting SCE members as well as members of the Society of Jewish Ethics (SJE) and the Society for the Study of Muslim Ethics (SSME) to address questions and topics about the relationship of law, religion, and morality.

While numerous paper and panel presentations engaged different facets of "Law and Christian Ethics," the annual meeting also included many papers and presentations that addressed other topics in religious and theological ethics. Current events, too, were palpably perceptible not only in these papers and panels but also in the plenary speeches, the working group and interest group sessions, the informal chats during coffee breaks in the book exhibit area, and on the wintry streets of the Windy City where members made their way to neighboring restaurants and cafés to continue conversations. From civil wars and revolutions in conflict-ridden areas of the world to cities around the United States where this past year protests and demonstrations have reminded us about festering injustices having to do with race, the use of force, and the police—the topic of ethics and the law proved to be timely for us. In addition to our usual wrestling with variations of what Athens has to do with Jerusalem, we reflected on and argued about what ethics and law have to do with Ferguson, St. Louis, New York City, Cleveland, and now, as these words are written, Baltimore. "Any law that degrades human personality is unjust," wrote Martin Luther King Jr. in his *Letter from Birmingham Jail*. The same can be said in our time as in his about the law's enforcement. Indeed, what is lawful is not always moral; but, on the other hand, as we sadly know, what is morally "justified" even by professional ethicists is sometimes actually immorally rationalized and perhaps even not lawful (civilly, if not criminally).

This issue of the *Journal of the Society of Christian Ethics* (*JSCE* 35, no. 2) includes the first set of essays delivered at this annual meeting that were accepted for publication. These essays relate to the annual meeting's theme. Many of the essays in this volume touch upon topics one might expect from a conference on "Law and Christian Ethics": biblical law, freedom from the law, natural law, civil law, and justice. The next issue, *JSCE* 36, no. 1, will contain essays on an assortment of topics that may or may not be tethered to the meeting's theme.

The first three essays in this volume address the dialogue between secular law and Christian ethics. In Kaveny's essay, "Law and Christian Ethics: Signposts for a Fruitful Conversation," which is based on her 2015 presidential address, she makes the case that Christian ethicists tend to draw moral conclusions based primarily on Christian sources and then turn to secular law to see if it is or is not upholding these normative judgments. She argues that "common law" has its own narrative accountability and methodological consonance. She ends the essay exploring a particular case that proved important in defining the "doctrine of unconscionability." In "The Just War Tradition and International Law against War: The Myth of Discordant Doctrines" Mary Ellen O'Connell, the Robert and Marion Short Professor of Law and Research Professor of International Dispute Resolution at the University of Notre Dame, criticizes many just war theorists (such as Jean Bethke Elshtain and Nigel Biggar) for ignoring or misinterpreting the international law of armed conflict, in particular Article 2(4) of the United Nations Charter. She is also critical of the contemporary practice of international law for an overreliance on positivism and a lack of understanding of the natural law foundations of just war theory. As an illustration of Kaveny's thesis that law and Christian ethics have much to learn from each other, O'Connell proposes that Christian just war theory and international law can mutually enrich each other. O'Connell's essay, which is based on her plenary address given at the meeting, is followed by Nigel Biggar's response. He opens by identifying points of agreement and then moves to five points of disagreement: different understandings of the complexity of peace; different interpretations of whether or not the just war tradition harbors a "peremptory norm against aggression"; different approaches to the interpretation of international law (i.e., "the hermeneutics of international law"); different understandings of the efficacy of the international legal system, especially in terms of authorizing the use of force in cases of humanitarian intervention; and different interpretations of the efficacy of military intervention.

The next set of essays address distinctly Christian analyses of the role of law in politics and society. Elise Edwards's essay, "When Law Does Not Secure

Justice or Peace: Requiem as Aesthetic Response" proposes poetry and liturgy as effective practices of Christian civic engagement when legal processes fail. In this timely piece she explores two jarring cases involving the bodies of black men: first, Marilyn Nelson's "Fortune's Bones: The Manumission Requiem," which was commissioned to honor the life of an eighteenth-century slave who was denied Christian burial for decades as his skeleton was used for display; and, second, the disruption of the St. Louis symphony in October 2014 by demonstrators responding to the acquittal of white police officer Darren Wilson, who had shot and killed Michael Brown, an unarmed black teenager, in August 2014. In both cases aesthetics was a tool of justice, affirming the value of two black bodies in racist contexts. In "The Return of Neo-Scholasticism? Recent Criticisms of Henri de Lubac on Nature and Grace and Their Significance for Moral Theology, Politics, and Law," Thomas J. Bushlack offers "an alternative correction" to contemporary neo-Scholastic interpretations of de Lubac's theology of nature and grace. For Bushlack, de Lubac's theology, which helped the Catholic Church adapt to the modern nation-state, remains a valuable resource for Christians seeking to "engage in a nuanced dialogue of affirmation and critique of human goods sought by late modern political and legal institutions." David VanDrunen's "The Protectionist Purpose of Law: A Moral Case from the Biblical Covenant with Noah" steers a course between "protectionist" and "perfectionist" interpretations of the purpose of law and government. Drawing on the Noahic Covenant, VanDrunen contends that the protectionist approach is not individualist, subjectivist, or indifferent to the common good, as many perfectionists claim, and that a "strong (yet rebuttable) protectionist presumption ought to govern Christian-ethical reflection upon the purpose of law and government."

The next set of essays address two instances of discord within the church, and like VanDrunen's essay, both essays look to scripture and its laws and norms for guidance. Karen V. Guth wrestles with the difficult question, "What are Christian ethicists to do with the legacy of John Howard Yoder in light of his sexual violence against women?" Guth identifies two approaches to this question: the "witness ethicists" camp, which argues that "his theology remains valuable despite his egregious actions," and the "feminist ethicists" camp, which condemns his behavior and ignores his work (in part because he leaves little room for "revolutionary subordination" in feminist ethics). For Guth, both of these approaches fail at "doing justice"; instead, she proposes restorative justice as a "common ground between these often antagonistic groups of ethicists." David P. Gushee tackles the debate over lesbian, gay, bisexual, and transgender (LGBT) rights in evangelical Christianity in his essay, "Reconciling Evangelical Christianity with Our Sexual Minorities: Reframing the Biblical Discussion." After chronicling a growing openness to considering LGBT rights in evangelical churches in recent years. Gushee compares and contrasts traditional evangelical positions on homosexuality (often citing the same six biblical passages) with perspectives of younger evangelicals, many of whom are critical of traditional condemnations. Gushee then frames the debate within a larger social context that considers the physical and emotional suffering and marginalization done to LGBT evangelicals by the traditionalist approach. In the end he concludes that "a tragic misreading of scripture has . . . hurt the evangelistic witness of the Church in culture, with LGBT persons, and in our churches."

The final pair of essays draws on aspects of tradition to interpret contemporary challenges of ethics and law. Celia Deane-Drummond's essay, "Natural Law Revisited: Wild Justice and Human Obligations for Other Animals," explores natural law and ethological accounts of "wild justice" to argue that "law, operative in all social species, including humans, can be interpreted as controlling functions of highly complex self-organizing social systems," which calls for different approaches "when considering human obligations to other animals." Paul Scherz, in "The Legal Suppression of Scientific Data and the Christian Virtue of *Parrhesia*" proffers the ancient virtue of *parrhesia* (truth telling) as a remedy to the practice of political interest groups and corporations that attack scientists' research and reputation in order to generate enough doubt in judicial hearings in order to protect profits and power. Instances of such behavior include research on smoking and cancer, climate change and the use of fossil fuels, toxic chemicals in consumer products, and pharmaceutical side effects. Drawing on Stoic philosophy, Michel Foucault, and Christian virtue theory, Scherz encourages scientists to be steadfast in their witness to the truth of their research (fully aware of the suffering they may endure), committed to the pursuit of their research in the name of the common good, and fully reliant on the grace of God to help them endure.

There were 151 proposals submitted for the 2015 meeting (including not only the SCE but also the SJE and the SSME), from which 20 were accepted for publication. This yields a competitive 13.2 percent acceptance rate for the journal. We are grateful to all of the anonymous referees and to the *JSCE*'s editorial board for their invaluable service to the journal and for their helpful feedback to the members of the SCE, the SJE, and the SSME who submitted papers for possible publication in it. This volume also includes the demographic data collected on the proposals submitted for the 2015 annual meeting in Chicago.

Demographic Distribution Results

Proposals Submitted for the 2015 Annual Meeting of the Society of Christian Ethics through Papers Accepted by the *Journal of the Society of Christian Ethics* (Demographic data 2014–2015; 59 of 151 proposals*)

	Gender		Membership			Ethnic–Racial Group							Education		Tradition			Total
	F	M	S	F	L	Ar	As	AA/A	HL	NA/A	W	O	DC	D	C	J	O	
Proposals Submitted*	17	42	16	42	1	1	3	3	1		53	1	14	45	59			59*/151
Submission Occurrence*																		
First																		20
Second																		15
Third or more																		24
Decisions**																		
Proposals Accepted																		67**
Papers Submitted	26	31	4	53			1	2	2		44		3	54	45			57**
Papers Accepted	8	12		19				1			19			20	19		1	20**
Gender**																		
Female																		17
Male																		42

Membership: S = Student, F = Full, L = Life

Ethnic-Racial Group: Ar = Arabic, As = Asian, AA/A = African American/African, HL = Hispanic/Latinoa, NA/A = Native American/Alaskan, W = White, O = Other (N.B.: per the survey, respondents could check all that apply)

Education: DC = Doctoral Candidate; D = PhD/STD (per the survey, respondents check highest degree earned)

Tradition: C = Christianity, J = Judaism, O = Other

*59 persons completed the demographic survey out of 151 proposals received (143 paper and 8 panel/interest/working group proposals); occurrence history and gender reflect this 39% rate of return.

**60 paper and 7 panel proposals were accepted out of 151 submissions. These decisions and gender information were established with the raw data from the survey, correlation of authors with proposals, correlation of authors with papers presented at the Chicago meeting, and papers subsequently accepted for publication (including authors from the SJE, and Pacific Section meetings).

Selected Essays

Law and Christian Ethics: Signposts for a Fruitful Conversation

M. Cathleen Kaveny

This essay invites Christian ethicists to engage in a mutually beneficial conversation with the secular law, particularly the common law. It argues that the common law's feature of narrative accountability provides a natural bridge to Christian ethics. It also points out contact points between the two fields regarding normative concepts of persons, actions, norms, and the common good. Finally, it illustrates the possibilities of a conversation between law and Christian ethics by delving into the leading case on the doctrine of unconscionability, which permits courts to refuse to enforce contracts that shock the conscience.

> I long for your salvation, O Lord,
>   and your law is my delight.
> Let me live that I may praise you,
>   and let your ordinances help me.
> I have gone astray like a lost sheep; seek out your servant,
>   for I do not forget your commandments.
>   (Ps 119:174–76, New Revised Standard Version)

IN A TYPICAL PASSAGE, THE PSALMIST HERE EXTOLLS THE loveliness of God's law; he praises the beauty of its sublime reconciliation of justice and mercy. Yet our ordinary experience of law, both human and divine, is far from sublime. The machinations of the legal system made by human beings are far from beautiful, as the recent harrowing and heart-breaking events of Ferguson, Missouri; New York; and Baltimore demonstrate.[1] Moreover, those who claim they love God's law are not infrequently lovers of their own will—which they scandalously impose on others *as if* they are imposing God's law. Furthermore, the very concept of law—even God's law—is not unproblematic or uncontested in Christian thought, as Paul's Letters to the Galatians

M. Cathleen Kaveny, JD, PhD, is the Darald and Juliet Libby Professor in the Law School and Department of Theology at Boston College, Stokes Hall N310, Chestnut Hill, MA 02467; cathleen.kaveny@bc.edu.

Journal of the Society of Christian Ethics, 35, 2 (2015): 3–32

and to the Romans demonstrate. Nonetheless, I make a case that contemporary Christian ethicists might find in the secular law a fruitful conversation partner.

The term "conversation partner" is crucial. I want to highlight a different facet of the relationship than the facet normally emphasized between Christian ethicists and secular law. Christian ethicists generally treat the law as an arena for the application of their normative insights. For example, we might use the resources of Christian ethics to come to a conclusion about some particular ethical matter and then turn to the question whether the law should enforce our moral judgment. Or we might use the resources of Christian ethics to critique a particular law or public policy on topics such as abortion, immigration, same-sex marriage, and climate change.[2]

These are extremely important tasks. But they also model a rather one-sided relationship in which the resources of Christian ethics are used to assess and critique the dictates of secular law, but the law is seen as having little to contribute to the study of Christian ethics. This essay proposes a more balanced and mutual dialogue between Christian ethics and secular law by suggesting how the law can raise questions for ethicists to consider and can provide insights for them to ponder, on the one hand, and by showing how insights from Christian ethics can contribute substantively to the legal conversation, on the other.

"Law," of course, is a very general term—rather like "religion" or even "theology." In order to make my case, therefore, I focus upon what I know best: the Anglo-American common law tradition and, within that, the law of contracts, which I have been teaching for nearly twenty years now. Some may wonder why I do not focus on constitutional law or even family law. After all, these subjects touch upon key ethical and religious controversies such as the permissibility of contraception, abortion, and same-sex marriage. Of course I do not wish to deny the importance of these matters. The aim of this essay, however, is to invite an encounter between the two fields that goes beyond neuralgic issues of applied ethics. I want to make a case that Christian ethicists may well find in the common law a worthy conversation partner on fundamental matters of ethical theory.

This essay proceeds through three sections. In the first section I describe the key normative feature of common law system—narrative accountability. In the second section I highlight some of the more specific points of methodological consonance that make the common law an attractive conversation partner for Christian ethics. The final section illustrates the claim that moral concepts continue to have a rich place in the law by delving into one particular case: *Williams v. Walker-Thomas Furniture*, which is the leading case in the articulation of the doctrine of unconscionability—the doctrine that a party may be able to avoid enforcement of an otherwise valid contract on the grounds that it shocks the conscience.[3]

The Common Law and Narrative Accountability

As I use the term here, "common law" refers to a body of legal norms law that is developed by judges over time, more or less organically, as individual judges decide the particular cases and controversies brought before them. The "common law" system of law originated in England in the Middle Ages and has expanded to follow the English colonial system. In 1154 King Henry II inaugurated the development of a more integrated and unified legal system throughout England, establishing practices that we still have today, such as trial by jury and investigation of witnesses under oath. Henry also set up a practice of circuit-riding judges. The "common" law was the law applied by these itinerant judges traveling around England delivering the King's justice rather than deciding according to local custom.[4]

As the English empire expanded, so did the reach of the common law, to the far corners of the globe. Yet the law outlasted the empire that initially implemented and enforced it. Significantly, most former colonies did not reject the English common law framework when they gained their independence; rather, they retained it as the basis for further development of their own independent legal systems. Approximately one-third of the world's population currently lives under a common law system—including forty-nine of the fifty states in the United States.[5] The common law transcends—or *infuses*—a variety of religious and cultural systems. For example, India, Israel, and Pakistan all maintain legal systems deeply indebted to the English common law.[6] At the same time, the influence of the norms of Christian ethics on the common law tradition is significant and undeniable. For this reason, Christian ethicists interested in questions of enculturation of moral norms and comparative ethics might find a valuable resource in the common law's global instantiations.

The common law tradition is not only broadly influential, it is also conceptually rich. It offers a complex and multifaceted tradition of moral reflection in which norms of justice and norms of practical rationality are deeply intertwined. Many Christian ethicists have been deeply influenced by the work of Alasdair MacIntyre, particularly his groundbreaking work *After Virtue.*[7] However, *Whose Justice? Which Rationality?* is equally important because it makes the case for the intimate connection between a tradition's view of justice and its view of practical reason.[8] While MacIntyre does not consider legal sources, he might well have done so: the cases comprising common law provide additional evidence for his argument.

Some object that the norms at stake in the common law are legal norms, which are distinct from, although related to, moral norms. It is certainly true that the law does not enforce all moral norms—it would be immoral for it to do so. At the same time, the common law tradition makes rich use of moral concepts in a thoroughly contextualized way. To put the point another way, the common law is an exercise in the critical preservation, retrieval, and correction of a normative political-moral tradition. It nicely coheres with MacIntyre's definition of a living tradition: "an historically extended, socially embodied argument, and an argument precisely in part about the goods which constitute the tradition."[9] Even today, in the highly pluralistic and contentious American context, the common law manages to adapt and even to thrive as it addresses the legal issues raised by a rapidly evolving culture.

The flourishing of the common law in the contemporary context is in part attributable to its remarkable combination of flexibility and epistemological humility. The tradition grows not by grand pronouncement but by humble accretion—the law builds up gradually, case by case, as each judge addresses the situations raised by the parties before the bench. American courts do not consider legal issues in the abstract; they require a relevant and real case in controversy before they consider a legal question. A strong preference for stability is built into the common law system through the doctrine of *stare decisis*, which calls upon courts to follow precedent by deciding the same cases the same way. At the same time, what counts as the same case is always debatable: because the facts are preserved along with the rule, it is often possible to distinguish the facts of a prior case and to decide that it is not relevantly similar to the current case at hand.[10]

Law's Narrativity

The key elements of moral analysis—person, action, norm, and community— are key elements of the common law tradition. As a tradition theorist indebted to MacIntyre would expect, these elements are integrated and ordered through narrative. This narrativity is ethically significant because it carries a certain kind of accountability that is important for law and the communities it regulates. The crucial features of that accountability follow from the fact that law's narrativity is not *realistic* narrative (pace Hans Frei); rather, it is *real* narrative. No hypothetical situation imagined in a seminar room can match the three-dimensional texture of an actual case, nor replicate the multitude of overlapping connections between the general and the specific, the traditional and the innovative. Precisely because the narratives of the common law are *real* and not merely realistic, the situations these narratives grapple with reveal the strengths and weaknesses of human nature as manifested in actual human beings living in particular times and places. Reading the cases that compose the common law allows us to see a thickly encultured set of legal, moral, and social norms. The opinions provide a snapshot of the dominant moral worldview operative in a particular time and place—in its broader historical and institutional context. I use the term "dominant" deliberately. Unlike moral philosophers, moral theologians, or even legal academics, common law judges make moral assessments that are enforced directly against the litigants themselves and indirectly by contributing to the body of legal precedent against which others in the community will measure their rights and responsibilities.

The narratives of the common law tradition shape the sensibilities and expectations of those who will be active participants in that tradition. There is a canon of stories (legal cases) that all persons learning to be lawyers read, just like there is a canon of stories (centrally, the synoptic Gospels) that all persons learning to be Christians read.[11] Among the crucial tasks facing budding lawyers is learning to distinguish between three distinct but overlapping narratives: the narrative *in* the case, the narrative *of* the case, and the narrative *made from* the case.

The Narrative in *the Case*

Legal cases are controversies—they narrate a human situation in which something went drastically wrong. Not surprisingly, then, these contested situations are described in different ways by various parties. The fact finder, either a jury or in some cases a trial judge, determines the facts of the case. Except in very rare instances, the judges hearing the case on appeal will not disturb the factual findings at the trial court level. Appellate court judges, however, can and do arrange, order, and frame those facts. The appellate court's narration of the facts is tied forever to its articulation of the law of the case. The appellate court's factual statement is preserved together with the law. Not surprisingly, the appellate court frequently tells the story in a way that makes sense of its ultimate legal decision—in manners large and small.

For example, consider *Wood v. Lucy, Lady Duff-Gordon* (1917), a famous New York contracts case from the first part of the twentieth century.[12] It was decided by Judge Benjamin Cardozo, the most distinguished jurist of his time, who took his place on the US Supreme Court after a long and illustrious career on the highest court of New York state. The defendant, Lucy, Lady Duff-Gordon, was a glamorous English fashionista. After surviving the wreck of the Titanic, she figured out how to market to starstruck Americans her savvy sense of style and the posh English title she acquired in her second marriage. The plaintiff, Otis F. Wood, was a prominent New York ad man whom Lucy hired to help her market her brand; he claimed that she wrongly cut him out of a deal that she made separately with Sears, Roebuck and Co.

To the attentive reader, it is clear that Lucy is going to lose her case by the first sentence of Judge Cardozo's opinion: "Defendant styles herself a creator of fashions." In this one sentence, Cardozo tacitly suggests that Lucy is a charlatan, someone who is merely styling herself as a posh lady, duping the gullible customers who pay for her name on the label of their dresses. One might also sense in his opinion some intellectual disdain for her endeavors. Yet that would be unjust; Lady Duff-Gordon is widely considered to be a pioneer in the development of both the international couture industry and mass-marketing of fashion trends. Reading the case nearly a century later, it is hard not to see both sexism and intellectual elitism in the judge's response to the activities of the innovative businesswoman. Yet Judge Cardozo probably reached the right result. Lady Duff-Gordon's sharp commercial sense was not matched by an equally sensitive perception of commutative justice. It does appear that she was cheating her marketing agent by making a separate deal with Sears, Roebuck without cutting him in on the profits. Her defense—that the contract was invalid because it lacked consideration on Wood's part—seems specious, as Cardozo recognized.

The Narrative of *the Case*

Many times courts do not reach the correct result. The stories told in appellate opinions are often rich enough for later readers to raise questions about the holding, to call it into doubt concretely, and thereby to raise questions about the law that it articulates. This is a crucial point where contemporary Christian ethicists might be able to contribute their insights to a broader conversation about the relationship of law and morality in contemporary American society. Feminist and liberation theologians have taught the entire field about the necessity of practicing a hermeneutic of suspicion when reading canonical texts in the Christian tradition.[13] As Elisabeth Schüssler Fiorenza has pointed out, a biblical hermeneutics of suspicion seeks to expose not only the biased or oppressive aspects of a text and the world that created it but also the biases and assumptions of the reader.[14] Liberation theologians have shown us that a text's authoritative status does not exempt it from critique. Their lessons apply not only to Scripture and religious tradition but also to foundational legal texts.

The law can liberate and protect. It can also serve as a tool for unjust oppression in ways that a Christian ethics of liberation can unmask. Furthermore, marginal status in the secular legal system often correlates to marginal status within the Christian community. For example, Daisy L. Machado has insisted that "the undocumented immigrant woman and her struggle cannot be omitted from what women are saying in their theological, ethical, and political discourse. . . . It seems that rarely, if ever, have undocumented women been treated as explicit subjects of the concerns of women in theology."[15] M. Shawn Copeland writes of her theologian's task to "draw back the veil" that conceals the suffering of enslaved black women and men, to remember and learn from their lives "for the sake of freedom."[16]

Whose voice is missing from the narrative? Whose perspective is missing from the analysis? These questions are as applicable to normative texts in the American legal tradition as they are to normative texts in the Christian theological tradition. In law, as in theology, problematic ethical issues reveal themselves not by asking who is in the story but by asking who is entirely left out of consideration. Consider, for example, *Rockingham County v. Luten Bridge Company* (1929), a contract case from North Carolina.[17] Rockingham County hired Luten Bridge Company to build a bridge over the Dan River. After disputes erupted on its governing board, the county repudiated the contract. Nevertheless, the company kept building the bridge, doubtless hoping that the county would change its mind. When that did not happen, Luten sued the county for the full contract price for the bridge. The US Court of Appeals for the Fourth Circuit held that although Rockingham County had breached its contract, Luten Bridge Company was not entitled to the full contract price in damages. It should have stopped work when it was clear that the county had repudiated the contract. Consequently, it was entitled to its profits plus expenses incurred up until the time of the breach as damages. According to the court, this amount would make the bridge company whole. That statement is doubtless true—as far as it goes.

But liberationist insights would invite us to press further. Who is not in the picture? Whose interests are not articulated, let alone taken into account, in the judicial analysis? When I ask students this question, it can take them a while to find the human beings—and human suffering—occluded by the shadows of the narrative. The controversy operates within the broad context of American employment law, which generally assumes at-will employment. This context means that Luten Bridge Company can cut its expenses after the breach by immediately terminating the workers it hired to build the bridge. They have no contractual claims against the bridge company for continued employment. Since the case was decided on the cusp of the Great Depression, we would not be wrong to wonder how long it took the employees to find another source of income.

The Narratives Made from the Case

As we broaden our perspective beyond one case, we can see that the law in general is articulated in and through the accretion and conversation of the narratives of particular cases. It would be fair to say that the narratives *incarnate* the law—the legal tradition has its life in the movement from case to case. When asked to reflect upon the state of the law on a current topic, lawyers and laypeople alike tend to think of the "rule" articulated across cases. But it is just as important to think in terms of "characters" and "roles." It is people who are incarnate—not rules. The narratives that operate normatively across the American legal tradition depend just as surely upon characters and roles as they do upon rules.

In teaching my students contract law, we use casebooks—books full of quasi-canonical legal narratives and newer cases meant to illustrate key legal points.[18] These narratives include character types that track scriptural ways of categorizing persons with surprising frequency. On the one hand, little old ladies and orphans are frequently treated as good, innocent, and vulnerable in judicial opinions. On the other hand, insurance companies and banks tend to be viewed with more than a little suspicion. There are sacred spaces, such as the family homestead, or even the newly purchased suburban tract house, the symbol of the mid-twentieth-century American dream. There are even invasive plagues—basically, any kind of icky bug that infests a dwelling place. The more legs on the bug, it seems, the more severe the plague.

One or two of my first-year contracts students have been heard to say, almost flippantly, "The little old lady always wins." I have been known to speak those words myself. They are not literally true, of course. But part of being a good lawyer is recognizing that one is not representing an abstract position in court but speaking on behalf of clients whose identity and whose concerns inevitably fit within a larger social narrative. For example, in one case I teach, the buyers were able to set aside a real estate contract because the sellers had failed to disclose that the house under contract had been infested with termites.[19] From the point of view of someone who ignores the role characters play in developing our legal tradition, this result was astonishing. The buyers, a married couple, admitted that they "half-knew" that the house might be so infected, but they went ahead with the deal anyway because they really liked the house. Since the buyers were given full opportunity to inspect the property, it would seem that the law ought to place the risk of termite infection on them. Such an analysis, however, misses a significant part of the equation. On a deeper level, the major character in this legal narrative is not a natural person but rather an American ideal: the idea of owning one's own little home, a little piece of heaven on earth. It is that dream that is sullied by the pestilence of termites.

Narrative and Naming

At the same time, and equally importantly, the characters in the paradigmatic cases taught to law students are not merely stock characters or social stereotypes; they are known by name. In the common law tradition, the practice of naming is rich and complex. It is also crucial to narrative accountability. It enables a legal narrative to be held accountable not only to the human beings whose controversy generated it but also to others affected by the norms it articulates.

"The law" is not an abstract and impersonal deliverance. As John Noonan has explored so well, it is made by and applied to human beings, whose dignity and responsibility are reflected in their unique names.[20] Names—particular names—are pervasive in the common law tradition. Consider, for example, the most infamous case ever decided by the Supreme Court of the United

States: *Dred Scott v. Sandford* (1857), the pre–Civil War Supreme Court case whose name lives in infamy in American jurisprudence.[21] The case is known by the names of the principal parties. Dred Scott was a slave who had been taken from a slave state to a free state. Mr. Scott was the plaintiff suing defendant, John Sandford, his current owner, for his freedom in federal court. Consequently, the case was not just about the "institution of slavery" in the abstract; it was also and centrally about a particular man—a man who had been born into slavery in Southampton County, Virginia, married a woman named Harriet Robinson, and raised two girls and two boys (who died in infancy) with her.[22]

By attaching names to cases, the common law tacitly presupposes that particular human persons stand at the center of the relevant moral and social analysis. As the *Dred Scott* case suggests, the institution of slavery is not understandable apart from its effects on the lives of unique individuals, people like Mr. Scott and his family. It does not, however, possess the resources to articulate powerfully and persuasively why this is so. The fundamental insights of Christian ethics can be used to explain, defend, and even deepen the pattern of naming in the common law. For example, the idea that each human being is an unrepeatable and irreplaceable icon of God, made in the divine image and likeness, and called to friendship with God, helps to explain why it is so important to link legal judgments permanently with the names and persons they first affected. Conversely, the common law practice of linking case holdings to the names and stories of the parties can assist Christian ethicists in thinking about what it might actually look like to place particular persons at the center of systematic normative analysis. For example, the process of naming the parties in common law cases can encourage—although not ensure—that we do not develop the normative frameworks governing our communities in a manner that is entirely abstracted from the persons whose lives those norms regulate and restrict.

It is also significant that the American common law tradition generally preserves the names of the judges who were involved in deciding the case. The authors of the majority opinions in appellate cases generally sign their opinions, making them publicly accountable for both the reasoning and the result. And so, writing for the *Dred Scott* majority, Justice Roger Brooke Taney held that African Americans, whether enslaved or free, could not be American citizens and therefore had no standing to sue in federal court. Dissents are preserved by name as well: Justice Benjamin Robbins Curtis offered a point-by-point refutation of the majority opinion, exposing its legal analysis as raw political pandering.

The practice of tying judges to their opinions and their votes by name facilitates accountability in three ways. First, it reminds judges that their work will be considered their personal work, not only in the immediate moment but also in the grand sweep of history. It acts as a counterweight to the desire for momentary popularity. Second, it reminds the reader that the law is not only applied to human beings, but it is also made by human beings who are no less flawed and limited in their perspective by virtue of their judicial office. There is no "view from nowhere"—there is no pure articulation of law that escapes being shaped, influenced, and even altered by the perspectives of the human beings who interpret it and apply it. Third, and most importantly, it reveals to us that the standard image of "blind justice" is deeply inaccurate both as a description of what actually happens and as a normative idea. Justice is not blind; nor, for that matter, is it deaf. It has partial sight and selective hearing. It sees and hears what the judges themselves see and hear. The challenge for wise judges is to open their eyes and ears, not to shut them further.

Law and the Building Blocks of Ethical Analysis: Persons, Actions, Norms, and Communities

Most contemporary Christian ethicists emphasize the social nature of human beings. Many members of our guild increasingly draw upon insights from social sciences to understand how we are formed in response to communal forces—sometimes for good, sometimes for ill. We increasingly recognize the significant influence that society and culture have upon our understandings of own agency, the range of actions permitted to us, and the claims that moral norms exert upon us. Moreover, these concepts are not unconnected themselves. An individual's self-worth and her worth in the eyes of others very much affect the scope she has for exercising agency and the way in which social norms are applied to her. The common law offers a unique opportunity to examine and critique the interaction among four key concepts—and realities—in ethical thought: persons, actions, norms, and community.

(Reasonable) Persons

The most fundamental and pervasive category in the law is the "reasonable person" standard.[23] It is the starting point for determining our social obligations to one another. In brief, the law holds that each person has a duty to others to behave as a reasonable person would under the same circumstances. The "reasonable person" standard critiques what we do. It also critiques what we fail to do. Refracted through different areas of the law, the reasonable person standard helps determine whether a defendant is guilty of criminal negligence, as well as negligence under tort law.

Most significantly for the purposes of Christian ethics, the "reasonable person" standard is communally defined. What is reasonable to do, or to neglect doing, is directly reflective of communal standards. It is the fact finder, in many cases the jury, that determines whether the defendant acted reasonably or not in the situation under examination. The "reasonable person" standard is not an abstract or academic standard. It is in many ways a test of a defendant's engrained cultural competence. It is an assessment of situational responsiveness demonstrated, often in a split-second decision, by embodied and socialized persons. This means, of course, that generally reasonable persons can and do act unreasonably on specific occasions. I very much doubt there is even one competent adult American who has never violated the reasonable person standard at any point in his or her life, just as I very much doubt there is one competent adult American who has never committed a sin. Most of the time, however, luck (or cosmic mercy) allows the legal transgression of the norms of reasonableness to fade into the past with a quick prayer of thanksgiving. A new driver neglects to observe a stop sign—but, fortunately, no other vehicle is entering the intersection at the time. She takes a deep breath, resolves to be more careful, and moves on—with the realization that her life would have been very different if she had actually hit another car.

Who, then, is this "reasonable person"? Do we have a model or a standard-bearer? This is a fascinating question, and one well worth the attention of Christian ethicists interested in applied anthropology. It raises issues regarding the relationship of our common human nature, and our specific characteristics. It also provides academic ethicists with a fascinating locus to examine how factors such as gender, age, level of ability, and social position affect one's moral standing, which goes hand in hand with one moral responsibility.

The "reasonable person" standard was originally called the "reasonable man" standard; as women began to claim social equality and participation, it was broadened, generalized, and homogenized to encompass both genders. So there is no "reasonable woman" standard that operates independently of a separate "reasonable man" standard. At the same time, the standard is tailored for some people. For example, children are required to act as a "reasonable person of like age, intelligence, and experience under the circumstances."[24] Persons with a physical disability are held to the standard applicable to a person with the same physical disability. Generally, however, all adults are held to a uniform standard of behavior. There is no separate and more lenient measure for, say, persons of slightly below-average intelligence who smoked a lot of weed in their youth. More problematically, there is no separate standard for persons with severe mental illness.[25]

The "reasonable person" standard, then, remains an abstraction to be fleshed out by the cases applying it. We are not thinking of either saints or sociopaths when we invoke the standard. The definition, to the extent there is one, is virtue-oriented: "A reasonable person is an ordinary, prudent person who normally exercises due care while avoiding extremes of both audacity and caution."[26] In the case law, the standard receives its fullest definition in a negative way, by decisions regarding what a reasonable person would *not* do.

- A reasonable person does not allow a friend with no experience to take the helm of a powerboat in crowded waters.[27]

- A reasonable person does not urinate on a coworker's belongings.[28]

- A reasonable person does not get on a freeway ramp going the wrong way, ignoring well-marked "DO NOT ENTER" signs, traverse three lanes of oncoming traffic, and then try to pull a U-turn to go the right way.[29]

Both Protestants and Roman Catholics interested in notions of a "natural morality" or a "common morality" may find a fruitful conversation partner with the case law developing the idea of a reasonable person.[30] Two features of the prospective conversation are important. First, it is significant that the case law generally defines a reasonable person's actions negatively—with reference to what such a person would *not* do. This aspect of the common law might contribute to an ecumenical project of articulating a modest but still helpful common morality. Roman Catholics have historically tended to refer to the precepts of such a morality as "natural law," a category that has been highly contested not only between Catholics and persons of other faith traditions but also among Catholics themselves. A chief sticking point of controversy is the charge that natural law theorists claim too much, with too much certainty, on the basis of natural reason. Critics say that natural law theorists have rigged the system, smuggling in the pronouncements of the Roman Catholic magisterium on particular matters, which they deem to be highly questionable.

Some natural law theorists may do just that. But an excess of certainty about contestable matters is not an inevitable trait of natural law theory, as Jean Porter has so well demonstrated in her ongoing work. That point can be made even more strongly in conversation with the common law. In *Nine Modern Moralists*, written more than half a century ago, the eminent Protestant ethicist Paul Ramsey explored the connection between natural law and positive law, finding in conversation partners Edmund Cahn (a secular legal theorist) and Jacques Maritain (a Catholic natural law theorist) the room for an inductive, epistemologically humble, and enculturated understanding of the natural law.[31]

Ramsey saw epistemological humility in a natural law whose defining mark is what Cahn called "a sense of injustice"—not a sense of justice.[32] It may in fact be easier to reach some agreement across confessional lines about what human beings and fellow members of our community should not do than rather than what we should do. Judging by the questions we address, our guild has long tacitly acknowledged this fact in its focus on debating and defining negative moral norms. For many years, the core of this debate has focused on the issue of negative moral absolutes: whether there are actions that are always and everywhere morally impermissible and, if so, how we can identify them. In both Catholic and Protestant circles over the past fifty years, much ink has been spilled over questions such as whether abortion, euthanasia, adultery, homosexual activity, the use of nuclear weapons, and even lying are *always* wrong. I do not mean to deny the importance of these debates. At the same time, I think that it is equally if not more important to analyze actions that are wrong not always but by reason of circumstance. The common law, particularly the law of torts, is rich with examples of acts that are wrong precisely because they were performed in the wrong circumstances.

Assessing whether a defendant's action is negligent by reason of circumstance is not conceptually tidy. It requires, first, immersing oneself in the point of view of a flawed human being, to see why (for example) pulling a U-turn on a busy highway "seemed like a good idea at the time" to the hapless defendant. For jurors tasked with deciding whether such an action was negligent, the qualities of judgment, imagination, and empathy are necessary. Why did the defendant act in that manner? What time of day did the event occur? What would a sensible person (but not a saint) have done in similar circumstances?

Second, making an assessment of negligence requires a rich and textured familiarity with the ways, means, norms, and tacit assumptions of the particular community in which the defendant acted. The morality articulated in case law is thoroughly enculturated morality. The common law method is not an abstract, deductive application of a moral norm to a neutrally described pattern of facts. Norm and context are mutually interpreting. A jury of the defendant's peers is able and empowered to draw upon that richly textured knowledge of how the community operates in evaluating whether or not the defendant's behavior was reasonable under the circumstances. Competent contemporary experts in American culture—jurors—know, for example, that persons driving down highways have little expectation and less protection against drivers going in the wrong direction. They would contrast this situation, for example, with someone driving the wrong way out of a department store parking lot, where speeds are slower and drivers are more accustomed to being on guard against unexpected events ranging from wrong-way drivers to runaway toddlers.

Actions

Generally speaking, the law concerns itself not with states of character considered in the abstract but rather with actions and omissions. A murderous heart, in and of itself, is not subject to a criminal indictment unless it issues in a murderous act. Moral philosophers and moral theologians alike have spent a great deal of time analyzing the morality of human actions. All too frequently the hypothetical examples they discuss in order to advance or to test their action theories are very thin; the characters and actions are often described in the most abbreviated and cursory terms. In contrast, in many important common law cases, human actions are presented in all their variegated complexity. Moreover, and more importantly, they are also presented as they commonly occur in real life: not as isolated actions issuing from the practical agency of an atomistic individual but as thoroughly *interactional*. We see in the case law how one action or omission by one person prompts a response by another person. We see as well the way in which human actions augment or undercut each other to create a situation that no particular person involved could have anticipated.

A case I teach in contract law exemplifies this phenomenon:[33] A testimony to the strand of American optimism that believes any idea can make money provided that it is thoroughly promoted, a group of investors decided to form "Hightower Productions"—designed to capture public interest in breaking the world record for flagpole sitting. They planned to build a tractor trailer specially equipped with a hydraulic lift, on top of which would be a small compartment with a bed and a bathroom. They would then ensconce the aspiring record-breaker, a man to be known as "Woody Hightower," in the compartment. He would ascend to his perch on April Fool's Day, spend the next several months being driven around the country to appear at county fairs and shopping malls, and descend to earth at the New Year's celebrations in Times Square, immediately following the dropping of the New Year's ball.

But there was a flaw in their plan, which was not of their own making. The law firm that legally incorporated Hightower Productions had failed to conform to the requirements of the federal securities laws. Because the corporation was unable to sell stock, the project fell apart due to lack of capitalization. Woody remained earthbound. The disappointed principals in Hightower Productions sued the law firm for breach of contract and negligence—and won. They received an amount equal to their startup costs as damages. In all likelihood, the stunt would have lost money if it had gotten off the ground (no pun intended). But since the defendant law firm could not prove that flagpole sitting *wouldn't* become the year's next popular craze, the investors in Hightower Productions got their startup money back. They may not have made money, but thanks to the legal missteps of their law firm, they didn't lose money either.

It seems to me that this comic and strange little scenario from real life raises interesting questions pertaining to action theory, which Christian ethics is poised to address. Our guild is accustomed to analyzing actions in Kantian terms, in which we ask whether the agent acted according to a maxim that conformed to the moral law. We are familiar with consequentialist analysis in which we consider whether the agent acted in a manner designed to maximize positive outcomes. We are also well acquainted with the methodological moves involved in viewing actions in terms of virtue theory, in which actions both reflect and develop the character of the agent who performs them. Despite their differences, all of these ways of analyzing human acts abstract them from the patterns of action and reaction in which they are generally embedded. A key belief of Christian anthropology is that human beings are essentially social.

Norms

Beginning in the mid-twentieth century, many members of our guild devoted much attention to the matter of "norm and context in Christian ethics," to borrow the title of a book edited by Paul Ramsey and Gene Outka.[34] This discussion, of course, involved the question of whether exceptionless moral norms exist and, if so, how they should be defined. In Protestant circles, the debate centered on "situation ethics," while in Roman Catholic discussions, the controversy arose around the method of proportionalism. Despite the differences, both discussions focused on whether it was possible to define any moral norm in a way that would reliably rule out further exceptions or qualifications based on the circumstances under which the agent was acting. The more straightforward debate surrounded whether an action—say, "torture"—could be justified on the basis of consequences—say, learning the location of a nuclear bomb set to explode in a modern metropolis. More complicated questions arose when participants began to question the definition of moral terms. It is one thing to ask, for example, whether "adultery" is justified by good consequences—for example, spicing up a marriage or relieving boredom. It is another thing to ask whether a married woman who, with the consent of her husband, has sexual relations with a concentration camp guard in order to secure the release of their child from custody actually commits "adultery." The nuances of these debates, it seems to me, might profitably be absorbed by legal scholars, who tend to operate with fairly wooden notions of the crimes and torts that they analyze.

Yet religious moralists might also find inspiration in the discussion of norms in the legal context. More specifically, it strikes me that the law has forthrightly addressed the pedagogical function of moral norms in a way that Christian ethicists might find a useful spur to further reflection. If we human beings recognize ourselves as essentially social beings, as I think a sound Christian anthropology requires us to do, how do we think about the process of articulating, applying, and following norms as a social practice? To what extent does the process of making, enforcing, and applying norms need to consider the first-order question of what is right in and of itself, and to what extent does that process need to look at how the rule, overall, will impact the social community? It strikes me that this issue is one of the questions that divides "moral progressives" from "moral conservatives" on many social issues. It is commonly said that conservatives focus on slippery-slope arguments; that is true, but it is also an incomplete understanding of their concerns. It is better to acknowledge that conservatives tend to be wary that the revising of a moral norm, even in a hard case, will weaken the intricate combination of social and moral norms that structure communal behavior and expectations. By contrast, moral progressives tend to be less worried that making exceptions in hard cases, or even articulating a new moral norm to cover a whole range of cases (e.g., same-sex relations), will produce a range of unhappy unintended social effects. It may be helpful if we pose the question in terms of moral ecology. How do we as ethicists advocate for the correction of unjust situations even while protecting the delicate relationships in a community's moral ecosystem?

A second and related issue that may merit more attention from Christian ethicists is the way in which rules of accountability serve as incentives for action. A key example here might be the concept of strict liability in tort law. That concept was one of the most difficult for me to accept as a new student of law. In fact, the very idea of "strict liability" struck me as a contradiction in terms. The word "tort" means "wrong" in French; much of tort law has historically dealt with wrongful acts that result in harm to private parties. Sometimes the wrong involved is intentional, as in the case of assault or battery. In other instances, the wrongfulness is not planned or purposeful but rather involves a failure to attend appropriately to the situation, as in negligence. In contrast, the essence of strict liability is that an agent can be held accountable for activity that causes harm even if that activity is not culpable—that is, even if it is not classifiable as an intentional tort or negligence. It is a "tort" (legal wrong) that is not the result of a tort (moral or social wrong).

First articulated in the California courts in the mid-twentieth century, the doctrine of strict liability began by holding anyone in the chain of manufacturing and distribution of an inherently dangerous product liable for any harm caused by such product—whether or not they were negligent.[35] Later the California courts extended strict liability to encompass any product introduced into the stream of commerce, whether or not it could be deemed "inherently dangerous."[36] The basic policy reasons justifying the imposition of strict liability are twofold. First, the manufacturer of any product is in the best position proactively to anticipate and stave off possible defects as well as continuously to improve quality. Second, manufacturers (and distributors) are in the best position to spread the loss inflicted by a product among all consumers. More specifically, they can institute pricing strategies that allow everyone who uses the product to share the costs of a mishap rather than leaving the few who were unfortunate enough to be actually harmed to bear the entire financial burden.

Many people imagine norms as functioning as a neutral framework, much like the rules of a game. On this view, a society's legal moral rules set the boundaries for fair play, shaping the reasonable expectations of social players. The example of strict liability calls this understanding of norms into question in at least three ways. First, it shows that a society's legal and moral rules do not stand over and apart from the persons whose actions they regulate. Norms have a pedagogical function, inculcating certain patterns of behavior. For example, the regime of strict liability teaches that the disparity in knowledge and power between manufacturers and distributors, on the one hand, and consumers, on the other, justifies a disparity in responsibilities. This message stands in marked contrast with the message of classical contract law, which was "caveat emptor"—let the buyer beware.[37] That message presumed that buyers were in a position to investigate and, if necessary, negotiate quality-control measures with sellers. That presumption was dubious at best two centuries ago; it is nothing short of delusional in our capitalist, globalized economy. Second, the strict liability regime highlights the incentivizing function of norms. Manufacturers of products to be introduced into the stream of commerce have a tangible financial incentive not only to search out and remedy any possible defects in their products but also to devote their creative efforts to designing ever newer and improved safety measures. Third, as more and more manufacturers strive to improve their products, the standard for "reasonable care" actually rises—strict liability can function to elevate the bar for non-negligent behavior.

It strikes me that the legal phenomenon of strict liability is an ideal locus for a mutually beneficial conversation between contemporary Christian ethics and secular law. Many Christian ethicists have devoted tremendous care and attention to uncovering and analyzing disparities in social power and social capital. They have called for a "hermeneutic of suspicion" with which to scrutinize the biases embedded in norms that appear neutral on their surface. They have advocated for a preferential option for the poor and the marginalized, motivated by a spirit of solidarity, based in the equal dignity of all persons. I believe that the insights developed by such scholars provide a rich way to articulate the moral basis for a legal innovation such as "products liability." Such an articulation is sorely needed; until the market crash of 2007, the dominant analytical and normative framework in American law schools was economic analysis of law, which maintains that the overarching purpose of legal rules is to maximize economic efficiency. It is true that certain aspects of the strict liability regime do reflect concerns for economic efficiency; one can say, for example, that the manufacturer of an item is in the best position to stave off preventable defects and to spread the costs of unpreventable ones among the entire class of purchasers. At the same time, however, a concern for economic efficiency does not entirely account for the view that preemptive attention to risk and risk-sharing are goods worth pursuing. One might argue, for example, that it is better to have cheaper product costs for everyone—leaving the unlucky few who have been injured by the product in question to bear the costs themselves. But Christian ethics offers a response to that argument. All purchasers stand in solidarity with each other; such solidarity requires that we take seriously the insight "there but for the grace of God go I" when contemplating the suffering of another consumer who purchased the same product. Viewed in light of the virtue of solidarity, a strict liability regime looks something like a mutual benefit or mutual insurance society.[38]

At the same time, however, I think that considering the phenomenon of strict liability may encourage Christian ethicists to advance and refine our own conceptual tools. Our moral tradition has a well-nuanced way of analyzing individual actions. It also possesses a nicely honed and powerful form of social analysis that takes an acute critical look at unjust social structures and institutions. But we are just beginning to develop the same level of sophistication in what I call "interactional" theory, an account of moral action that takes seriously the way human beings and corporate human agents act in response to, and in anticipation of, the actions of others. Game theory and the insights of psychology, sociology, and economics are all relevant to understanding these issues. At the same time, the common law tradition has developed concepts and tools that may prove useful in making normative assessments about which sorts of incentives are morally permissible, which are impermissible, and why.

Furthermore, our society is increasingly aware that many socially harmful situations are precipitated by contexts in which one agent wrongfully predicts the future actions of another agent. Sometimes these predictions are fueled by unjust prejudice, as the mounting number of cases in which police officers shoot young African American men demonstrates. Combining the insights from the legal tradition and the tradition of Christian moral analysis may help give a fuller account of how and where patterns of action and reaction go so lethally awry.

Communal Bonds

Finally, I want to offer a few words about the role of community in both ethics and law. The past thirty years have witnessed what we might call a communitarian turn in Christian ethics. Protestant and Catholic theorists have emphasized the essential sociality of every human being. The many ethicists indebted to Alasdair MacIntyre and Stanley Hauerwas have focused on the church as a particular type of community that forms human beings in a particular way. Moreover, many social ethicists, especially those concerned with the plight of the most marginalized and vulnerable members of the human community, have focused on the problems of structural sin in our pluralistic society. An emerging issue, however, is how to formulate a differentiated and nuanced chain accountability that integrates individual responsibility and structural responsibility. One question we need to face is how to think about the nature of group action. What, exactly, does it mean to talk about what Exxon did? Or what the CIA did? Or what the Ferguson grand jury did? A second essential question pertains to the relationship of individual responsibility and group responsibility? How do we think, more broadly, not merely about questions of personal culpability for the wrongful actions of groups but about a more broad sense of responsibility? Because human beings are essentially social, it is important to acknowledge that we all may have a responsibility for addressing and ameliorating harms for which we were not personally culpable. How do we construct a unified theory of agency that takes into account not only the actions of individual persons and the actions of groups but also relates the two in a nuanced and sensible way?

Theological ethicists are now turning their attention to these problems with tremendous vigor. They may find helpful resources in the secular law. The entire subject matter of corporate law is devoted to the action taken by collective bodies that have a life apart from their individual members: corporations. Corporations have rights as well as responsibilities, as demonstrated in *Citizens United*, the recent Supreme Court case recognizing broad corporate rights to free speech.[39] Judicial decisions that expand the rights of corporations (artificial persons) at the expense of natural persons have been subjected (in my view, rightly) to trenchant critique. At the same time, the existence of these cases ought not to deter Christian ethicists from turning to the less workaday and less controversial aspects of corporate law that work out what it means for a group of persons to be responsible for a collective action.

Moral Concepts in the Law: The Example of Unconscionability

Important strands of contemporary legal theory have tried to marginalize the place of moral analysis in law. Adherents of the economic analysis of law, for example, have argued that the purpose of law is to promote economic efficiency.[40] I may be wrong, but I sense some dimming of enthusiasm for attempts to use this approach after the Great Recession of 2007—although it would be wrong to deny that concern for economic efficiency still has a place in assessing the strengths and weaknesses of law, particularly the law relevant to market transactions. I do think the time is right, however, for Christian ethicists to retrieve, extend, and highlight the undeniably normative aspects of the common law tradition. A sensible place to start would be the idea of "unconscionability," which was first fleshed out in *Williams v. Walker-Thomas Furniture*, a case decided by the US Court of Appeals for the District of Columbia in 1972.[41]

The lead plaintiff, Ora Lee Williams, lived with her seven children in Northeast Washington, DC. Between 1957 and 1962, she purchased a number of household items from the defendant, Walker-Thomas Furniture, which was a local rent-to-own store marketing to the low-income, largely African American population in its neighborhood. Mrs. Williams handled her finances responsibly; by April 1962, she had brought her account with Walker-Thomas down to $164. But then she made a major purchase: she bought a stereo for $514.95, which would be about $4,000 in today's dollars. That amount proved too heavy for her to carry; she defaulted on her payments in the fall of that year. Walker-Thomas Furniture had a reputation as a very impatient creditor; the store obtained a writ of replevin and sent in federal marshals to repossess the goods. This is the key to the story: the marshals repossessed not only the stereo but also nearly everything else she had ever purchased from them. They took a bed and a chest that she had bought in 1958 along with a washing machine and the stereo. In short, they made Dr. Seuss's Grinch look tenderhearted.

Mrs. Williams, together with other plaintiffs, defended against the enforcement of the sale agreements on the grounds that they were unconscionable. Walker-Thomas won at the lower court level; the judge held that the defense of unconscionability was not available to the plaintiffs because the Uniform Commercial Code (which codified the defense) had not yet been enacted in the District of Columbia.[42] The federal appellate court, however, reversed the lower court and remanded for further proceedings. It found that the doctrine of unconscionability was part of the common law and therefore available to Mrs. Williams as a defense even before the enactment of the Uniform Commercial Code.

What exactly does it mean to say that an agreement is "unconscionable"? The traditional account, articulated in the late nineteenth century, maintains that an unconscionable agreement is "such as no man in his senses and not under delusion would make, on the one hand, and as no honest or fair man would accept, on the other."[43] That definition is powerful. It is, alas, also vague. How can we give it further specificity? Christian ethicists can offer some help to legal theorists. The four basic categories of person, act, norm, and community can facilitate the analysis of specific aspects of the situation in *Williams v. Walker-Thomas Furniture* while also helping to relate them to broader social patterns of injustice. Furthermore, the Christian commitment to seeing the situation from the perspective of the least advantaged allows ethicists to focus on aspects of the case that are often ignored or downplayed.

Person

The lower court noted that Mrs. Williams was a social worker and earned $218 a month.[44] It went on to suggest that the unconscionable act was the sale of the stereo *to a person such as Mrs. Williams:* "With full knowledge that appellant had to feed clothe and support both herself and seven children on this amount, appellee sold her a $514 stereo."[45] Mrs. Williams has been configured as a quasi-child at best, as a Welfare Queen at worst—as someone who is spending her precious government stipend (*our* precious government stipend?) on luxuries. But this portrayal of her is just false—she had been purchasing from Walker-Thomas for years; and, as the federal court of appeals notes, she had steadily paid back about $1,400 of the $1,800 she had owed them for her purchases. Her record is not that of an irresponsible spendthrift. It rather suggests that she is a person who ran into unexpected bad luck. Perhaps she was taken ill—or perhaps one of her children fell sick. Perhaps she ran into other unexpected expenses without the benefit of a "rainy-day fund" or a safety net. We don't know. And configuring Mrs. Williams as an irresponsible child squelches the desire to ask more questions. It allows us to alleviate our consciences in this case while wrongly absolving ourselves of the duty of investigating more systemic issues in our economic system.

Action

Some might say that what was unconscionable in the case was the act by which—and the manner in which—the contract was made, and in particular the way in which the contractual term allowing repossession of previously pur-chased goods made its way into the agreement. The federal court of appeals quotes the relevant contractual provision:

> The amount of each periodical installment payment to be made by (pur-chaser) to the Company under this present lease shall be inclusive of and not in addition to the amount of each installment payment to be made by (pur-chaser) under such prior leases, bills or accounts; and all payments now and hereafter made by (purchaser) shall be credited pro rata on all outstanding leases, bills and accounts due the Company by (purchaser) at the time each such payment is made.[46]

I ask my first-year law students what this provision means. Many of them do not understand it. In essence, it states that Walker-Thomas Furniture retains a security interest in every item ever purchased until all items are paid off. So, for example, if I bought a table for $200 in March 1960, a bed for $300 in May 1960, and a sofa for $500 in July 1960, my $100 September payment would be applied as follows: $20 to table, $30 to the bed, and $50 to the sofa. No item would be paid off until all are paid off.

This provision would be hard enough to grasp if a customer had an opportu-nity to review the agreement at her leisure. But Mrs. Williams wasn't afforded that opportunity. Walker-Thomas Furniture Company did a great deal of its business through door-to-door salespeople. Very frequently they didn't leave their clients with completed contracts—the price term was often filled out back at the office. Under these conditions, one could argue that the payment term, coupled with the repossession term, constituted "unfair surprise" because Mrs. Williams did not have an opportunity to read or understand a key element of her contract with the furniture company. A situation in which one party is deprived of the opportunity to review and consider contractual terms is often described as "procedural unconscionability."

But what if Mrs. Williams did have an opportunity to read the contract but decided not to do so? Shifting to the contemporary context, think about the ubiq-uitous "iTunes" agreements, which most people don't read. For all you know, you might have agreed to sacrifice your first-born child in exchange for the privilege of downloading the new Taylor Swift song. But you don't know because you didn't read the agreement—you simply scrolled through and impatiently clicked the "I ACCEPT" button. Under this scenario, at least you could claim you didn't actually know what could happen to you—and so could Mrs. Williams.

Suppose, however, that Mrs. Williams *did* know what happened if a customer didn't keep current with Walker-Thomas Furniture's payment schedule. That scenario, of course, is not beyond the realm of possibility; she could very easily have heard of a friend or neighbor who was faced with repossession of their goods. Perhaps Mrs. Williams simply didn't think that what happened to them would happen to her—she thought she would be able to keep up with the payments. Or perhaps she had no other practical choice; credit cards at department stores were not (and are not) commonly made available to persons in her economic situation. Moreover, knowing about the prospect of repossession would not really put her in a better position to negotiate with Walker-Thomas Furniture Company, which would insist upon the payment and repossession terms as a condition of the sale. Is it really fair to protect those who couldn't or at least didn't read the agreement, while leaving in the lurch those who did know about the terms but wouldn't be able to do anything about them? To put the question another way, is not the problem also a matter of substantive unconscionability as well as procedural unconscionability?

Norm

So we move on to the norm. Should we bite the bullet and say what shocks the conscience in this particular agreement is not mainly the circumstances under which this contract was made but the very contract itself, and in particular its payment and repossession provision? Should we have a norm, therefore, that prohibits this type of provision in every contract—no matter who signs it and what they knew about it? This is a very tempting approach, but it is not a solution without its own problems. Economic theorists of law have argued that businesses such as Walker-Thomas would only find it financially viable to serve populations at high risk of default if they have a way of protecting their investment and making profit.[47]

It is true, of course, that in our fallen world, those who have the most need of favorable credit terms are the least able to obtain them. But as Anne Fleming has persuasively recounted, Walker-Thomas Furniture went far beyond commercially reasonable practices in a number of respects, in essence making intimidation, including governmental intimidation through the writ of replevin, part of its business plan. In the mid-1970s Walker-Thomas had deleted the offending clause in response to Mrs. Williams's successful claim. Not much else changed, however. It continued to solicit business and collect payments using a door-to-door sales force. It continued to overprice merchandise and to sell repossessed goods as new. In many cases the sales people did not disclose the price term to customers until they were already committed to purchase an item. Far more ominously, Walker-Thomas continued to employ six men, known as "pimps," who were tasked with investigating their customers to uncover information that might be used to intimidate them so they wouldn't complain about its unfair business practices. One might say that Walker-Thomas had complied with the "letter" rather than the "spirit" of the law against unconscionability.[48]

Community

It is impossible, therefore, to consider the relationship of Ora Lee Williams and Walker-Thomas Furniture in a way that is hermetically sealed from broader issues of social and economic justice. Sometimes one case—one face—can trigger social reform. In fact, Fleming documents how Mrs. Williams's plight became something of a cause célèbre that prompted Congress to pass a retail installment sales act that required lenders to apply payments to old debts first.[49] But the industry rebounded, restructuring their contracts as leases that do not fall within the scope of the relevant legislation. Even today, rent-to-own operations such as Rent-a-Center charge elevated prices and affix exorbitant interest rates to people who cannot afford to buy on credit at conventional stores.[50]

A single judicial opinion, and even a single piece of legislation, will be insufficient to address the plight of Ora Lee Williams and countless others similarly situated—then and now. A federal commission charged with studying the problem of consumer credit concluded that the basic problem was twofold: first, poor customers lived in areas that were not competitive marketplaces; and second, the poor were not aware of their rights to the same degree as more affluent customers.[51]

This is all true. In my view, however, it ignores a problem that Christian ethics refuses to ignore—the problem of human sin, particularly when it takes the form of greed. Walker-Thomas Furniture didn't merely adjust for the financial and social weaknesses of its clients; it made those weaknesses the centerpiece of its business model. Greed is not merely an individual sin; it is also a key ingredient in social sin.[52] As Kristin Heyer observes, social sin "encompasses the unjust structures, distorted consciousness, and collective actions and inaction that facilitate injustice and dehumanization."[53] The investment bankers who created economic havoc forty years later by selling subprime mortgages not only are a symbol of personal greed but also exemplify systemic greed.[54] The personal and the social are mutually influencing; indeed, they are inseparable. Sri Lankan liberation theologian Aloysius Pieris writes,

> Mammon is more than just money. It is a subtle force operating within me, an acquisitive instinct driving me to be the rich fool whom Jesus ridicules in the passage of the harvester who wanted to tear down his grain bins and build

larger ones. Or again, mammon is what I do with money and what it does to me; what it both promises and brings when I come to terms with it; security and success; power and prestige—acquisitions that make me appear privileged. I may even experience an irresistible satisfaction in . . . being chosen to exert great influence over others.[55]

Christian ethicists have long recognized that key building blocks of ethical analysis are the concepts of person, act, norm, and community. We have devoted much attention to critiquing and nuancing these concepts. It is tempting, however, to treat these concepts in isolation, abstracting them from their dynamic relationships with each other and from real-life situations. Engagement with the common law can help us overcome this temptation toward abstraction, as my analysis of *Williams v. Walker-Thomas Furniture* suggests. Ethicists who engage with case law can explore dynamic connections between and among concepts of person, act, norm, and community. Precisely because those concepts are embedded in real narratives, they cannot be treated in an abstract and isolated fashion, but take on a multi-dimensional and relational quality.

More generally, the case law dealing with unconscionability can profitably engage the rich tradition of Christian reflection on what it means to act according to one's conscience. Many contemporary Christian ethicists have reflected powerfully upon the primacy of conscience vis-à-vis the externally imposed norms of state and church. The legal framework of unconscionability can generate a fruitful discussion on pressing related questions, such as what counts as appropriate formation of conscience and how do we account for and confront seriously erring consciences? Both of these questions are important and difficult in themselves; they become even more complicated and pressing in our increasingly pluralistic society. Moreover, they point to an emerging moral challenge: how do we go about forming the conscience not of an individual but of an entire community? The reflections that Christian moralists develop on these issues should have broader relevance in the public square because our country's history includes myriad examples where morally egregious behavior has failed to "shock the conscience" of the populace.[56] The legal doctrine of unconscionability is of little use in a land where consciences have been lulled into somnolence.

Conclusion

Christian ethics and the contemporary common law have much in common. Both fields take seriously the social nature of human beings. Both understand that human actions are not simply expressions of a person's internal will but are shaped by myriad social forces. Both must grapple with the consequences of deliberate wrongdoing, negligence, bad luck, and bad circumstances on the lives of human agents, those who interact with them, and the society at large. And both fields must grapple with the tension between fostering communal values and protecting the moral integrity of individuals.

My goal in this essay has been to spark a wide-ranging conversation between the two fields, not to provide an exhaustive outline of suitable topics for discussion.[57] At the same time, of course, my own normative commitments have shaped my presentation of the options. First, I have stressed the real narrativity of common law cases not only because of its resonances with narrative theology and ethics but because that type of narrativity honors the fact that what happens to particular people in the course of their particular lives is of the highest relevance. Each of these persons, signified by each name in each case, is created in the divine image and likeness. Second, I have lingered in the particularities of the cases I have discussed not only because doing so resonates with methodologies ranging from casuistry to feminist ethics to liberationist ethics but also because it is in those particularities that the dynamic relations between person, action, norm, and community are to be found. It is by paying attention to those dynamisms, I believe, that both legal scholars and Christian ethicists can best use our minds and hearts to build up the common good.

Notes

I would like to thank Bill Werpehowski for his generosity in reading and commenting on a draft of my presidential address under very tight time constraints, as well as the two anonymous *JSCE* reviewers for their helpful suggestions about how to turn the address into an essay. I would also like to express my gratitude to Kate Ward for both her editorial assistance and substantive suggestions to improve the manuscript. Finally, many thanks to Mark Allman and Tobias Winright for their insights and improvements to the text.

1. On August 9, 2014, a white police officer fatally shot Michael Brown, an unarmed African American eighteen-year-old man, in Ferguson, Missouri. The event precipitated a series of protests and civil unrest. In November 2014, a Missouri grand jury decided not to indict the police officer. In March 2015, the US Justice Department also declined to prosecute the police officer on the grounds that his use of force could not be shown to be "objectively unreasonable." Nonetheless, the Justice Department also charged the Ferguson Police Department with systemic discrimination against African Americans. Erik Eckholm and Matt Apuzzo, "Darren Wilson Is Cleared of Rights Violations in Ferguson Shooting," *New York Times*, March 4, 2015, A1. On July 17, 2014, a white police officer placed Eric Garner, a 350-pound African American man, in a choke hold, ignoring his cries that he could not breathe. Garner later died en route to the hospital. J. David Goodman and Al Baker, "Waves of Protest After Grand Jury Doesn't Indict Officer in Eric Garner Chokehold Case," *New York Times*, December 3, 2014, A1. Freddie Grey, a young African American man, died after falling into a coma while being transported in a police van on April 12, 2015. Baltimore's chief prosecutor charged six police officers with criminal wrongdoing in connection with the transport. Alan Blinder and Richard Pérez-Peña, "6 Baltimore Police Officers Charged in Freddie Grey Death," *New York Times*, May 1, 2015, A1.

2. See, e.g., Beverly Wildung Harrison, *Our Right to Choose: Toward a New Ethic of Abortion* (Boston: Beacon Press, 1984); Martin Rhonheimer, *The Ethics of Procreation and the Defense of Human Life: Contraception, Artificial Fertilization, and Abortion* (Washington, DC: Catholic University of America Press, 2010); Kristin Heyer, *Kinship across Borders: A Christian Ethic of Immigration* (Washington, DC: Georgetown University Press, 2012); Anthony Esolen, *Defending Marriage: Twelve Arguments for Sanity* (Charlotte, NC: Saint Benedict Press, 2014); David P. Gushee with Brian D. McLaren, Phyllis Tickle, and Matthew Vines, *Changing Our Mind* (Canton, MI: Read the Spirit Books, 2014), and James B. Martin-Schramm, *Climate Justice: Ethics, Energy, and Public Policy* (Minneapolis: Fortress Press, 2010).

3. *Williams v. Walker-Thomas Furniture Co.*, 350 F.2d 445 (C.A. D.C. 1965).

4. For a more detailed introduction, see, e.g., John H. Langbein, Renee Lettow Lerner, and Bruce P. Smith, *History of the Common Law: The Development of Anglo-American Legal Institutions* (Aspen, CO: Aspen Publishers, 2009); and Thomas Lund, *The Creation of the Common Law: The Medieval Year Books Deciphered* (Clark, NJ: Talbot Publishing, 2015).

5. Philip R. Wood, *Maps of World Financial Law*, 6th ed. (London: Sweet and Maxwell, 2008). Louisiana, settled by the French rather than the English, operates with a code-based system more common in continental Europe. See, e.g., George Dargo, *Jefferson's Louisiana: Politics and the Clash of Legal Traditions* (Clark, NJ: Lawbook Exchange, rev. ed. 2009).

6. See a complete list of common law countries at this University of Exeter website: "Common Law Countries," *University of Exeter*, http://socialsciences.exeter.ac.uk/law/undergraduate/commonlawcountries/, accessed July 14, 2015. For a complete list of countries and legal systems, see Central Intelligence Agency, World Factbook (Legal Systems), https://www.cia.gov/Library/publications/the-world-factbook/fields/2100.html. For a more nuanced account, see Christian Hertel, "Legal Systems of the World—An Overview," Notarius International, no. 1–2 (2009), http://www.notarius-international.uinl.org/DataBase/2009/Notarius_2009_01_02_hertel_en.pdf.

7. Alasdair MacIntyre, *After Virtue: A Study in Moral Theory*, 3rd ed. (Notre Dame, IN: University of Notre Dame Press, 2007).

8. Alasdair MacIntyre, *Whose Justice? Which Rationality?* (Notre Dame, IN: University of Notre Dame Press, 1988).

9. MacIntyre, *After Virtue*, 222.

10. An older but still helpful account is Edward H. Levi, "An Introduction to Legal Reasoning," *University of Chicago Law Review* 15, no. 3 (Spring 1948): 501–74.

11. There are differences between the Gospel stories and canonical cases. One law professor notes that "the decisions best remembered by our students are largely freaks—that is, single instances unlikely ever at any time to be repeated in the same form." Marvin Chirelstein, "Teaching Contracts," *Journal of Legal Education* 63, no. 3 (February 2014): 429–30, at 429.

12. *Wood v. Lucy, Lady Duff-Gordon*, 222 N.Y. 88, 118 N.E. 214 (1917).

13. For current perspectives, see, for example, María Pilar Aquino, "Latina Feminist Theology: Central Features," in *A Reader in Latina Feminist Theology: Religion and Justice*, ed. María Pilar Aquino, Daisy L Machado, and Jeanette Rodriguez, 134–60 (Austin: University of Texas Press, 2002); Cheryl Townsend Gilkes, "'Go and Tell Mary and Martha': The Spirituals, Biblical Options for Women, and Cultural Tensions in the African-American Religious Experience" (217–36); and Renita J. Weems, "Re-Reading for Liberation: African American Women and the Bible" (51–63), both in *Womanist Theological Ethics: A Reader*, ed. Katie Geneva Cannon, Angela D Sims, and Emilie M. Townes (Louisville, KY: Westminster John Knox Press, 2011). See also the following classic feminist and liberation texts: James H. Cone, *Black Theology and Black Power* (Maryknoll, NY: Orbis Books, 1997);

Gustavo Gutiérrez, Caridad Inda, and John Eagleson, *A Theology of Liberation: History, Politics, and Salvation*, 15th ann. ed. with new introduction (New York: Orbis Books, 1988); Elizabeth A. Johnson, *She Who Is: The Mystery of God in Feminist Theological Discourse* (New York: Crossroad, 1992); Elizabeth A. Johnson, *Truly Our Sister: A Theology of Mary in the Communion of Saints* (New York: Continuum, 2003); Aloysius Pieris, *An Asian Theology of Liberation* (Maryknoll, NY: Orbis Books, 1988); Elisabeth Schüssler Fiorenza, *But She Said: Feminist Practices of Biblical Interpretation* (Boston: Beacon Press, 1992); and Elisabeth Schüssler Fiorenza, *In Memory of Her: A Feminist Theological Reconstruction of Christian Origins*, 10th ann. ed. with a new introduction (New York: Crossroad, 1994); Juan Luis Segundo, *Liberation of Theology* (Maryknoll, NY: Orbis Books, 1976); and Elsa Tamez, *Bible of the Oppressed* (Maryknoll, NY: Orbis Books, 1982).

14. Schüssler Fiorenza, *But She Said*, 53.

15. Daisy L. Machado, "The Unnamed Woman: Justice, Feminists, and the Undocumented Woman," in *A Reader in Latina Feminist Theology: Religion and Justice*, ed. María Pilar Aquino, Daisy L. Machado, and Jeanette Rodriguez, 161–76 (Austin: University of Texas Press, 2002), 173.

16. M. Shawn Copeland, *Enfleshing Freedom: Body, Race, and Being* (Minneapolis: Fortress Press, 2010), 3.

17. *Rockingham County v. Luten Bridge Company*, 35 F.2d 301 (4th Cir. 1929). The case actually involved a struggle for control of the county board of commissioners. For background, see Barak D. Richman, "The King of Rockingham County and the Original Bridge to Nowhere," in *Contract Stories*, ed. Douglas G. Baird, 306–36 (New York: Foundation Press, 2006).

18. I have long used as my textbook Charles L. Knapp, Nathan M. Crystal, and Harry G. Prince, *Problems in Contract Law: Cases and Materials*, 7th ed. (New York: Wolters Kluwer, 2012).

19. *Hill v. Jones*, 725 P.2d 1115 (Ariz. Ct. App. 1986).

20. John T. Noonan Jr., *Persons and Masks of the Law: Cardozo, Holmes, Jefferson, and Wythe as Makers of the Masks*, rev. ed. (Berkley: University of California Press, 2002). Noonan writes: "No person itself, the law lives in persons. Rules of law are formed by human beings to shape the attitude and conduct of human beings and applied by human beings to human beings. The human beings are persons. The rules are communications uttered, comprehended, and responded to by persons. They affect attitude and conduct as communications from persons to persons. They exist as rules—not words on paper—in the minds of persons" (4).

21. *Dred Scott v. Sandford*, 60 US 393 (1857).

22. For a fuller account, see Paul Finkelman, *Dred Scott v. Sandford: A Brief History with Documents* (New York: Bedford/St. Martin's, 1997).

23. For a helpful overview, see Mayo Moran, "The Reasonable Person: A Conceptual Biography in Comparative Perspective," *Lewis & Clark Law Review* 14 (Winter 2010): 1233–83. See also Christopher Jackson, "Reasonable Persons, Reasonable Circumstances," *San Diego Law Review* 50 (August–September 2013): 651–706.

24. American Law Institute, Restatement (Second) of Torts §283A.

25. For a critique, see Kristin Harlow, "Applying the Reasonable Person Standard to Psychosis: How Tort Law Unfairly Burdens Adults with Mental Illness," *Ohio State Law Review* 68 (2007): 1733–60.

26. See BusinessDictionary.com. Black's Law Dictionary (10th ed.) has a similar definition: "A hypothetical person used as a legal standard, esp. to determine whether someone acted

with negligence; specif., a person who exercises the degree of attention, knowledge, intelligence, and judgment that society requires of its members for the protection of their own and of others' interests. The reasonable person acts sensibly, does things without serious delay, and takes proper but not excessive precautions." Henry Campbell Black, *Black's Law Dictionary*, ed. Bryan A. Garner, 10th ed. (St. Paul, MN: Thomson Reuters, 2014).

27. *Tillman v. Singletary*, 865 So.2d 350 (Miss. 2003).

28. *Gilbert v. Daimler-Chrysler*, 685 N.W.2d 391 (Mich. 2004).

29. *People v. McGrantham*, 56 A.D.3d 68 (NY Appellate Div., 2nd Dept., 2008).

30. Three helpful anthologies are Gene Outka and John P. Reeder, eds., *Prospects for a Common Morality* (Princeton, NJ: Princeton University Press, 1993); Lawrence S. Cunningham, ed., *Intractable Disputes about the Natural Law: Alasdair MacIntyre and Critics* (Notre Dame, IN: University of Notre Dame Press, 2009); and John Berkman and William C. Mattison III, eds., *Searching for a Universal Ethic: Multidisciplinary, Ecumenical, and Interfaith Responses to the Catholic Natural Law Tradition* (Grand Rapids, MI: Eerdmans, 2014).

31. Paul Ramsey, *Nine Modern Moralists* (Englewood Cliffs, NJ: Prentice Hall, 1962).

32. Edmond Cahn, *The Sense of Injustice* (Indianapolis: Indiana University Press, 1975).

33. *Wartzman v. Hightower Productions, Ltd.*, 456 A.2d 82 (Ill. Ct. Spec. App. 1983).

34. Gene H. Outka and Paul Ramsey, eds., *Norm and Context in Christian Ethics* (New York: Scribner, 1968).

35. For a history, see Fred W. Morgan and Karl A. Boedecker, "A Historical View of Strict Liability for Product-Related Injuries," *Journal of Macromarketing* 16, no. 1 (Spring 1996): 103–17. See also Kenneth W. Simons, "The Restatement (Third) of Torts and Traditional Strict Liability: Robust Rationales, Slender Doctrines," *Wake Forest Law Review* 44 (Winter 2009): 1355–82.

36. The key architect was Richard Traynor, widely acknowledged to be the most distinguished judge in California. Crucial cases include *Greenman v. Yuba Power Products*, 377 P.2d 897 (Cal. S.Ct.1963), *Vandermark v. Ford Motor Co.*, 391 P.2d 168 (Cal. S.Ct. 1964), and *Elmore v. American Motors Corp.*, 451 P.2d. 84 (Cal S.Ct.1969).

37. For an analysis of the doctrine before the rise of products liability, see Walton H. Hamilton, "The Ancient Maxim Caveat Emptor," *Yale Law Journal* 40 (June 1931): 1133–87.

38. For a discussion of solidarity and the law, see Cathleen Kaveny, *Law's Virtues: Fostering Autonomy and Solidarity in American Law* (Washington, DC: Georgetown University Press, 2012). For other recent discussions of solidarity, see, e.g., Meghan J. Clark, *The Vision of Catholic Social Thought: The Virtue of Solidarity and the Praxis of Human Rights* (Minneapolis: Fortress Press, 2014); Rebecca Todd Peters, *Solidarity Ethics: Transformation in a Globalized World* (Minneapolis: Fortress Press, 2014); and Miguel A. De La Torre, *Doing Christian Ethics from the Margins*, 2nd ed. (Maryknoll, NY: Orbis Books, 2014).

39. *Citizens United v. Federal Election Commission*, 558 U.S. 310 (2010).

40. For a helpful, although dated, introduction, see Steven Shavell, *Foundations of Economic Analysis of Law* (Cambridge, MA: Belknap Press of Harvard University Press, 2004).

41. *Williams v. Walker-Thomas Furniture*, 50 F.2d 445 (D.C. Cir. 1965). My account of the facts is taken from the majority opinion as well as from a fascinating recent article that delved extensively into the broader context of the case: Anne Fleming, "The Rise and Fall of Unconscionability as the 'Law of the Poor,'" *Georgetown Law Journal* 102 (2014): 1383–1441. See also Philip Bridwell, "The Philosophical Dimensions of the Doctrine of Unconscionability," *University of Chicago Law Review* 70 (Fall 2003) 1513–31; Eben Colby, "What Did the Doctrine of Unconscionability Do to the Walker-Thomas Furniture Company," *Connecticut Law Review* 34 (Winter 2002): 625–60; and Russell Korkobkin, "A

'Traditional' and 'Behavioral' Law-and-Economics Analysis of *Williams v. Walker-Thomas Furniture Company*," *University of Hawai'i Law Review* 26 (Summer 2004): 441–68.

42. *Williams v. Walker-Thomas Furniture Co.*, 198 A.2d 914 (D.C. C.A. 1964).

43. See the discussion of unconscionability in *Hume v. United States*, 132 U.S. 406 (1889).

44. *Williams v. Walker-Thomas Furniture Co.*, 198 A.2d at 916.

45. Ibid.

46. *Williams v. Walker-Thomas Furniture*, 50 F.2d at 447.

47. The most influential article in this vein is Richard Epstein, "Unconscionability: A Critical Reappraisal," *Journal of Law and Economics* 18, no. 2 (October 1975): 293–315.

48. Fleming, "Rise and Fall of Unconscionability," 1433–34.

49. Ibid., 1424–29.

50. See, e.g., "Consumer Reports Investigation: Would You Pay the Equivalent of 311 Percent Interest to Own a Big-Screen TV?," ConsumerReports.org, June 2011, http://www.consumerreports.org/cro/money/shopping/rentacenter/overview/index.htm.

51. Federal Trade Commission, Economic Report on Installment Credit and Retail Sales practices of District of Columbian Retailers (1968).

52. For background on social sin from Catholic and Protestant perspectives, see John Paul II, *Reconciliation and Penance* (apostolic exhortation), December 2, 1984, 15–16. http://w2.vatican.va/content/john-paul-ii/en/apost_exhortations/documents/hf_jp-ii_exh_02121984_reconciliatio-et-paenitentia.html, accessed May 1, 2015; Hormis Mynatty, "The Concept of Social Sin," *Louvain Studies* 16 (1991): 1–26; Jamie T. Phelps, "Joy Came in the Morning Risking Death for Resurrection: Confronting the Evil of Social Sin and Socially Sinful Structures," in *A Troubling in My Soul: Womanist Perspectives on Evil and Suffering*, ed. Emilie Maureen Townes, 48–64 (Maryknoll, NY: Orbis Books, 1993); Stephen G. Ray, *Do No Harm: Social Sin and Christian Responsibility* (Minneapolis: Fortress Press, 2003); Stephen G. Ray, "Embodying Redemption: King and the Engagement of Social Sin," in *Bonhoeffer and King: Their Legacies and Import for Christian Social Thought*, ed. Willis Jenkins and Jennifer McBride, 163–74 (Minneapolis: Fortress Press, 2010); Daniel J. Daly, "Structures of Virtue and Vice," *New Blackfriars* 92 (2011): 341–57; and Heyer, *Kinship across Borders*, chap. 2.

53. Heyer, *Kinship across Borders*, 37. See also Jamie Phelps, OP, who writes "Those who consciously participate in the construction and perpetuation of socially sinful institutions, which mediate existential and physical suffering and death, are participating in what is designated morally as social sin." Phelps, "Joy Came in the Morning," 49.

54. For a readable account of what transpired in the mortgage market collapse, see Kathleen C. Engel and Patricia A. McCoy, *The Subprime Virus: Reckless Credit, Regulatory Failure, and Next Steps* (New York: Oxford University Press, 2011).

55. Pieris, *Asian Theology of Liberation*, 16.

56. See, e.g., James F. Keenan, SJ, "Redeeming Conscience," *Theological Studies* 76 (2015): 129–47. See also Julie Clague, "Christian Conscience, Catholic Teaching and Lay Participation in Public Life," *International Journal of Public Theology* 5, no. 3 (2011): 296–313; Anthony Egan, "Conscience, Spirit, Discernment: The Holy Spirit, the Spiritual Exercises and the Formation of Moral Conscience," *Journal of Theology for Southern Africa* 138 (2010): 57–70; Kenneth R. Himes, "The Formation of Conscience: The Sin of Sloth and the Significance of Spirituality," in *Spirituality and Moral Theology*, ed. James Keating, 59–80 (New York: Paulist Press, 2000); Richard Rwiza, *Formation of Christian Conscience in Modern Africa* (Nairobi: Paulines Publications Africa, 2001); William Schweiker, "Responsibility and the Attunement of Conscience," *Journal of Religion* 93 (2013): 461–72; and Theron F.

Schlabach, *War, Peace, and Social Conscience: Guy F. Hershberger and Mennonite Ethics* (Harrisonburg, VA: Herald Press, 2009).

57. I am deeply hopeful for the future of the conversation between Christian Ethics and law. Gustavo Maya, a graduate student at Princeton, is working on the issue of unconscionability and domination. Andrew Forsyth, a graduate student at Yale, is writing a dissertation on the relationship of Christian ethics and the development of the common law. Daniel DiLeo, a PhD candidate at Boston College, is deeply involved in legal and theological issues related to climate change. And Conor Kelly, a BC graduate who is taking up a faculty position at Marquette this fall, has conducted research on the ethical issues involved in the Supreme Court decision on corporate free speech and campaign donations.

The Just War Tradition and International Law against War: The Myth of Discordant Doctrines

Mary Ellen O'Connell

The international law regulating resort to armed force, still known by the Latin phrase, the *jus ad bellum,* forms a principal substantive subfield of international law, along with human rights law, international environmental law, and international economic law. Among theologians, philosophers, and political scientists, just war theory is a major topic of study. Nevertheless, only a minority of scholars and practitioners know both *jus ad bellum* and just war theory well. Lack of knowledge has led to the erroneous view that the two areas are in conflict. This article responds to this misapprehension, explaining the deep compatibility of international law and just war theory. Today's *jus ad bellum,* especially the peremptory norm against aggression, is not only the law; it also forms the minimum threshold of a just war under just war theory. In other words, for a war to be morally just, it must at least be lawful. To go to war in violation of the *jus ad bellum* is both a legal and a moral wrong. Compliance not only fulfills the general moral good of obedience to law; it forms the first step toward fulfilling moral obligations in the grave area of war. This characterization of the relationship between law and morality is seen in the history of the legal prohibition on force and in the actual set of rules that make up the contemporary regime. Comprehensive and persuasive accounts of the *jus ad bellum* and just war theory consistently reflect this thesis.

AS I WRITE, THE WORLD IS AWASH IN WAR: AFGHANISTAN, THE Central African Republic, Colombia, Darfur, the Democratic Republic of Congo, Kashmir, Iraq, Libya, Mali, Pakistan, Somalia, Sudan, South Sudan, Syria, Ukraine, Yemen . . . These are places where organized armed groups are engaged in intense, sustained fighting. The list signifies unfathomable suffering in the form of mass death, physical and mental injury, dislocation, disease,

Mary Ellen O'Connell is the Robert and Marion Short Professor of Law and Research Professor of International Dispute Resolution—Kroc Institute for International Peace Studies, at the University of Notre Dame, 3104 Eck Hall of Law, Notre Dame, IN 46556-5677; MaryEllenOConnell@nd.edu.

Journal of the Society of Christian Ethics, 35, 2 (2015): 33–51

sexual violence, poverty, wildlife and habitat destruction, property damage, and loss of cultural heritage.

In the parallel world of ideas, we might expect to see major efforts toward ending this litany of tragedy. International law has a well-known rule at the heart of the United Nations Charter, Article 2(4), which imposes a broad, general prohibition on the use of armed force by states. Yet, instead of working to promote awareness and respect for Article 2(4), a major effort in the academy is toward finding exceptions to it. Few advocate compliance with the prohibition, let alone expanding its reach to, for example, prohibit civil war.[1]

Many international law scholars today advocate diluting the prohibition on force. They are joined by a number of prominent just war scholars.[2] Jean Bethke Elshtain is one who paid scant attention to the international law against war in her many publications on just war theory.[3] Omitting the law conflicts with the view that law is important to moral life and should be valued for its support of human flourishing.[4]

The theologian Nigel Biggar demonstrates the importance of international law in his book *In Defence of War*. Nevertheless, he is willing to dismiss international law when he determines that war is justified as a moral matter. His analysis omits the understanding that today's international legal regime against the use of force, especially the peremptory norm against serious violations of Article 2(4), is not only the law; it also forms the minimum threshold of just war theory. In other words, for a war to be just, it must at least be lawful. Thus, to go to war in violation of the UN Charter is both a legal and a moral wrong. This means that the peace regime of international law is a rare set of rules that is not only helpful as a general matter for fulfilling moral obligations; it also forms the first step toward fulfilling those obligations when it comes to war.

This characterization of the relationship between the law and morality of war is seen in the history of the legal prohibition on force and in the actual set of rules that make up the contemporary regime. Several reasons exist to explain how some just war theorists came to see the law and morality of war as separate and even discordant. Two explanations will be examined here. One concerns the effort to reduce international law to a system solely of positive law stripped of moral content. The other concerns the heavy influence of the political science theory of realism with its reliance on military force. Realism's normative support of war has filled the gap left by reliance on amoral positivism.

Common Origins

Many just war theorists are familiar with the history of just war theory but may be less aware that today's international law on force, the *jus ad bellum*, shares much of that history. The *jus ad bellum* of international law is generally traced to St. Augustine (354–430), who drew on earlier thinkers such as the Roman jurist Cicero to develop a concept of just war for his moral argument against the pacifism of early Christians.[5] International law historian Stephen Neff has written that the early Christians along with Confucians uniquely developed the concept that peace is the normal condition of human life and war the abnormal.[6] The Christian insistence on "the existence of a residual or background condition of peace in world affairs" was owing to "a powerful strain of radical pacifism inherent in Christian doctrine."[7] The "early Christian Church refused to accept war as moral in any circumstances and until AD 170 Christians were forbidden to enlist. This period of extreme pacifism lasted for three centuries after Christ."[8] Then Augustine introduced his just war theory, building on the work of St. Ambrose and others.[9] In a letter to St. Boniface, Augustine wrote: "Peace should be the object of your desire; war should be waged only as a necessity and waged only that God may by it deliver men from the necessity and preserve them in peace. For peace is not sought in order to [be] the kindling of war, but war is waged in order that peace may be obtained."[10] In addition to self-defense, Augustine considered it just to fight to restore stolen property, to deter future wrongs, and to promote Christianity.[11]

This last cause, the promotion of Christianity, helped to transform pacific Christians into persons for whom fighting to preserve and promote the faith and the interests of the church became a noble and virtuous thing.[12] Fighting in the Crusades or fighting to conquer and colonize all became justified under the argument that, once the world was converted to Christianity, peace would prevail and all fighting would end.

The list of just causes of war continued to grow, but some Christians sought to keep the ideal of pacifism alive. The "Peace of God" movement, for example, began in eleventh-century France and sought to protect the weak in time of war and to limit the days for warfare.[13] Faithful Christians respected the church's restrictions on war and its authority to enforce them. Historian Geoffrey Parker has found evidence that the rules against resort to war were effective, to an extent, in part because church teaching could be enforced through various sanctions. Bishops could compel obedience through the threat of excommunication or the withholding of sacraments. "We know, by the example of Henry IV, who knelt upon the snowy ground at Canoss before Gregory VII, how heavily such sanctions could weigh upon a rebel."[14]

Thomas Aquinas (1225–74) systematized the church's teaching on war into a set of law-like principles that famously included a declaration by a right authority, a just cause, and the right intention on the part of the authority.[15] Aquinas's restrictions on resort to war are part of his wider, general view of the importance of human law in the flourishing of humanity. As Cathleen Kaveny explains, "in considering human law, he shows how it can lead men and women to virtue in order to promote the common good."[16]

The fact that Aquinas had codified the just war theory proved helpful in preserving it through the long, bitter years of the Protestant Reformation and the era of imperial conquest of non-Christian people. As the Roman Catholic Church began to lose adherents, scholars like Francisco de Vitoria (1480–1546), a member of a group known as the Spanish Scholastics, built on Aquinas's work and began to see how the law itself could substitute for the authority of the pope and the Holy Roman emperor in intercommunal affairs.[17] However, Vitoria also promoted the idea that all parties to a conflict could be fighting with the right intentions and, therefore, doing nothing morally wrong.[18] This argument might be entirely appropriate when considering the fate of an individual's immortal soul. For constraining resort to war, however, it removed the just war theory's major objective constraint. If a leader deciding for war needed only to make up his own mind that his cause was just rather than consulting with authorities about whether the cause was objectively just and the opponent's cause unjust, the constraint of just war was lost. Another Scholastic, Francisco Suárez, pointed out the absurdity of considering all parties to a conflict as having a permissible just cause based on a leader's personal belief about his own cause. Suárez, however, still insisted on the ultimate authority of the pope to decide between competing claims of justice and had no ready solution when a party rejected the pope's authority.[19]

The idea of a subjectively just cause appealed to Protestant leaders. They believed they could rely on individual conscience when deciding for war, just as they had come to do when interpreting the Bible or in understanding their personal relationship with God. Alberico Gentili (1552–1608), an Italian Protestant who fled Italy for England and held the first Chichele professorship of public international law at the University of Oxford, is particularly associated with the individual leader's right to decide for oneself on the justness of a cause of war and the concomitant possibility that all sides in a conflict could be fighting lawfully. Writing in 1593, he said: "It is true, the prince is still considered as bound to examine the justice of his cause before he engages in war; . . . whatever the result of his decision may be, it never affects the legality of his action, since war is nothing more than a procedural device that may be resorted to even for the redress of a probable wrong without exposing either party to the blame of injustice."[20]

Hugo Grotius (1583–1645), the renowned Dutch Protestant legal scholar, theologian, and diplomat, argued strenuously for law as the substitute for the pope and the emperor. Grotius rejected the thinking of those, like Gentili, who wanted to leave each prince supreme in his own realm, relying on his own conscience as to the justice of his cause of war or the need to comply with a treaty.[21] Grotius disliked the results of leaving matters to the consciences of European leaders of his day. The devastating Thirty Years' War (1618–48) was, at least on the surface, about clashing consciences—Catholic versus Protestant and Protestant versus Protestant. For Grotius, resort to war could be judged against objective standards, as he argued in his seminal work, *On the Law and War and Peace* (1625). He wanted to help end the Thirty Years' War and mitigate its barbarism. He hoped to inspire greater humanity in the conduct of the war and encourage the establishment of a legal order superior to the warring factions after the war. A group of legally coequal sovereign states did in fact emerge in western Europe under the treaties known as the Peace of Westphalia (1648). Grotius's comprehensive treatise provided the legal blueprint for the new world order.

To have an impact, Grotius responded to those who shared Gentili's view as well as to those who took seriously the advice of Niccolò Machiavelli (1469–1527) in his book *The Prince*.[22] Machiavelli's prince, like Gentili, saw no law above sovereigns, rejecting even the restraint of listening to conscience. For the prince, no action was unjust if a ruler found it expedient. Grotius, by contrast, according to Hersch Lauterpacht, saw "an intimate connexion between the rejection of the ideas of 'reason of State' and the affirmation of the legal and moral unity of mankind. [Grotius] insist[ed] that if no association of men can be maintained without law, 'surely also that association which binds together the human race, or binds many nations together, has need of law.'"[23] Grotius saw law as possible in every type of human community because he understood human beings as "being intrinsically moved by a desire for social life, endowed with an ample measure of goodness, altruism, and morality, and capable of acting on general principle and of learning from experience."[24]

By contrast, law above nations was impossible for Machiavelli's prince and the prominent seventeenth-century political theorist Thomas Hobbes because of their view that, again in the words of Lauterpacht, "man is essentially selfish, anti-social, and unable to learn from experience."[25] For them, "the basis of political obligation is interest pure and simple; the idea of a sense of moral duty rising supreme over desire and passion is a figment of imagination. . . . This is the typical realistic approach of contempt towards the 'little breed' of man."[26] Grotius felt no such contempt. He believed in the Christian law of love and held the optimistic view of people's capacity reflected in Christianity. He built his conception of international law on the Spanish Scholastics, moving further in the direction of a secular understanding of natural law than they had in order to avoid the religious controversies swirling as he wrote. He emphasized the use of human reason to understand the law ordained by nature and the universal principles of morality. He explained that while much of international law is positive law, natural law is the more important part because it provides the basis of positive authority of law and is the measure of the aspirations of law.

After Grotius, Emmerich de Vattel has had the greatest influence on international law. His principal work, *The Law of Nations* (1758), was widely read for decades. He shared with Grotius an understanding that a higher law governed human affairs, but he left it to each individual sovereign to judge his own compliance. No sovereign could sit in judgment of another. Vattel preceded and inspired Jean Bodin (1530–96) and others usually given credit for the rise of the idea of absolute state sovereignty. Vattel's vaunted view of states and their leaders was also aligned with the rise of science and the importance of objective evidence. The combination undermined natural law theories supporting the authority of international law as law over states, leaving positivism as the dominant theory. Positivism holds that binding law comes through the affirmative acts of states and other international actors. Treaties, which require affirmative consent, and customary international law, which is built on state practice and state expression of *opinio juris*, can be explained by positivism. General principles and rules of *jus cogens*, however, require natural law explanations. Despite Vattel, natural law explanations persisted for decades to explain the legally binding nature of law against war.[27]

In many accounts of the nineteenth century, however, international legal historians write that the rise of positivism and the concept of absolute state sovereignty meant the end of legal restraint on force. In fact, scholars and government officials in Europe as well as North and South America continued to recognize just war theory. Few European governments failed to justify the use of force in terms of some lawful end. Prominent international law scholars in Britain and the United States crusaded to eliminate natural law jurisprudence from the "science" of international law, but natural law played too central a role and continues to do so.[28] Indeed, in recent years, new interest has emerged in understanding the place of natural law in the international legal system.[29]

Even as just war theory continued to play a role in international law, Christians committed to Christ's teaching of peace and love of neighbor continued to oppose war as immoral and to demand alternatives for the settlement of disputes. In the United States, pacifist Christians (including Quakers, Mennonites, and the Amish) who sought refuge from Europe inspired a significant secular peace movement. That movement, which spread back to Europe, made the advancement of peace through law a major goal.[30] By the time of the First World War, the global peace movement had grown to impressive size, calling for international law and tribunals to replace war. Largely through pressure from the peace movement, alternatives to war were added to the agenda of the first Hague Peace Conference of 1899. That conference resulted in multilateral treaties requiring states to attempt alternatives to war and led to the founding of the Permanent Court of Arbitration.

Many in the mass peace movements of Europe and North America, however, wanted more. They wanted robust legal obligations prohibiting resort to war, and they wanted an international court of law, not just arbitral tribunals.

Leaders of the movement reasoned that if the US Supreme Court could keep the peace among semisovereign states, a world court could do the same for the international community. In 1905 and 1906, techniques of mediation and fact-finding were used to good effect to end the Russo-Japanese War and to prevent a war between Russia and Britain. All of these factors and others led to the convening of another Hague Peace Conference in 1907. No court was established then either, but a treaty outlawing resort to force to collect debts was an important positive law step supporting the just war theory's restriction of war to just causes only.

Christians such as Jane Addams (1860–1935), of Hull House fame, advocated mediation and arbitration among European states as the first signs of impending war emerged prior to the outbreak of the First World War.[31] She and other campaigners were ignored, but following the disaster of the First World War, states agreed to far stricter positive limits on the right to resort to war in the Covenant of the League of Nations. League members also decided to finally form a world court. The United States, having not joined the League, worked to promote peace in another form, the Kellogg-Briand Pact, a treaty that comprehensively prohibited resort to war as an instrument of national foreign policy: "The High Contracting Parties solemnly declare in the names of their respective peoples that they condemn recourse to war for the solution of international controversies, and renounce it as an instrument of national policy in their relations with one another."[32]

It was at this time that the great Austrian jurist Hans Kelsen (1881–1973) began to lend his considerable talent to international law and the legal problem of war. He wrote that the contemporary just war theory was found in the Treaty of Versailles, the Covenant of the League of Nations, and the Kellogg-Briand Pact. He cited Augustine, Aquinas, and Grotius as the founders of the doctrine and identified nineteenth-century political theories of absolute state sovereignty as responsible for its decline. Kelsen argued against absolute sovereignty as destructive not only of the just war theory's limitations on war but of all of international law.[33]

During the Second World War, Kelsen fled to the United States where he continued to write on law against war and international organization. He wrote treatises promoting the United Nations and recognized the just war tradition in the UN Charter's prohibition on the use of force.[34] Within a few years following the end of the Second World War, however, it was not Kelsen but his intellectual rival, Hans Morgenthau (1904–80), who rose to greater and more enduring prominence. Morgenthau was a disciple of Hobbes; Kelsen, of Grotius. Morgenthau founded the realist school of American foreign policy and that school's view that a US president should not, as a normative matter, heed the UN Charter restrictions on the use of force.[35]

Contemporary Convergence

In the United States today and increasingly in other countries, Morgenthau's view of the charter is dominant. This is a curious development when it comes to just war theorists since the contemporary legal regime on the use of force continues to reflect its origins in the teaching of Augustine and Aquinas. The charter, like just war theory, generally prohibits war, requiring an affirmative showing that resort to armed force is on the basis of one of the exceptions to the prohibition.[36] In the case of the charter, force is permitted in only two cases: when needed for self-defense and when authorized by the Security Council.

The international legal regime on the use of force includes other rules, most importantly the principles of necessity and proportionality.[37] These principles apply to uses of force in self-defense or with Security Council authorization. Necessity requires a demonstration that force is a last resort and has a good chance of success in achieving the lawful objective as defined by the charter.[38] If states can demonstrate necessity, they must also demonstrate that the method of force used will not result in disproportionate loss of life or destruction compared to the value of the legitimate objective. Necessity and proportionality are not expressly mentioned in the charter, but the International Court of Justice has held that they are a binding part of the law restricting resort to force.[39]

The principles of necessity and proportionality also apply to states taking part in civil war. Most states do not interpret the UN Charter as reaching the use of force within states, and we have many examples of states citing a right to assist governments in suppressing internal rebellion by organized armed groups. France, for example, has intervened in its former colonies more than twenty times since 1962 on the basis of an invitation by a government.[40] There is an argument, however, that Article 2(4) should prohibit outside intervention in civil war even on the side of a government. Assisting rebels is already prohibited as a violation of the principle of nonintervention, if not a violation of Article 2(4).

Other rules that may be relevant include the law of state responsibility and human rights law. State responsibility says that a state acting in self-defense may only attack a state responsible for the armed attack that gave rise to the right of self-defense.[41] Similarly, the Security Council would violate a state's rights if the council authorized resort to force against a state that bore no responsibility for a threat or breach of the peace. In addition to rules on responsibility, it is increasingly clear that human rights law has a wide and pervasive reach. In international armed conflict, a use of force without a right to resort to force means that the right to life of those killed would be violated.[42] Those who take up arms in a civil war violate the right to life of the people they kill.

Attempts to get around this comprehensive law on resort to force, the *jus ad bellum*, have centered on three groups of arguments: creative reinterpretation of the meaning of self-defense, criticism of the Security Council for "inaction" when the council does not authorize force, and moral arguments for force asserted to be superior to the legal restrictions.[43] All three categories of arguments continue to be made despite the fact that in 2005, the United Nations' entire membership came together for a world summit. The purpose of the summit was to consider a three-year review of the charter and the United Nations as a whole following the 2003 invasion of Iraq. The preliminary report of the panel carrying out the review concluded that for the international community, the measure of legitimacy must be international legality. Law is the common code of all humanity. It is not the moral discernment of any particular national or religious leader, ethicist, or theologian. The UN's membership unanimously re-endorsed the charter's rules for peace in 2005. The only significant change was a clarification that the Security Council could consider serious human rights violations within one country to be a threat to international peace.[44]

UN members agreed to continue to support the Security Council as the only body with the legal right to authorize force in a situation other than emergency self-defense. No other institution presently exists that could command similar support. Biggar argues that only a world government is an adequate institutional substitute for unilateral assessment of the right to go to war.[45] Against this view, theologian Esther Reed writes that, in positing a requirement of world government that will never come to pass, Biggar deflects "attention from the need for laws to restrain and regulate armed conflict, and fail[s] adequately to expose the political 'loves' of great world powers in the determination of the laws of war."[46] Indeed, since Aquinas, just war restraint has relied on concepts of law, not government.

Biggar's view draws on a popular impression borne of accounts concerning the massacres in Rwanda (1994) and Srebrenica (1995): that the Security Council does not authorize military force when it should.[47] This impression has led some to conclude that states may disregard the Security Council because the council does not authorize force often enough. In fact the council had authorized "peace enforcement" missions for both Rwanda and Srebrenica, but the United Nations was never able to attract sufficient numbers of troops or the type of weapons specified by the UN's experts.[48] The presence of these inadequate troop deployments gave people a false sense of security. In Srebrenica, Bosnians would not have crowded into "safe areas" where they were slaughtered in large numbers. In Rwanda, Tutsis would not have trusted their Hutu neighbors as Tutsi rebels rolled back into the country to renew the civil war and oust the Hutu government. In these cases, as in so many others, the council failed to consider whether by authorizing this sort of force it did the United Nations would do more good than harm.[49]

Further, the argument for ignoring the council rests on the view that states will do a better job by deciding unilaterally or outside the council process for war. The facts do not support this claim either. The abject failure of the 2003 Iraq invasion is well known. The results in Kosovo were little better. The failure of states to heed the limits a Security Council resolution placed on the use of force in Libya by outside states is another stark example. In March 2011 the council authorized the protection of civilians as the Libyan leader, Col. Muammar Gaddafi, sought to suppress an insurrection in Benghazi. The council authorized the use of military force by NATO countries and others to protect civilians. The United Kingdom and France quickly escalated the conflict on the legal argument that the only way to protect civilians was to remove Gaddafi. That was a wholly unreasonable interpretation of the resolution. Proponents of force argued that civilians in Benghazi were threatened imminently by Gaddafi's forces; they made no mention of their interest in ending the Gaddafi regime. Over thirty thousand people died in the four months of the NATO intervention. Violence, revenge attacks, and widespread fighting have continued ever since. Today Libya is spoken of as a failed state. Ample evidence demonstrates that outside intervention in civil wars does not lead to the positive outcomes predicted by unilateral intervention advocates.[50]

Even if states had a better track record, it would be no basis for ignoring the Security Council's authority. Discussing efficacy and the alleged need to use military force for various desiderata is reminiscent of the debate about the efficacy of torture. Jeremy Waldron believes that discussions of the law and morality against torture should not consider whether torture could be effective in generating intelligence.[51] He is correct that efficacy is irrelevant to the absolute legal and moral ban on torture. Still, academics with access to relevant facts have a responsibility to share them.

Too few people seem to be aware, for example, of the Statement on Interrogation Practices drafted and signed by twenty of the US Army's most accomplished interrogators with a combined two hundred years of interrogation experience.[52] Their statement rejects the use of coercive interrogation practices as unreliable. The statement is consistent with much of the academic literature on torture.[53] Similarly, the use of military force for various humanitarian purposes is unlawful and immoral; it is also a counterproductive tool of change.[54]

If the Security Council rejects a request for force, the law requires compliance with the decision and attention to lawful and effective alternatives for responding to the problems of human rights, governance, arms control, and terrorism. Invasions by superior military powers of weaker ones, such as in 1990 when Iraq invaded Kuwait or in 2014 when Russia occupied Crimea, are the sort of cases where military force might be justified to reverse unlawful outcomes.[55] Even for these cases and certainly for more complex ones, international law offers multiple forms of nonviolent response. The UN Charter calls on states to respect international law, to participate in global economic development, to protect human rights, and to rely on peaceful mechanisms for the resolution of disputes. Charter Article 33 recommends negotiation, mediation, arbitration, adjudication, and the use of international institutions to resolve disputes.

By the 1980s the charter's prohibition on the use of force came to be spoken of as *jus cogens*—a norm of peremptory character. A standard account explains that "some rules of international law are recognized by the international community of states as peremptory, permitting no derogation. These rules prevail over and invalidate international agreements and other rules of international law in conflict with them. Such a peremptory norm is subject to modification only by a subsequent norm of international law having the same character."[56] Peremptory norms need to be explained according to natural law theory because positivism is inadequate to explain how a norm that has no basis in consent is binding and superior to consent-based rules.[57] The perception that Article 2(4) is a peremptory norm acknowledges the rule's origin in just war theory and its connection to fundamental moral teaching.

Indeed, the general contemporary regime of international law restricting the use of force bears close resemblance to the moral teaching of the Roman Catholic Church on resort to war as restated in the Catechism:

> The strict conditions for *legitimate defense by military force* require rigorous consideration. The gravity of such a decision makes it subject to rigorous conditions of moral legitimacy. At one and the same time:
>
> - the damage inflicted by the aggressor on the nation or community of nations must be lasting, grave, and certain;
>
> - all other means of putting an end to it must have been shown to be impractical or ineffective;
>
> - there must be serious prospects of success;
>
> - the use of arms must not produce evils and disorders graver than the evil to be eliminated. The power of modern means of destruction weighs very heavily in evaluating this condition.
>
> The evaluation of these conditions for moral legitimacy belongs to the prudential judgment of those who have responsibility for the common good.[58]

The Catechism sets the bar above international law's minimum requirements. The injury must be "lasting, grave, and certain" and the response must not inflict "evils and disorders graver than the evil to be eliminated." Moreover, the Catechism only refers to "aggression" and "defense," not force in response to human rights violations, arms control, or terrorism.[59] Logically, therefore, an ethical leader in a case of self-defense or in seeking or giving Security Council authorization needs to first consider the law on resort to force and then, if resort would be lawful, consider whether it would also be moral. The World

Council of Churches reached this conclusion in 2011 when it developed its doctrine of "Just Peace," which is founded on considerations of international law as well as respect for the United Nations and grassroots peace activism.[60]

In one important respect, contemporary international law and the just war theory of Aquinas do differ. For the state *qua* state, international legal responsibility for wrongful conduct is generally found by looking at objective facts and not at what a leader intends. "In the conditions of international life, which involve relations between complex communities acting through a variety of institutions and agencies, the public law analogy of the *ultra vires* act is more realistic than a seeking for subjective *culpa* [fault] in a specific natural person."[61] In international law, if a state violates the prohibition on the use of force, it does not matter if the state's leader did not intend to violate the law. International law works more as a strict liability system than one based on fault. The response to such a violation, however, does not take the form of punishment. Force today is lawful only to counter force to end a continuing violation. Reprisals and force to deter future violations are strictly unlawful.

Since the Nuremberg Tribunal, however, international law has concerned itself with the intentions of national leaders. A national leader who violates the prohibition on the resort to force might be found guilty of the crime of aggression. Thus, Biggar's moral argument for waging wars to punish is morally retrograde when compared with the contemporary legal regime. Individuals may be punished for aggression in national and international courts. There is no right to use war to punish a whole people for a leader's wrongful conduct.[62]

Ideological Division

How did it come to be, therefore, that so many just war theorists fail to take international law into account, do so imprecisely, or argue it is moral to override the rules against resort to force? We can find prominent examples of these positions in the just war literature assessing NATO's 1999 war against Serbia over Kosovo, the 2003 invasion of Iraq, and the use of military force on behalf of Syria's antigovernment rebels. Important causes of this disconnect are the tendency to rely only on positivism as the single explanatory theory of international law, excluding natural law, as well as the rise of realism as the dominant school of political science.

Positivism, based as it is on material evidence, is adequate to explain much of international law. It holds that treaties bind because of express consent, and rules of customary international law bind on the basis of tacit consent indicated by state practice and *opinio juris*. Positivism, however, does not explain why consent should bind a party that wishes to withdraw consent. Nor does positivism explain how rules, including certain general principles of law (e.g., good faith) and international law's peremptory norms (e.g., against torture), bind without consent. These aspects of the international legal system are better explained by natural law theory.

Few international lawyers still have access to natural law explanations, however, owing to the dominance of positivism. Positivism today has no overt connection to religious and ethical traditions. It has no means of explaining why rules supporting peace might be morally superior to other rules or state interests—positivism is famously "amoral."[63] Realism has largely filled the normative gap left by the suppression of natural law. Realism provides evidently secular foundations for *raison d'état*, in particular, the amassing of military strength. Hans Morgenthau taught that a national leader's decision to use military force cannot be fettered, as a normative matter, by international law against war.[64]

Morgenthau deserves credit for beginning the decisive turn of political science and international relations toward realism and away from classic international law.[65] In Morgenthau's world, international law does play some role in the decisions of national leaders respecting trade, diplomacy, and the like—just not in the area of war.[66] He remains inordinately influential. His book *Politics among Nations* is read by every student of international relations, certainly in the United States.[67] Morgenthau's view of power and the importance of using military force is reflected in the work of his contemporary, theologian Reinhold Niebuhr. Niebuhr's "Christian realism" is also based on a dark view of human nature and advocates the use of military force against communism without much apparent regard for international law.[68] The theologian Paul Ramsey also wrote during the Cold War on the moral use of force.[69]

Certainly other scholars sought to retain a central role for international law. David Hollenbach, for example, warned in the 1980s that just war theory was moving away from Aquinas's position, presuming that war is sinful, to one presuming war is just so long as it is waged by legitimate authorities.[70] Elshtain was one who persisted in ignoring international law. In the spring of 2001 she was invited to give one of the prestigious "Grotius Lectures" at the opening session of the annual meeting of the American Society of International Law. In a twenty-six-page article developed from the lecture, she never uses the term "international law" and refers to the UN Charter only once when discussing a reference to it by Michael Walzer.[71] Yet Elshtain said she was analyzing the "*jus ad bellum*," the term used by contemporary international law scholars to refer to the international law on the use of force. She concludes that invading other countries to remove dictators or for other "humanitarian" reasons could meet the just war requirement of a just cause. She has nothing to say about the charter's prohibition on such a use of force. She omits any consideration of the morality and rationality of law compliance. Yet, as discussed above, international law on the use of force is the common code used by all states and intergovernmental organizations—regardless of the religious or ethical views of individual leaders. International law is what the world shares in addressing the normative issue of resort to force. Failing to consider international law, even to explain why she found it unimportant to do so, before an audience of hundreds who explore international law as their principal scholarly discipline, underscores the point here of how isolated just war theory has become from international law.

A few years later in an interview in which she defended the morality of the 2003 invasion of Iraq, Elshtain did mention international law but got it wrong. She said, "Given the history of that regime [of Saddam Hussein], the violation of UN resolutions, the material breach of protocols at the end of the 1991 Gulf War—in international law, a material breach is a *casus belli*, a legitimate occasion for war—I can't think of anyone who said no case could be made."[72] The only just cause of war according to the consensus of the international community is reflected in the charter, which does not include "material breach." In using the term, Elshtain likely picked up on part of the attenuated argument of the United States and the United Kingdom for invading Iraq without a Security Council resolution. Lawyers for the two governments proposed that resolutions from 1991 provided authorization because Iraq was in "material breach" of them. As the world learned during the United Kingdom's inquiry into the decision to go to war in Iraq, Britain's experts on international law clearly advised that "fresh" authority was needed. The 1991 resolutions could not authorize force in 2003. While Elshtain was right that some sort of case for legality could be made, the great weight of opinion was that the invasion was unlawful.[73]

Some may argue that expecting Elshtain to know the international law on the use of force is asking too much. An academic, however, who publicly seeks to justify or advocate for the use of violence on the scale of war needs to have knowledge of the world's law on the subject. As set out above, to know the morality of war is to know the international law on the use of force.

Philosopher Jeff McMahan supplies a more worrying example. While Elshtain either ignores international law or gets it wrong, McMahan goes as far as saying that the UN Charter rules against resort to war are "crude," "simplistic," and "largely obsolete."[74] The only international law of any relevance to just war scholars is, in his view, the law on the conduct of war, such as the Geneva Conventions. Yet even this law, for McMahan, is "quite distinct" from morality, diverging in important ways.[75] This means apparently there is no moral duty to comply with international law on the use of force. He seems unaware of the points raised above concerning the convergence of just war theory and international law on the use of force. Given that the international community just recommitted to these rules in 2005, they are obviously not "obsolete." His other characterizations have no bearing on whether this law is binding. In fact, no state in the world officially denies that these rules bind.

Biggar has a more sophisticated understanding than McMahan of the international law on the use of force and the moral arguments in support of international law. He writes: "There are good moral reasons of a prudential sort why we should be loath to transgress positive law even for the noblest of motives."[76] Nevertheless, he is willing to defend as moral the unlawful resort to force by NATO over Kosovo and the 2003 invasion of Iraq. These were cases, he says, of "natural justice" trumping positive law.[77] As discussed above, however, Biggar's conclusion about Kosovo and Iraq rests on his misperception that positive law relies on punishment, which he believes is lacking in the international system, and on factual errors respecting the Rwanda and Srebrenica tragedies. His comment regarding "natural justice" indicates a failure to appreciate that the international law against the use of force incorporates the natural law peremptory norm against aggression. The resort to unlawful war violates both positive and natural law. The content of Biggar's "natural justice" may differ from the moral reasoning leading to the natural law norm against the use of force, but the analysis above urges caution in adopting any theory in conflict with twenty-one centuries of legal and moral teaching on war.

Conclusion

Since the adoption of the UN Charter in 1945, respect for the general prohibition on the use of force appears to be in decline. Reasons include the rise of the political ideology of realism, which places great confidence in military power; the concomitant decline in knowledge of international law; and the development of just war theory that either ignores or rejects the legal prohibition on force. This last reason rests in some cases on failure to realize that the international law against war and just war theory today have the same roots in early Christian teaching. Today's legal prohibition of aggression is a peremptory norm explained on the basis of ancient natural law. Complying with the law as a general matter is thus consistent with moral conduct. To be moral, any resort to war must also be lawful, and—even if lawful—war may still not meet additional moral objections. In short, humanity has placed its most powerful normative barriers against the "madness" of war.[78]

Notes

1. Two notable exceptions are Christine Gray of Cambridge University and Olivier Corten of the Free University of Brussels. See Olivier Corten, *The Law against War: The Prohibition on the Use of Force in Contemporary International Law* (Oxford: Hart Publishing, 2010); and Christine Gray, *International Law and the Use of Force*, 3rd ed. (Oxford: Oxford University Press, 2008).

2. For a recent example of such scholarship, and citations to Paul Ramsey and James Turner Johnson, who also promote greater resort to force with little regard for international law, see Johnathan Stonebraker and Sarah Irving, "The Just War Tradition Reconsidered: Protestantism and International Law," *Oxford Journal of Law & Religion* 3, no. 3 (2014), 373–92, doi:10.1093/ojlr/rwu043.

3. See, e.g., Michael J. Matheson, "Just War and Humanitarian Intervention: Comment on the Grotius Lecture by Jean Bethke Elshtain," *American University International Law Review* 17 (2001): 27–33; Richard Falk points to a similar weakness in Michael Walzer's promotion of humanitarian intervention in Michael Walzer, "On Humanitarianism," *Foreign Affairs*, July–August 2011, http://www.foreignaffairs.com/author/michael-walzer. See also Richard Falk, "Can Humanitarian Intervention Ever Be Humanitarian?" August 4, 2011, http://mwcnews.net/focus/editorial/12577-humanitarian-intervention.html?tmpl=component.

4. See, e.g., Cathleen Kaveny, *Law's Virtues: Fostering Autonomy and Solidarity in American Society* (Washington, DC: Georgetown University Press, 2012), 29, citing Aquinas, *Summa Theologica*, I-II, q. 91, art. 4. See also the famous defense of the morality of law, Lon Fuller, *The Morality of the Law* (New Haven, CT: Yale University Press, 1964). For a connection between international law and morality, see Jean Porter, *Ministers of the Law: A Natural Law Theory of Legal Authority* (Grand Rapids, MI: Eerdmans, 2010), 339–51; and for international legal restraints on resort to war and morality, see Esther Reed, *Theology for International Law* (London: Bloomsbury Publishing, 2013), chap. 4.

5. See also Wilhelm G. Grewe, *The Epochs of International Law*, trans. Michael Byers (Berlin: De Gruyter, 2000), 108–11; and Arthur Nussbaum, *A Concise History of the Law of Nations*, rev. ed. (New York: Macmillan, 1954), 35.

6. Stephen C. Neff, *War and the Law of Nations: A General History* (Cambridge: Cambridge University Press, 2005), 31, 39. See also his masterful newer treatment of the history of international law generally, *Justice among Nations* (Cambridge, MA: Harvard University Press, 2014).

7. Neff, *War and the Law of Nations*, 39–40.

8. Ian Brownlie, *International Law and the Use of Force by States* (Oxford: Clarendon Press, 1963), 5 (citation omitted). Of course these are complex social facts. The critical issue for international law is that a persuasive argument began to develop supporting war as sometimes moral.

9. Ibid.

10. Leon Friedman, ed. *The Law of War: A Documentary History* (New York: Random House, 1972), 7.

11. Joachim von Elbe, "The Evolution of the Concept of the Just War in International Law," *American Journal of International Law* 33 (1939): 665.

12. Geoffrey Parker, "Early Modern Europe," in *The Laws of War: Constraints on Warfare in the Western World*, ed. Michael Howard, George J. Andreopoulos, and Mark R. Shulman (New Haven, CT: Yale University Press, 1994), 43.

13. Ibid., 41.

14. Jacques Dumas, "Sanctions of International Arbitration," *American Journal International Law* 5 (1911): 937.

15. Grewe, *Epochs of International Law*, 109; see also Von Elbe, "Evolution of the Concept," 669; and Brownlie, *International Law*, 6.

16. Kaveny, *Law's Virtues*, 29.

17. Von Elbe, "Evolution of the Concept," 674–75; and Nussbaum, *Concise History of the Law of Nations*, 79–91.

18. See Nussbaum, *Concise History of the Law of Nations*, 80.

19. Ibid., 87–90.

20. Quoted in von Elbe, "Evolution of the Concept," 678.

21. Mary Ellen O'Connell, *The Power and Purpose of International Law: Insights from the Theory and Practice of Enforcement* (New York: Oxford University Press, 2008), chap. 1.

22. Hersch Lauterpacht, "The Grotian Tradition in International Law," *British Yearbook of International Law* 23 (1946): 31. For an argument that *The Prince* was intended as satire, see Garret Mattingly, "Machiavelli's The Prince: Political Science or Political Satire," *American Scholar* 27 (1958): 482–91.

23. Ibid., citing Grotius, *De jure belli ac pacis* (1623), Proleg., 23.

24. Ibid., 24.

25. Ibid.

26. Ibid., 24–25.

27. Neff, *Justice among Nations*, 261–69.

28. O'Connell, *Power and Purpose of International Law*, 57–98.

29. See, e.g., opinions of Judge Antonio Cançado Trindade, especially his dissenting opinion in *Jurisdictional Immunities of the State (Ger. v. Italy)* 2012 I.C.J. 179 (February 10).

30. David Cortright, *Peace: A History of Movements and Ideas* (Cambridge: Cambridge University Press, 2008).

31. J. C. Farrell, *Beloved Lady: A History of Jane Addams' Ideas on Reform and Peace* (Baltimore: Johns Hopkins University Press, 1967), 140–41, 150–53.

32. Kellogg-Briand Pact 1928, http://www.yale.edu/lawweb/avalon/imt/kbpact.htm.

33. O'Connell, *Power and Purpose of International Law*, 48–51.

34. Douglas Johnston refers to the charter as the "sacred text of the world community." Douglas M. Johnston, *The Historical Foundations of World Order: The Tower and the Arena* (Leiden: Martinus Nijhof, 2008), 164, 708.

35. See Martti Koskenniemi, *The Gentle Civilizer of Nations: The Rise and Fall of International Law 1870–1960* (Cambridge: Cambridge University Press, 2004), 454–55.

36. UN Charter Art. 2(4): "All Members shall refrain in their international relations from the threat or use of force against the territorial integrity or political independence of any state, or in any other manner inconsistent with the Purposes of the United Nations."

37. Judith Gardam, *Necessity, Proportionality and the Use of Force by States* (Cambridge: Cambridge University Press, 2004).

38. Ibid.

39. Legality of the Threat or Use of Nuclear Weapons, Advisory Opinion, 1996 I.C.J. 226, 245 (July 8).

40. See Andrew Hansen, "The French Military in Africa," Report to the Council on Foreign Relations, February 8, 2008, http://www.cfr.org/france/french-military-africa/p12578. More interventions have occurred since the report was issued.

41. The International Court of Justice has ruled on this point in a number of important cases, in particular, *Military and Paramilitary Activities in and against Nicaragua (Nicar. v. U.S.)*, 1986 I.C.J. 14 (June 27), and *Armed Activities on the Territory of the Congo (Dem. Rep. Congo v. Uganda)*, 2005 I.C.J. 168, paras. 146, 301 (December 19).

42. See, e.g., William Schabas, "*Lex specialis*? Belt and Suspenders? The Parallel Operation of Human Rights and the Law of Armed Conflict, and the Conundrum of *Jus ad bellum*," *Israel Law Review* 40 (2007): 592–613.

43. "Military action for humanitarian purposes or to counter acts of terrorism is not easily accommodated within existing legal rules on the use of force." Ian Johnstone, "The Plea of 'Necessity' in International Legal Discourse: Humanitarian Intervention and Counter-Terrorism," *Columbia Journal of Transnational Law* 43 (2005): 337.

44. 2005 World Summit Outcome, GA Res. A/60/L.1, September 15, 2005, 22–23.

45. Nigel Biggar, *In Defence of War* (Oxford: Oxford University Press, 2013), 241.

46. Esther Reed, "In Defence of the Laws of War," *Society of Christian Ethics*, 2013 (unpublished remarks on file with the author).

47. For accurate accounts of both tragedies, see Report of the Secretary-General Pursuant to General Assembly Resolution 53/55 (1998) (Srebrenica Report), UN Doc. November 15, 1999; and Report of the Independent Inquiry into the Actions of the United Nations During the 1994 Genocide in Rwanda, UN Doc. December 15, 1999 (Rwanda Report).

48. See the Srebrenica and Rwanda Reports.

49. In addition to Rwanda and Srebrenica, consider the authorization of French interventions in Ivory Coast and other former colonies, peacekeeping missions to Haiti over many years, and the new Peace Intervention Brigade that has used offensive force in the complex conflict of the Democratic Republic of the Congo.

50. See, e.g., Goran Peic and Dan Reiter, "Foreign-Imposed Regime Change, State Power and Civil War Onset, 1920–2004," *British Journal of Political Science* 41, no. 3 (2011): 453–75; and Maria Stepan and Erica Chenoweth, *Why Civil Resistance Works: The Strategic Logic of Nonviolent Conflict* (New York: Columbia University Press, 2008).

51. These views were shared with the author during a four-year consultation sponsored by the Center of Theological Inquiry (2006–10) on the subject of theology and international law. The particular concern of the group was the use of torture by the United States after 9/11. For Waldron's wider views, see *Torture, Terror, and Trade-Offs: A Philosophy for the White House* (Oxford: Oxford University Press, 2010).

52. The Statement on Interrogation Practices by 20 Former US Army Interrogators for the US Congress Committee on Armed Forces, July, 2006, http://www.law.cam.ac.uk/faculty-resources/summary/statement-on-interrogation-practices-by-20-former-us-army-interrogators-for-us-congress-committee-on-the-armed-services-jul-2006/4848.

53. For a general overview, see Mary Ellen O'Connell, "Affirming the Ban on Harsh Interrogation," *Ohio State Law Journal* 66 (2005): 1259–64.

54. Stonebraker and Irving are among those who see war as efficacious, despite the facts, when they write, "churches speak out against evil, but do not advocate any form of effective means to stop that evil," by which they mean military intervention. Stonebraker and Irving, "Just War Tradition Reconsidered," 17.

55. Nor is the case as clear as that of Kuwait's liberation, given the questionable way the Ukraine government took power at the time Russia moved to occupy Crimea.

56. American Law Institute, Restatement (Third) of the Foreign Relations Law of the United States § 102, cmt. k (1987).

57. For a more detailed discussion, see Mary Ellen O'Connell, "*Jus cogens:* International Law's Higher Ethical Norms," in *The Role of Ethics in International Law*, ed. Donald Earl Childress III (Cambridge: Cambridge University Press, 2011), 78–100.

58. *Catechism of the Catholic Church*, Part 3, *Life in Christ*, sec. 2, ch. 2, art. 5, para. 2309, http://www.vatican.va/archive/ccc_css/archive/catechism/p3s2c2a5.htm.

59. In a May 2013 letter to the Obama administration, Bishop Richard E. Pates expressed doubts that drone attacks against terrorism suspects could meet the requirements of para.

2309. See Richard E. Pates, Letter to Mr. Thomas E. Donilon, May 17, 2013, available at http://www.usccb.org/issues-and-action/human-life-and-dignity/war-and-peace/arms-trade/upload/letter-to-administration-congress-on-drones-2013-05-17.pdf.

60. World Council of Churches, *An Ecumenical Call to Just Peace* (2011), http://www.overcoming violence.org/fileadmin/dov/files/iepc/resources/ECJustPeace_English.pdf.

61. James Crawford, *Brownlie's Principles of Public International Law*, 8th ed. (Oxford: Oxford University Press, 2012), 556.

62. Biggar's view conflicts with the law.

63. This was H. L. A. Hart's argument in the famous debate with Lon Fuller, published in the *Harvard Law Review* in 1958.

64. Hans Morgenthau, *Politics among Nations: The Struggle for Power and Peace*, 5th ed. (New York: Knopf, 1978), 281.

65. See Christoph Frei, *Hans J. Morgenthau: An Intellectual Biography* (Baton Rouge: Louisiana State University Press, 2001), chap. 1–4.

66. Morgenthau was also influenced by the positivist-realist perspective of the anti–natural law international law scholar Lassa Oppenheim. Benedict Kingsbury, "Legal Positivism as Normative Politics: International Society, Balance of Power and Lassa Oppenheim's Positive International Law," *European Journal of International Law* 13 (2002): 435.

67. The first edition was Hans Morgenthau, *Politics among Nations: The Struggle for Power and Peace* (New York: McGraw-Hill, 1948). See also note 65 above for a citation to Morgenthau's fifth and final edition. Later editions revised by Morgenthau's students and followers have also appeared.

68. Reinhold Niebuhr, *Moral Man and Immoral Society: A Study in Ethics and Politics* (New York: Charles Scribner's Sons, 1932), 111.

69. Ramsey omits discussion of international law in his major work on war, *The Just War: Force and Political Responsibility* (New York: University Press of America, 1968).

70. David Hollenbach, *Nuclear Ethics: A Christian Moral Argument* (New York: Paulist, 1983), 14–16. See also John W. Lango, *The Ethics of Armed Conflict: A Cosmopolitan Just War Theory* (Edinburgh: Edinburgh University Press, 2014); and Michael W. Brough, John W. Lango, and Harry van der Linden, eds., *Rethinking the Just War Tradition* (Albany: State University of New York Press, 2007).

71. Jean Bethke Elshtain, "The Third Annual Grotius Lecture: Just War and Humanitarian Intervention," *American University International Law Review* 17, no. 1 (2001): 10, http://digitalcommons.wcl.american.edu/cgi/viewcontent.cgi?article=1211&context=auilr.

72. Elshtain quoted in Ken Trainor, "Just War: Divinity School Professor Considers the Moral Necessities for War," *University of Chicago Magazine*, May–June 2010, http://magazine.uchicago.edu/1006/investigations/just-war.shtml.

73. Even a long-time US government lawyer who often defends US uses of force, Sean Murphy, concluded the invasion was unlawful; see Sean Murphy, "Assessing the Legality of Invading Iraq," *Georgetown Law Journal* 92 (2004), 173.

74. Jeff McMahan, "Laws of War," in *Philosophy of International Law* 493, ed. Samantha Besson and John Tasioulas (Oxford: Oxford University Press, 2010), 496.

75. Ibid., 494.

76. Biggar, *In Defence of War*, 216.

77. Ibid.

78. Pope Francis referred to war as "madness." "War Is Madness," *New York Times*, September 13, 2014, http://www.nytimes.com/video/multimedia/100000003112598/pope-francis-war-is-madness.html.

Just War and International Law: A Response to Mary Ellen O'Connell

Nigel Biggar

The following remarks were prepared as a response to Mary Ellen O'Connell's plenary address, "The Just War Tradition and International Law against War: The Myth of Discordant Doctrines," at the 2015 annual meeting of the Society of Christian Ethics. O'Connell's essay appears in this issue of the *Journal of the Society of Christian Ethics* (vol. 35, no. 2). After noting some points of agreement, the response discusses five main issues: the moral complexity of "peace," the consonance of a peremptory norm against aggression with just war thinking, the formative role of controversial political convictions in the interpretation of international law, the political defects of the current international legal system, and the efficacy of military intervention.

Points of Agreement

Let me begin by noting important points of qualified agreement between Mary Ellen O'Connell and me. First of all, we both follow Grotius in preference to Machiavelli and Hobbes. We both deny that the state of nature is a morality-free zone. Even where there are no social contracts or positive laws, the natural moral law applies.[1] However, whereas I use this to argue that sometimes natural law trumps positive law, O'Connell argues that positive law incorporates natural law completely and that no gap remains between them.

Second, we both agree upon the importance of international law—and my appreciation of international law certainly owes a lot to reading O'Connell and talking with her over the past five years. Nevertheless, we give different accounts of that importance. I think it is important as a means of developing a common understanding of the norms that should govern relations between states and thus of fostering international trust and reducing unpredictability in international relations—the kind of unpredictability, for example, that allowed

Nigel Biggar is regius professor of moral and pastoral theology and director of the McDonald Centre for Theology, Ethics and Public Life, University of Oxford, Christ Church, Oxford OX1 1DP, United Kingdom; nigel.biggar@chch.ox.ac.uk.

a local Balkan crisis in 1914 to escalate into the First World War. I do not expect the common understanding to be at all perfect; I believe only in tense consensus. O'Connell is more optimistic and ambitious. She sees the importance of international law lying in its being the means of achieving, ultimately, such perfect international consensus as to make war redundant.

Third, we both agree that war involves grave evils, that it is better to resolve conflicts by nonbelligerent means if we can *and if we may*, and that some kinds of injustice are better endured than removed by armed force.

Before I proceed to discuss some topics on which we disagree, let me clarify one misunderstanding. I argue that just war is basically punitive in form. O'Connell reads this as implying that I approve of a belligerent state engaging in "acts of reprisal." I do not: I have been explicit in making a distinction between the waging of just war and the meting out of discriminate justice by postwar courts.[2]

Points of Disagreement

Now I turn to five topics on which O'Connell and I disagree.

Peace Is Not Simple

In my view O'Connell has too uncomplicated a view of peace, tending to set peace as simply good against war as simply bad. This is my first main point of critical engagement: peace is not simple. Like war, it too involves evils, tragedies, ambiguities, risks, and uncertainties. The fact that the United Kingdom and the United States stayed at peace in 1994 left Ratko Mladić at peace to seriously disturb the peace of the seven thousand men and boys he slaughtered at Srebrenica; the fact that we, the international community, stayed at peace in 1995 left the Hutu at peace to seriously disturb the peace of the eight hundred thousand Tutsis they hacked to death in Rwanda; and, were we to stay at peace in 2015, we would leave the self-styled Islamic State at peace to atrociously disturb the peace of the Yazidis, Kurds, and Iraqis. Peace is not simple: peace here does not spell peace there. I cannot take "peace" at face value. I need to know what kind of peace, whose peace, and at whose cost. And because peace is not simple, I do not accept the novel notion of a presumption against war. Those who argue for "not-war" have to justify themselves, too.

Just War Thinking

I have a couple of quibbles with O'Connell's reading of its history. I think it is misleading to say that "the early Christian Church refused to accept war as moral in any circumstances"—as I explained in the first chapter of *In Defence of War*.[3] I also think it misleading to imply, without any qualification, that just war thinking helped to justify the Crusades.[4]

But my main quarrel concerns O'Connell's statement that contemporary international law's "peremptory norm against aggression" is a restatement of Christian just war doctrine. I disagree. Unlike some modern philosophical accounts of just war, the Christian tradition from Augustine to Grotius does not denigrate aggression and sanctify defense. Both aggression and defense can be just or unjust depending on the circumstances of motive, intention, and proportion. A tyrant's self-defense might well be unjust; a Christian prince's aggressive (or offensive) intervention to stop widespread cannibalism or human sacrifice might well be just. Whereas for post-1945 international law the paradigm of justified war is self-defense, for *classical* Christian just war thinking, it is the rescue of the innocent—and rescue can take both defensive *and* aggressive forms. The fact that the doctrine of the Responsibility to Protect as a whole has not yet received sufficient international support to achieve undisputed status as international law means that the law and classical Christian just war thinking remain at odds with one another.[5] The claim that there is a gap between them is no myth.

However, O'Connell's argument is that the "just war" as now interpreted by the *Catechism of the Catholic Church* and by the World Council of Churches (WCC) in its doctrine of "just peace" *does* endorse a "peremptory norm against aggression." When I first read what O'Connell says about this, I found myself stopped in my tracks: after all, why should *my* reading of just war prevail over the combined authority of Rome and Geneva? Eventually, however, I managed to reassemble my nerve and then I remembered that I am a Protestant and that, with all due respect, I am not bound to agree with the Catholic Catechism. As for the WCC, ever since it bought uncritically into left-wing ideology in the 1970s, its authority in my own Church of England lies somewhere between negligible and zero.

But maybe I should listen anyway. Maybe it makes good sense that the classical tradition of just war should be so developed as to affirm a novel "peremptory norm against aggression." After all, there is no intrinsic merit in remaining classical. Well, I have listened, and I just do not think that it makes sense.[6] Either the norm is wrong or it is formal and vacuous. As I explained immediately above, "aggression" need not be unjust if it comprises military intervention to rescue the victims of grave injustice. If one believes, as O'Connell seems to, that such intervention can never be proportionate and thus prudent, an absolute norm against it would make sense.[7] However, as I shall argue at the very end of this essay, I do not think that O'Connell has made a cogent case for the universal inefficacy of humanitarian intervention. Therefore, I think that an absolute norm against it is wrong. But maybe "aggression" here is supposed to mean not merely an offensive or interventionist mode of action but an unjust attack. If so, the very definition involves a norm against it, but not one that tells us anything useful about what makes it unjust. Therefore it is formal and vacuous.

The Hermeneutics of International Law

Those of us who have long labored in the fields of Christian theology are well acquainted with the notion that the meaning of a sacred text depends on the manner of its interpretation. While the words on the page do constrain the ways in which they may be taken, their interpretation is bound to involve extra-textual factors such as the moral and political assumptions of the interpreter. That is all very familiar—at least to anyone who is not a biblical literalist.

So when I, as a Christian ethicist, come to the interpretation of the sacred texts of international law, I expect the same. And in examining disputes about the legal status of military intervention for humanitarian purposes that has not been authorized by the UN Security Council, I have found what I expected. For example, on the one hand, Ian Brownlie argued (as O'Connell now argues) that international law's prohibition of unauthorized military intervention is unequivocal. Its meaning is plain. In support, Brownlie cited, inter alia, the text of the UN Charter and the statements of a variety of national legal authorities. He also denied that the history of state practice evidences an informal international consensus about a unilateral right to intervene, which could be held to constitute customary international law.[8]

Against Brownlie, Richard Lillich argued that the doctrine of humanitarian intervention can claim the authority of jurists such as Hugo Grotius and Emer de Vattel; that pre-charter history furnishes ample evidence of relevant state practice; that the charter does not "specifically abolish the traditional doctrine"; that the charter attributes *two* main purposes to the postwar international legal regime, the maintenance of peace *and* the protection of human rights; and that humanitarian intervention serves the latter.[9]

Brownlie implied that such a "flexible and teleological interpretation of treaty texts" is weak, while Lillich approvingly cited another commentator's view of Brownlie's interpretation as "an arid textualist approach."[10]

The struggle between textualist and contextualist lawyers for the true meaning of international law resembles nothing so much as the struggle between conservative and liberal theologians for the true meaning of the Bible. In both cases, while the text itself does constrain what can plausibly be attributed to it, the variety of plausible interpretations is considerably determined by extratextual factors. In the case of the interpretation of international law, prominent among these factors are the empirical, political, and moral assumptions that legal interpreters bring to the texts of treaties and to the "text" of the history of state practice.

Accordingly, I observe that Brownlie assumed a generally cynical view of the motives of governments when he wrote of "the near impossibility of discovering an aptitude of governments in general for carefully moderated, altruistic, and genuine interventions to protect human rights" and that "the whole field [of humanitarian intervention] is driven by political expediency and capriciousness."[11] In response, I would argue that the claim that genuinely moral action is altruistic and entirely lacking in self-interest is a particular ethical view, that it wrongly claims the authority of Kant, and that it is false. There is nothing wrong with the pursuit of self-interest, provided that it is constrained by duty to others. As Yves Simon wrote, "What should we think, truly, about a government that would leave out of its preoccupations the interests of the nation that it governs?"[12] We need a far more ethically discriminate understanding of national interest.[13]

Similarly, it is not necessary to attribute the selectivity of humanitarian intervention to grubby expediency and capriciousness. Sometimes the decision to intervene in one place rather than another is an expression of the moral virtue of prudence. And besides, even when it is a symptom of inconsistency, surely it is better to be inconsistently responsible than consistently irresponsible.

Brownlie also expressed skepticism about the efficacy of military action, arguing that civil conflicts "cannot be 'solved' by a use of force," and that those advocating military intervention "need to produce more evidence" that such action achieves benefits greater than the costs it imposes.[14] Whatever its truth, this is not a textual claim but an empirical one—and an empirical claim that involves an inarticulate and controversial moral ranking of the values that comprise costs and benefits (for example, bare lives, a just political environment, and the maintenance of international order), together with an opaque and spurious "calculation" of them.

Such skepticism about military action also fuels O'Connell's opposition to unilateral humanitarian intervention, which determines her interpretation of international law. In her 2008 book, *The Power and Purpose of International Law*, she reckons that one of the two main objections to military intervention for humanitarian purposes is "the severe pragmatic difficulty of protecting human rights through war."[15] She suggests that the desire to see more military force used to enforce human rights "*may* result from an unrealistic understanding of the good that can actually be accomplished by major armed force."[16] She writes, "*One can question* whether the US attack [on Libya in 1986] was proportional."[17] And she suggests that the continued use of massive aerial bombardment after the fall of the Taliban regime in 2001 "was *arguably* disproportionate."[18]

The issue that Brownlie and O'Connell raise is an important one, but it is a moral-empirical issue, not a legal-textual one. Moreover, as is bound to be the case, their judgments of proportionality are necessarily less than scientific, highly controversial, and difficult to substantiate. O'Connell herself signals this by the consistently tentative manner of her assertions: "may result," "one can question," "arguably." I shall return to the crucial empirical issue of the efficacy of military action shortly.

The interpretation of international law offered by Richard Lillich is, of course, no less influenced by extratextual considerations. However, unlike the textualists, Lillich thought that international law *should* be interpreted with reference to such factors. Thus, he quoted with approval Michael Reisman's comment that Brownlie lives "within the paper world of the Charter," and he complained that "there is little evidence that Brownlie has contemplated the costs in terms of life and dignity his construction of the Charter demands," and that he makes no mention of the problem of "the obvious procedural defects" of the UN.[19] Reisman's and Lillich's view of Brownlie's position is roughly my own view of O'Connell's.

The Defects of the Current International Legal System

O'Connell acknowledges that the UN Security Council process has been subject to heavy criticism. But she does not tell us what the criticisms have been, nor does she respond to them. I do not disagree that the current arrangement might be the best available means of negotiating international agreement about the use of force—or, to be more honest, the best way of containing unresolved *dis*agreement. Nevertheless, I think that the process does have serious deficiencies, that the Security Council's refusal to authorize force should not always be regarded as the final word, and that therefore we need a more subtle *and political* understanding of the authority of international law. I am certainly not alone in thinking this.

The basic problem with the current arrangement under the UN Charter is this. Should a future tyrant embark upon a Final Solution for a minority group within the sovereign borders of his own state, *should* he not be dissuaded from this policy by diplomatic or economic pressure, *should* he restrain himself from invading a neighbor and posing a threat to regional peace, and *should* the politics of the Security Council preclude agreement to authorize armed intervention, *then* international law would end up presiding over the next Holocaust. To me that seems to be a problem—but not, as far as I can tell, to O'Connell.

I think that international legal arrangements that can prevent effective sanctions against genocide or massive and systemic atrocity serve to undermine the law's authority. That is why international lawyers such as Richard Lillich and Christopher Greenwood have felt the need to qualify the interpretation of the text of the UN Charter by appeal to other authorities such as customary law or state practice. Other international lawyers prefer to take their legal cue strictly from the UN Charter but nevertheless to acknowledge a higher moral authority. Thus, commenting on NATO's 1999 intervention in Kosovo, Martti Koskenniemi, who is "widely considered to be one of the leading historians and philosophers of international law,"[20] has written that "most lawyers—including myself—have taken the ambivalent position that it was both formally illegal and morally necessary."[21] Moreover, dissatisfaction with current textual law is what has driven Kofi Annan and others to try and have the doctrine of the Responsibility to Protect (R2P) formally recognized as international law—so far with limited success. O'Connell would have us accept the verdict of the United Nations' 2005 World Summit as final. But it cannot be. According to the UN Special Adviser on R2P, Jennifer Welsh, as currently represented on the UN's own website, *should* a state manifestly fail to protect its own people against genocide and ethnic cleansing, that responsibility would then fall to the international community.[22] The question of what should happen if the Security Council were to fail to act remains, as ever, a nettle ungrasped.

It seems to me that any adequate account of international law has to take into account its political character and the fact that political interests will continue to conflict and political agreement often remain out of reach. Adam Roberts, professor emeritus of international relations at Oxford and former president of the British Academy, puts it thus: "the era since 1945 has witnessed—alongside the new institutions of the United Nations and the multilateral diplomacy that it embodies—the continuation of all the classical institutions of the international system: great powers, alliances, spheres of interest, balances of power and bilateral diplomacy."[23] The vision of a comprehensive security system based on the United Nations is an "impossible ideal," and the aspiration to create it is "hopelessly optimistic."[24] This is because the fault lies not simply with the unruly behavior of particular states, nor even with the right to veto in the Security Council, but with "deep and enduring problems of world politics."[25] "The Security Council," he writes, "is not an impartial judicial body, but a deeply political organisation" whose members have "very different perspectives on the world and the threats it faces."[26]

The Efficacy of Military Intervention

I think that the root of the disagreement between O'Connell and me is not legal but moral and empirical. I do not accept her claim that her legal case is ultimately independent of her reading of "the facts" about the efficacy of military intervention. I believe that she reads the law in the way she does—and in a way that not all lawyers do—*because* of her reading of the facts; and she reads the facts selectively. So she tells us that defenders of humanitarian intervention have yet to respond to "the expert studies showing that outside intervention in civil wars does not lead to the positive outcomes predicted . . . quite the opposite." And she adds that this data "clearly supports" the legal and moral case against intervention.[27]

While it is true that I have not yet read the particular literature she invokes in support, I have read enough to know that there are very considerable voices that disagree with O'Connell, three of whom I cite in *In Defence of War*, each of them with front-line experience in Bosnia or Iraq or Afghanistan, each properly chastened by their experience, yet each still adamant that intervention *can* work. Over these, O'Connell passes in complete silence.[28] I also know that assessing the consequences of action is an enormously problematic and complex affair, which is not just a matter of piling up "objective facts" but of weighing and ordering them in a careful argument. So it seems quite clear to me that the data does not "clearly support" O'Connell's legal position—or if it does, that she has not clearly shown it.

Notes

1. By "natural moral law" I mean simply a set of moral principles that are given in and with created human nature, and that therefore apply even in a "state of nature," where human customs, conventions, or laws are lacking. This is what Grotius espoused in the seventeenth century. On this occasion I do not mean any more specific concept, and certainly not the twentieth-century one asserted in Pope Paul VI's infamous encyclical *Humanae vitae*, according to which all forms of contraception are immoral.

2. See Nigel Biggar, *In Defence of War* (Oxford: Oxford University Press, 2013, 2014), 170–71.

3. Ibid., 27.

4. According to conversation with Christopher Tyerman, medieval historian and author of *God's War: A New History of the Crusades* (Cambridge, MA: Harvard University Press, 2009), the rationale of the earliest Crusades was that of Holy War, namely, obedience to divine command. This was quite different from the "just war" reasoning later developed in the late twelfth and early thirteenth centuries by the schools in Bologna and Paris, and epitomized by Thomas Aquinas, which invoked Augustine and operated in terms of moral norms prescribed by natural law and the law of nations. By the fifteenth and sixteenth centuries, the popes (e.g., Eugenius IV in the 1430s on the Portuguese conquest of the Canary islands, and Innocent IV in the 1500s on the conquest of the Indies) no longer gave a crusading justification at all for the conquest of the Americas but sought to justify it in terms of natural law and the law of nations as necessary to protect free trade or missionaries. That is to say, scholastic just war thinking actually *replaced* "Holy War" thinking. It was used to justify "crusades," but at the same time it constrained them by legal norms and so changed what they were about. Thus, in the sixteenth century, Francisco de Vitoria contradicted the conquistadors' claim that they were warranted in waging war to force the benefits of the Gospel upon the Caribbean natives and to civilize them, arguing that war could only be justified by the need to stop egregious sins "against nature" such as the practices of cannibalism and mass human sacrifice.

5. As I explain later in this essay, since the 2005 World Summit, international law has recognized a sovereign state's responsibility to protect its own people against genocide and ethnic cleansing and has affirmed that, should a state fail to do what it should, the responsibility would fall to the international community. What is not yet widely accepted—and so not yet part of international law—is the right of states to exercise the responsibility to protect by intervening, should the Security Council fail to authorize action.

6. Actually, the *Catechism of the Catholic Church* does not explicitly affirm any such peremptory norm. See part 3, section 2, chapter 2, article 5.iii.2307-17 (London: Geoffrey Chapman, 1994), 496–98. It is true, however, that some recent papal statements, if taken at face value,

are pacifist. Thus, for example, Pope Francis wrote in September 2014: "War is never a necessity, nor is it inevitable. Another way can always be found: the way of dialogue, encounter and the sincere search for truth" ("War Is Not Inevitable: Message to the International Meeting Organised by Sant' Egidio," *L'Osservatore Romano*, September 10, 2014, http://www.osservatoreromano.va/en/news/war-not-inevitable). While in the previous month he was widely reported as affirming the use of (armed?) force against the Islamic State of Iraq and Syria (ISIS), he did not quite do that. What he said on August 18, 2014, was this: "In these cases, where there is an unjust aggression, I can only say that it is licit to stop the unjust aggressor. I underscore the verb 'stop.' I'm not saying 'bomb' or 'make war,' just 'stop'." Alan Gomez, "Pope Backs Military Force to Protect Iraq Minorities," *USA Today*, August 18, 2014, http://www.usatoday.com/story/news/world/2014/08/18/pope-oks-protecting-iraq-minorities-wants-un-ok/14241193/. Quite what it could mean to "stop" ISIS without waging war against them, I have absolutely no idea.

7. Since a "peremptory" norm is one that brooks no contradiction, I take it to be the same as an "absolute" one.

8. In his 1974 exchange with Richard Lillich, Brownlie argued that, before 1945, history can be found to yield only "one possible genuinely altruistic action," namely, the 1860 intervention in Syria to prevent further massacres of Maronite Christians. The collective intervention in Greece in 1827, he said, did not use a legal justification; and the American intervention in Cuba in 1898 was justified by the Joint Resolution of Congress in terms of American interests. In the period between the UN Charter and 1974, Brownlie found state practice of humanitarian intervention "totally lacking." Ian Brownlie, "Humanitarian Intervention," in *International Law and the Use of Force: Cases and Materials*, ed. Mary Ellen O'Connell (New York: Foundation Press, 2005), 301.

9. Richard Lillich, "Humanitarian Intervention: A Reply to Ian Brownlie and a Plea for Constructive Alternatives," in *International Law and the Use of Force: Cases and Materials*, ed. Mary Ellen O'Connell (New York: Foundation Press, 2005), 307–8. As evidence of pre-Charter state practice of humanitarian intervention, Lillich cited collective action against Ottoman suppression of the Greeks in 1827; against Ottoman persecution of Christian Cretans in 1866–68; against Turkish oppression in the Balkans in 1877–78; and against Turkish oppression in Macedonia in 1903–8.

10. Brownlie, "Humanitarian Intervention," 300; and Lillich, "Humanitarian Intervention: A Reply to Ian Brownlie," 308.

11. Brownlie, "Humanitarian Intervention," 303, 304.

12. Yves R. Simon, *The Ethiopian Campaign and French Political Thought*, ed. Anthony O. Simon, trans. Robert Royal (Notre Dame: University of Notre Dame, 2009), 55.

13. For a fuller discussion of the morality of national interest, see Biggar, *In Defence of War*, 231–33.

14. Brownlie, "Humanitarian Intervention," 304.

15. Mary Ellen O'Connell, *The Power and Purpose of International Law: Insights from the Theory and Practice of Enforcement* (New York: Oxford University Press, 2008), 181. The other main objection is that intervention weakens the legal regime for peace (ibid.).

16. Ibid., 148.

17. Ibid., 183. Emphasis added.

18. Ibid., 188. Emphasis added.

19. Lillich, "Humanitarian Intervention: A Reply to Ian Brownlie," 313, 311. Martti Koskenniemi agrees: a formalistic, strictly textual reading of international law "seems arrogantly insensitive to the humanitarian dilemmas involved." Koskenniemi, "'The Lady Doth

Protest Too Much': Kosovo and the Turn to Ethics in International Law," *Modern Law Review* 65, no. 2 (March 2002): 163.

20. Claus Kreß, professor of international security law and the law of armed conflict at the University of Köln, in personal email correspondence, January 3, 2014.

21. Koskenniemi, "'The Lady Doth Protest Too Much'," 162.

22. See Jennifer Welsh on the video mounted in March 2014 at www.un.org/en/preventgeno cide/adviser/responsibility.shtml.

23. Adam Roberts and Dominik Zaum, *Selective Security: War and the United Nations Security Council since 1945*, Adelphi Paper 395 (London: International Institute for Strategic Studies, 2008), 24.

24. Ibid., 76, 18.

25. They point out that no veto prevented the Security Council from addressing the Khmer Rouge's auto-genocide in Cambodia from 1975–79, and that council members have sometimes acted in spite of a veto, for example, over the Suez crisis in 1956. Ibid., 37, 19.

26. Ibid., 20, 28. Edward Luck concurs: "As an innately political body composed of member states with individual interests . . . , the [Security] Council's determinations about . . . whether a government's . . . suppression of some of its population . . . threaten[s] its neighbors or more distant states . . . may often be controversial." *UN Security Council: Practice and Promise*, Global Institutions Series (London: Routledge, 2006), 82–83.

27. Mary Ellen O'Connell, "The Just War Tradition and International Law against War: The Myth of Discordant Doctrines," *Journal of the Society of Christian Ethics* 35, no. 2 (Fall–Winter 2015), 33–51.

28. I refer to Rory Stewart and Gerald Knaus, *Can Intervention Work?* Amnesty International Global Ethics Series (New York: W. W. Norton, 2011); and Paddy Ashdown, *Swords and Ploughshares: Bringing Peace to the 21st Century* (London: Weidenfeld & Nicholson, 2007).

When the Law Does Not Secure Justice or Peace: Requiem as Aesthetic Response

Elise M. Edwards

This essay assesses the possibilities for poetic-liturgical compositions, such as requiems, to promote Christian public engagement when legal frameworks are perceived to be inadequate for securing justice. This essay addresses the perception that legal statutes and procedures failed to honor the personhood of two particular African American males and discusses how aesthetic responses have been used to counter the devaluing of their lives. One such response, Marilyn Nelson's poem *Fortune's Bones: The Manumission Requiem,* questions the law's failure to protect an eighteenth-century enslaved man. Another requiem memorializes Michael Brown after the teen's killing by a police officer in 2014. This essay discusses these particular aesthetic responses and then evaluates the possibilities for the requiem as a Christian practice of civic engagement by appropriating Charles Mathewes's articulation of hopeful citizenship. In cases when the law is perceived to be complicit in devaluing African American personhood, liturgy can be a meaningful Christian response.

IN THE SECOND HALF OF 2014, SOCIAL MEDIA USERS ADOPTED the hashtag (#) #BlackLivesMatter to affirm the value of African American life in response to legal decisions that many people perceived to be racist. Hashtags are keywords, concepts, or commentary about statements posted on blogs and social media sites that can then be used as a way to search for related items and group them. Feminist Alicia Garza explains that she, along with Patrisse Cullors and Opal Tometi, created #BlackLivesMatter "as a call to action for Black people. . . . Black Lives Matter is an ideological and political intervention in a world where Black lives are systematically and intentionally targeted for demise. It is an affirmation of Black folks' contributions to this society, our humanity, and our resilience in the face of deadly oppression."[1] On November 24, 2014, the frequency of #BlackLivesMatter tweets increased dramatically by those angered by the grand jury decision in Ferguson, Missouri, to not indict police officer Darren Wilson for shooting and killing Michael Brown, an

Elise M. Edwards, PhD, is a lecturer in the Department of Religion at Baylor University, One Bear Place #97284, Waco, TX 76798-7284; elise_edwards@baylor.edu.

Journal of the Society of Christian Ethics, 35, 2 (2015): 63–81

eighteen-year-old African American male. The popularity of the hashtag and, more importantly, the sentiment behind it convey anger and frustration at the way black lives are mistreated. Varied forms of protests are used to counter the devaluing of black bodies and lives evident throughout US history. As a Christian ethicist, it is my conviction that these protests belong not only in the streets and social media but in Christian communities like churches, Christian universities, and academic guilds.

This essay assesses the possibilities for particular kinds of artistic responses to contribute to social transformation. Poetic and liturgical compositions like the requiem can enable Christians to respond to the subversion of justice. The perception that unjust legal statutes and procedures have too often failed to honor African American personhood is addressed by referencing the tragic ends of two particular African American males, Fortune (ca. 1740–98) and Michael Brown (1996–2014). The sections that follow introduce two specific requiems and discuss their historical context, content, and artistic form and the ethical issues highlighted by each. Focusing particular attention to perceived inadequacies of legal frameworks to secure justice, this essay examines how these requiems offer a counter response to the devaluing of the men's lives. First is *Fortune's Bones: The Manumission Requiem,* a poem commissioned in 1996 to memorialize the life and legacy of an eighteenth-century enslaved man. This composition by Marilyn Nelson draws elements from a traditional funeral mass to honor Fortune (full name unknown), whose skeleton had been on display in the Mattatuck Museum in Waterbury, Connecticut. The poem was developed into a cantata and choral work composed by Dr. Ysaye M. Barnwell, a musician formerly part of the ensemble Sweet Honey in the Rock and a researcher in African American communities, musical traditions, and health initiatives.[2] The next section of the essay discusses the requiem that commemorated Michael Brown's life after Darren Wilson's grand jury acquittal. The final section offers a theological analysis that engages both requiems. Drawing on the concept of hopeful citizenship articulated by ethicist Charles Mathewes, the final section articulates theological warrants and concerns for artistic responses to injustice and encourages their use in Christian communities as a form of civic engagement.

Analysis of requiems alone does not provide solutions to moral issues concerning violence and the value of black life. It does, however, suggest that particular liturgical forms have the power to memorialize and thereby publicly acknowledge the injustice of devaluing particular lives. Although the specific cases here are focused on the mistreatment of black male bodies, the devaluing of personhood also occurs with female, transgender, and queer bodies, and with bodies identified as belonging to other people of color. Sadly, the cases surrounding Fortune and Brown can be described as particularly gendered in the way they draw upon negative perceptions of black males, but they are also representative of a wider pattern of violence and mistreatment that falls along broader racial and class lines.

Learning from *Fortune's Bones*

Requiems are written and performed to honor the dead and lay their souls to rest. In the Roman Catholic Church, a requiem is a mass that is spoken or sung. *Fortune's Bones: A Manumission Requiem* is a poetic work written in 2001, commissioned to honor a man who had died over two hundred years prior. This particular requiem was not created for a mass in a church setting but instead was created as part of an aesthetic and civic engagement response within the Waterbury, Connecticut, community, which had to decide what to do with a skeleton that had been on display in its museum for years. The poem was composed in 2001, developed into a musical composition shortly thereafter, and published with notes about Fortune's life in 2004. The cantata for *Fortune's Bones* premiered in Waterbury in 2009, and it has been performed three times since then. Barnwell, who arranged the music, also curated a year-long project about *Fortune's Bones* that included workshops, performances, and community talks about art, race, and medical ethics for the Clarice Smith Performing Arts Center at the University of Maryland in 2011.[3] When the cantata of the requiem was performed at the University of Maryland, it featured a full symphony orchestra, three choirs, seven soloists, and a chorus of African bells.[4]

The history of Fortune's bones raises ethical issues about autonomy and consent, "postmortem racism," the display of bodies, and unequal protection of African American life under the law.[5] The poetic and musical works for his bones suggest ways that artistic civic engagement strategies might be used to acknowledge the tragedy of the devaluing of human life and personhood, specifically those of African Americans. In Fortune's case, a community museum collaborated with universities and other research initiatives to uncover the story of a black man who had been mistreated in life and death and to respond in ways that would confer a sense of dignity to the man's remains. The requiem was a key element. Barnwell explains: "A requiem is really a process, an artistic process through which we celebrate the life of someone who has died and memorialize that person in some way. We all hope for some closure at the end of a life. Fortune didn't have that, so that is what we are trying to do."[6]

Although Fortune's skeleton was on display for decades in the museum, little was known about the man. In recent years, examination of the skeleton yielded evidence for reconstructing some details of Fortune's life.[7] He was born in the 1740s. According to the 1790 census, Fortune, his wife, Dinah, and their four children were the legal property of Dr. Preserved Porter. Fortune worked on Porter's seventy-five-acre farm. Dinah likely cooked and cleaned in the Porter home. He died in 1798, but there are no records indicating the actual date or cause of death.[8] These words, from the first poem, "Preface" in *Fortune's Bones*, describe what the scant information recovered cannot reveal:

> Was Fortune bitter? Was he good or bad?
> Did he sometimes throw back his head and laugh?
> His bones only say that he served and died,
> that he was useful, even into death,
> stripped of his name, his story, and his flesh.[9]

The requiem, at its outset, provokes readers to consider that from his owner's perspective, Fortune's value resided in his usefulness, not his character, inner life, or disposition. Fortune was baptized in Waterbury's Episcopal Church on December 20, 1797, but while his baptism may have indicated spiritual change, it did not provoke a change in the social status or physical conditions of his life. Before 1729, Connecticut law allowed manumission of baptized slaves, but by the year Fortune was baptized, the ecclesial practice did not disrupt the legal ownership of persons. Any kinship in Christ between master and slave affirmed in the baptismal rite was strictly spiritual, without practical implications. After his baptism, and even after his death, Fortune's body remained more valuable to his owner than his soul.

When Fortune died, his owner boiled down pieces of the body, prepared Fortune's skeleton for anatomical study, and reportedly opened a "School for Anatomy." For generations to follow, local doctors and all of the doctors in the Porter family studied anatomy with Fortune's skeleton.[10] The bones were valued at fifteen dollars in Porter's will and passed down through the family until 1933 when Dr. Sally Porter Law McGlannan donated the skeleton to the Mattatuck Museum. By then the story about Porter preparing the skeleton for medical use had become a legend in Waterbury, but the details were confused and Porter's personal connection to the body (his ownership of Fortune) was historically erased.

Nelson's requiem points to the law's failure to protect Fortune's body, autonomy, and dignity in life and death. Pamela Espeland, who authored notes for the published version of Nelson's requiem, states the obvious—Fortune's body was the property of his owner. The overwork that led to his death at sixty years old was legally sanctioned. Moreover, Porter could dissect the body and use Fortune's bones for anatomical research because there were no laws governing the use of cadavers for research to forbid it. Yet even without laws forbidding it, rendering Fortune's body into a skeleton and displaying it in the doctor's office was morally wrong. Instead of allowing the man's body to be laid to rest by his loved ones and buried (which would have been customary at the time), Fortune's body remained his owner's property even in death, and its display in Porter's office would have remained a visible indication of that.[11] Fortune's family's consent to such practices was irrelevant. In "Dinah's Lament," words from the widow convey the moral wrong being done to her:

Miss Lydia doesn't clear the Doctor room
She say she can't go in that room: she scared.
She make me take the dust rag and the broom
and clean around my husband, hanging there.
Since she seen Fortune head in that big pot
Miss Lydia say that room make her feel ill,
Sick with the thought of boiling human broth.
I wonder how she think it make me feel?[12]

The requiem, by its very form, voices the pain of mourners left behind. Dinah remains a slave, and her husband's body, too, remains in bondage. As an enslaved woman, Dinah would not have had the power to make a claim to her husband's body against her owner's claim and his intent to use Fortune's bones for medical training. That Fortune and his family belonged to a racial group of persons denied rights to protect their own corpses is indicative of "postmortem racism," a term used by ethicist Harriet Washington. In *Medical Apartheid: The Dark History of Medical Experimentation on Black Americans from Colonial Times to the Present,* Washington exposes the challenges that medical practitioners and schools faced in procuring bodies for medical dissection up until the twentieth century. The use of bodies for medical training was seen to be necessary but socially abhorrent in previous centuries, which means that these bodies were rarely obtained with the willing consent of the deceased or their families. "As a result, physicians appropriated the bodies of enslaved persons with no legal rights or those of free blacks with no rights that a white man was obligated to respect."[13] The unequal rights of black slaves and white slave owners that were codified into law enabled a disproportionate use of black bodies for anatomical study.

Although in contemporary medical ethics we do not condemn using a cadaver for medical training or research as long as the body is procured through legal and morally sound means, we do criticize the use of a human body in a way that instrumentalizes it to a degree that violates the deceased person's dignity. Washington's description of the attitudes about anatomical dissection and display around 1800 makes it clear that Porter indeed violated Fortune's dignity. The passage is worth quoting at length:

The invasive violation involved in the anatomical dissection of a corpse ran counter to very strong nineteenth-century sentiments regarding the sanctity of the body. Today, a dead body is an alien entity that we encounter briefly in a hospital, funeral home, or place of worship, but in the eighteenth and nineteenth centuries, people tended to die at home rather than in hospitals, and the body, imbued with religious and social significance, was lovingly cared for in a way that balanced the dead person to his family and society. The corpse was kept fully bathed and groomed and postmortem photographs, portraits, or other images were often created and distributed. This care of the body certified the person's meaning and status as a member of a family and community. Dissection, however gave the corpse a very different meaning, limiting him to a bit of useful flesh, an object to be surgically severed from his community, treated with disdain, then discarded like trash.

For blacks, anatomical dissection meant even more: it was an extension of slavery into eternity, because it represented a profound level of white control over their bodies, illustrating that they were not free even in death.[14]

When Dr. Porter rendered Fortune's body into a skeleton, he denied Fortune's family the rituals of burial, a headstone or placard marking his presence, and an opportunity to arrange his remains with dignity and respect. Moreover, Porter's treatment and subsequent display of the body was morally problematic. The postmortem display of skeletal, stuffed, or mummified black bodies in "doctor's offices, anatomy laboratories, museums, traveling sideshows, and even private businesses" was also a manifestation of racism.[15] It signified not only possession and control of black bodies but also a threat to them. "Blacks' skeletons hanging in doctors' offices . . . constituted the same kind of warning to African Americans as did the bodies of lynched men and women left hanging on trees where blacks would be sure to see them."[16]

In the 1940s the Mattatuck Museum began to display Fortune's skeleton. While it was a popular exhibit, the museum removed the skeleton from public display in response to community concerns in 1970.[17] They began to investigate Fortune's life and death in the 1990s.[18] It was then that the museum created new exhibits to tell the true story of Fortune's bones and commissioned the poem that was turned into a musical requiem, which provoked the numerous performances and community activities around *Fortune's Bones*. On September 12, 2013, Fortune's remains were finally laid to rest after a funeral service at St. John's Episcopal Church in Waterbury, Connecticut, in a ceremony that recognized his worth as a whole person. In this church setting the value of his soul was finally affirmed, no longer sublimated to his body in value. Fortune is no one's property anymore.

Michael Brown and the Continuing Violence against Black Bodies

Although Fortune's story has its resolution, disturbing acts of violence against black men continue to occur. Michael Brown's death in Ferguson, Missouri, is just one of the numerous incidents in recent years that have prompted protests against injustices by law enforcement officials and courts. A Department of

Justice investigation into the Ferguson police department found routine discrimination and stereotyping in a "pattern or practice of unlawful conduct."[19] The names of several African American men killed throughout the United States have become rallying cries against injustice: Trayvon Martin, Jordan Davis, Eric Garner, Freddie Gray.[20] Protesters and activists have expressed outrage and concern over their deaths and the investigations and outcomes that exonerated or excused their killers. Brown died in August 2014 after being shot six times by police officer Darren Wilson.[21] The violent altercation occurred after Wilson stopped Brown and his friend because Brown fit the description of the perpetrator of a convenience store theft. Brown was unarmed, but Wilson and some eyewitnesses reported that Brown attacked him. The altercation began when Wilson was in his police SUV, but after Wilson fired the first shots, missing Brown, the teen ran away. Wilson followed him on foot. Brown then stopped and turned toward Wilson. When he made movements to come toward Wilson again, the police officer fired the fatal shots.[22] Some witnesses said Brown's hands were in the air when he was shot, although others had conflicting accounts. Reports also say that Brown's body was left lying in the street for four and a half hours after officers arrived on the scene to investigate. His shooting prompted protests in August 2014 and more civil unrest, investigations, and recommendations for police reform following Wilson's grand jury acquittal on November 24, 2014. The US Department of Justice investigated Wilson for violating Brown's civil rights but cleared him on March 4, 2015.[23]

The circumstances around Brown's death raise issues of racial profiling, officers' use of deadly or extreme force, and distrust between police and communities exacerbated by economic and racial disparities.[24] Although many people believe that the US criminal justice system is mostly fair and nondiscriminatory, scholars such as Michelle Alexander have demonstrated that racial disparities exist and cannot be explained away by crime rate data.[25] Statistics from the Human Rights Watch support this argument:

> Blacks comprise 62.7 percent and whites 36.7 percent of all drug offenders admitted to state prison, even though federal surveys and other data detailed in this report show clearly that this racial disparity bears scant relation to racial differences in drug offending. There are, for example, five times more white drug users than black. Relative to population, black men are admitted to state prison on drug charges at a rate that is 13.4 times greater than that of white men. In large part because of the extraordinary racial disparities in incarceration for drug offenses, blacks are incarcerated for all offenses at 8.2 times the rate of whites. One in every 20 black men over the age of 18 in the United States is in state or federal prison, compared to one in 180 white men.[26]

Alexander argues that although our system may be "formally colorblind," law enforcement officials have such discretion about who to stop, arrest, and charge that racial bias goes unchallenged. The system itself is then protected from legal challenges by those who would claim racial discrimination because the courts "demand that anyone who wants to challenge racial bias in the system offer, in advance, clear proof that racial disparities are the product of intentional racial discrimination—i.e., the work of a bigot."[27] Because racism is so widely believed to be morally wrong, proof of conscious racial discrimination is practically unobtainable.[28] Those who have experience with racial bias in this system and those who are convinced by the analysis offered by Alexander and others believe that too often the law does not secure justice but rather enables the proliferation of stereotypes that demonize African Americans as criminals and thereby legitimizes mass incarceration and excessive violence against them. The altercation between Brown and Wilson only lasted a few minutes, and many believe that the quick judgments the officer made were influenced by racial stereotypes about the harm Brown could inflict.

In the weeks following Brown's shooting, numerous protests in Missouri and around the United States publicized the perceived injustices surrounding his death. The early protests in Ferguson were tense and controversial and led to the deployment of the National Guard and visits by the US attorney general.[29] Protests resurged after the announcement that a grand jury failed to indict Wilson. The failure to indict indicated that the grand jury found no probable cause to charge him with a crime.[30] Was Brown's life so insignificant that Wilson should not even have had to stand trial to justify his decision to use deadly force? Although protests in the street along with images of looting, fires, and destruction garnered most of the news coverage about communities' responses to the perceived shortcomings of law and law enforcement, protesters used other creative responses.[31] On October 4, 2014, demonstrators disrupted a performance of the St. Louis Symphony with a "Requiem for Mike Brown." On the evening that the symphony was performing Brahms' *Requiem*, approximately fifty protesters began singing. The *St. Louis American* newspaper describes the protest, which began right after intermission:

> As symphony conductor Markus Stenz stepped to the podium to begin the second act of *German Requiem*, one middle-aged African American man stood up in the middle of the theater and sang, "What side are you on friend, what side are you on?"
>
> In an operatic voice, another woman located a few rows away stood up and joined him singing, "Justice for Mike Brown is justice for us all." Several more audience members sprinkled throughout the theater and in the balcony rose up and joined in the singing.
>
> Those in the balcony lowered white banners about 15 feet long with black spray-painted letters that said, "Requiem for Mike Brown 1996–2014" and

"Racism lives here," with an arrow pointed to a picture of the St. Louis Arch. Another banner said, "Rise up and join the movement."

Stenz stood stoically and listened to the demonstrators' performance. Some onlookers were outraged and start spewing expletives. Others stood up and started clapping. Most seemed stunned and simply watched.

The singing only went on for about two minutes before the demonstrators started chanting, "Black lives matter." They pulled up their banners and dropped red paper hearts over the edge of the balcony onto the main floor orchestra seats, which stated "Requiem for Mike Brown." Then they all voluntarily marched out together and left the theater. While they marched out, they received a round of applause from many of the audience members—as well as the musicians on stage.[32]

Unlike *Fortune's Bones*, this requiem did not have an institution like a community museum or university supporting it. This protest was a grassroots effort coordinated by Sarah Griesbach, a forty-two-year-old white woman from the St. Louis area. The shooting precipitated her awakening to the racial disparities that exist in her community. She had been protesting since August 9, 2014, to call attention to white privilege.[33] The group of protesters assembled for the requiem was diverse in ages, racial identifications, and occupations, intended to be representative of the larger community. Although dissimilar to the productions of *Fortune's Bones* in its scale, the requiem for Mike Brown was similar in its use of community voices to call for justice so that moral wrongs might be exposed and remedied. Both requiems memorialized a man who had died too soon and disputed the claims of "justice" of the legal frameworks that held no one accountable to their offenses. This requiem disputed the idea that justice for Brown, an African American male, is different from justice for anyone else. "Justice for Mike Brown is justice for us all," protesters sang, expressing solidarity.

Theologian M. Shawn Copeland explains that solidarity is "no mere commonsense identification among members of the same group" but is an "intentional moral and ethical task" that can be grounded in theological anthropology and Christology.[34] Jesus, in the flesh, was despised, derided, and killed. He shares in the suffering and anguish of all of God's children who are assaulted and denigrated in their fleshly being. Yet Christ also, through his body, his incarnate love, and his self-sacrifice, redeems sin, including the sin of those who fail to honor the humanity of others.[35] He says "Father forgive them," modeling a praxis of solidarity that acknowledges human complicity in evil yet endeavors to save both its perpetrators and victims. Copeland affirms the interconnectedness of all human creatures while maintaining God's particular concern for the particular bodies targeted for abuse, exploitation, and murder.[36] This understanding of solidarity goes beyond affirmation of the universality of God's love to insist that love manifests itself in action on behalf of the sufferers. Solidarity, as an ethical task, "begins in the intentional remembering of the dead, exploited, and despised victims of history."[37] The requiem for Mike Brown intentionally provokes us to not only remember this young man but protest the injustices perpetrated against his body as crimes against our own. Indeed, if all our suffering is bound up in the body of Christ, injustice for Mike Brown is injustice for us all.

Liturgy as Christian Response

The requiems for Fortune and Brown, their funeral services, and the countless other songs, poems, essays, and performative acts created to protest their treatment and mourn the injustice of the loss of their lives use imagery to move us past intellectual assent of moral wrongs. Theologian David Jasper writes:

> In the creative power of the word and in the power of images and music, the impossible does not cease to be impossible, but can present itself to us in all its moments of utter beauty, or awe and terror; in those moments of searing consciousness in a world in which we too often prefer to pretend, to close our eyes and not to see the ugly and the disfigured. But finally, in that marvel of consciousness . . . we are prompted to dare to be what we have not been.[38]

African American musical traditions including spirituals, blues, and jazz often include cries about injustice to God and those gathered in the community to hear, but these kinds of laments have a place beyond African American contexts in various racialized Christian communities. Using the concept of "hopeful citizenship" from Charles Mathewes's *A Theology of Public Life* as a framework, this section discusses the possibilities for adopting aesthetic responses as a public Christian exercise to counter the way law devalues life.[39] Using artistic practices to specifically protest the devaluing of people of color by communities that do not comprise people of color warrants caution against false sincerity or co-opting others' experience, but it does not make the use of artistic responses imprudent.

Mathewes discusses hopeful citizenship as one aspect of a theology of public life. Hope, as Mathewes describes it, is necessary for Christians who seek to engage in public life but are confronted by the realities of politics and become despairing, disillusioned, or resentful of them.[40] For Christians, this hopefulness must be based on a religious obligation to be witnesses and prophets to a fallen social order. An active, religious community is essential for providing the language of fallenness and cohesion needed to support an alternative "public" who takes a stand.[41] A Christian community should act out of response to God, made distinctive from other types of communities by its sense of calling. It enacts its liturgy as a way of life, embodying its response to God's call.[42] Bruce Ellis Benson encourages us to think of liturgy more expansively than what Christians do in worship services. He notes that all uses of the term *leitourgia* in the New Testament include actions of service and ministry. Liturgy is the *life* of worship, extending far beyond Sunday rituals.[43] It is the way we live our lives as a community of God's followers. Moreover, liturgy constitutes particular embodied beings as the body of Christ, which makes solidarity possible.

Similarly, Copeland argues that as we become the body of Christ, we do not minimize our particularities but instead claim that the flesh of the particular "others" next to us is, too, the flesh of Christ. It is because we are made new as Christ's flesh that we examine and renounce position, power, racial and cultural superiority, and repressive codes of gender and sexuality that privilege some of our particular bodies over others.[44]

> The only body capable of taking us all in as we are with our different body marks . . . is the body of Christ. This taking us in, this in-corporation, is akin to sublation, not erasure, not uniformity: the *basililea* [Kingdom of God] praxis of Jesus draws us up to him. Our humble engagement in his praxis revalues our identities and differences, even as it preserves the integrity and significance of our body marks. At the same time, those very particular body marks are relativized, reoriented, and reappropriated under his sign, the sign of the cross. Thus, in solidarity and in love of others and the Other, we are (re)made and (re)marked as the flesh of Christ, as the flesh of his church.[45]

Although Copeland writes specifically about the Eucharist in this passage, the argument could also apply to the liturgy of the requiem and to Fortune's baptism. If such practices are silently complicit with the slaveocracy that held Fortune in bondage or if they fail to confront the racism that exonerates the killers of black lives, the practices intended to form us as the unified body of Christ become distorted. The liturgy is intended to reorient us to God's ways. Instead of mediating God's grace and the freedom of living in Christ, a distorted, "desiccated antiliturgy hands us all over to consumption by the corrupt body of the market."[46]

One risk of using artistic-liturgical mediums as a response to injustice is that they might produce spectators who feel better about themselves for having viewed a performance or work of art, and may even have been moved by it, but ultimately remain unchanged and unwilling to change the world around them.[47] In other words, art could fail to provoke authentic interactions and the intended active response in its audience. Discussing the moral intuitions that guide people's responses, ethicist Rebecca Todd Peters identifies three categories that form a continuum of moral agency: sympathy, responsibility, and mutuality.[48] In the first stage people are moved by pictures and images they see and react with a feeling of sympathy, pity, or guilt. Their emotions are genuine, and the desire to help may be also, but what is lacking is a consideration of systemic factors that contribute to the moral problem and how their own privilege may be complicit in those systems.[49] Peters reminds us that "gut reactions and intuitions are not synonymous with ethical reflection and action"; as ethicists, we should be concerned with the latter.[50] Recalling Mathewes's assertion that hopeful citizenship requires *communities* of action, we must consider whether aesthetic responses effectively build bonds between people and motivate them to act in solidarity. Christians are by no means any more monolithic than society at large. Is art capable of provoking an authentic mutuality, a solidarity that Beverly Harrison describes as involving "concrete answerability" to oppressed people and the capability of being changed by them?[51] The answer depends on the art itself.

Art is a process, not merely a product. The process that went into creating the numerous manifestations of *Fortune's Bones* spanned decades and included career artists; a range of scholars from varied disciplines; residents in the town of Waterbury, Connecticut; musicians from the Washington, DC, metropolitan area; visitors to public libraries; and countless others possessing varied interests and areas of expertise. As gathered communities, they wrestled with the issue of who should speak for Fortune. How could they be held accountable to a man who died in 1798? Despite lacking a conclusive answer, the museum and its partners held themselves accountable to residents of Waterbury. They honored the community's wishes by burying the bones. By their faithful efforts to uncover the story behind the skeleton, share Fortune's plight, and discuss its implications for medical ethics and issues of racial justice, the community participants became accountable to each other and enablers of each other's growth despite their differences in social location. The requiem for Mike Brown was a much shorter piece assembled in a shorter time frame, but there, too, we see an attempt to be accountable to the community through the representation of its performers.

Another approach to the concern about community formation and the pitfalls of sympathy is to reconsider who we intend to reach with artistic works. We ought to expand the conception of "audience" to include the community of participants because art is a transformative process for those who participate in its making. The very process of performing a requiem puts one in community, and listening to the voices of those in the community is not optional but essential for the work to be done. Composing a piece, directing a choir, singing one's part, and playing one's instrument requires attentiveness to multiple parts at the same time. And for musicians to convincingly convey the sentiment of a piece, they must spend time with the work to understand its meaning. The performers embody the voices inside the music, bringing life to words and notations on a page. That is transformation. Transformation also occurs when the words the performers sing are the sentiments of someone like Fortune, who was denied a story and a legacy for too long. The type of artistry involved in productions like Barnwell's cantata of *Fortune's Bones* may limit opportunities for participation to those with specialized skills and musical talents. However, the series for *Fortune's Bones* at the University of Maryland included other events like a community sing and a ring shout, expanding the opportunity for others in the community to participate. Undoubtedly, aesthetic responses should intend to transform its viewers, but these types of events do not fail if some audience members are not moved past sympathy. With a Christian requiem, the art is not for the audience alone; it is for the praying community, the mourners left behind, and the souls of the departed.

A requiem is aesthetic response and spiritual form. As such, it can orient Christians to cultivate the proper frame of mind, putting this world, its evils, and our place in it in perspective, which relates to another aspect of Mathewes's articulation of hopeful citizenship. For Mathewes, proper Christian engagement in public life cannot be escapist, cynical, or limited to criticism.[52] Christians shirk moral responsibilities for life in this world if we overlook the conditions that need to be remedied while anticipating their correction in an afterlife or spiritual release. Faithful Christians must resist escapism, which is why Nelson's requiem is inadequate as a Christian response despite its rich meaning and relevance as a *model for* Christian response. In "Not My Bones," the voice of the deceased Fortune says, "I was not this body, I was not these bones. This skeleton was just my temporary home."[53] The concluding lines of Fortune's song about his bones, which is the high point of the entire requiem, reads:

> Well, I woke up this morning just so glad to be free,
> Glad to be free, glad to be free.
> I woke up this morning in restful peace.
> For I am not my body,
> I am not my bones.
> I am not my body,
> Glory hallelujah, not my bones,
> I am not my bones.[54]

Despite the tone and phrases here that resonate with Negro spirituals, the bodily negation in these lines makes it problematic from a Christian theological perspective—at least a liberationist one. Nelson did not intend for *Fortune's Bones* to be a Christian response to injustice, and she intentionally draws from Buddhist elements and the teachings of Thich Nhat Hanh.[55] In Nelson's description of the meaning behind "Not My Bones," she quotes the Vietnamese Buddhist leader's reply to a question about the most helpful thing to say to a person who is dying. Thich Nhat Hanh is reported to have responded, "We have learned . . . that the most helpful thing we can say is, 'Don't worry. The body that is dying here is not you.'"[56] While this sentiment undoubtedly provides peace in dying to many who hear it, the body-denying logic seems inappropriate for a requiem commemorating a man whose remains had been misused. Fortune was much *more* than his body, more than skeleton put on display. But it is because he *was* his body that the treatment of his bones reflects the value his society placed on his life and personhood. It is because his body is due the care and dignity of a person and child of God that we find its mistreatment morally wrong.

A Christian requiem must not sever the connection between body and the spirit, even though that disconnect commonly enters our discussions of death.[57] A person's soul, his or her very essence of being, is integrally linked to the body because it inhabits the body and is influenced by its experiences, its subjections, and its perceptions. If the soul continues to exist, it remains informed by the body even after death. As Margaret Farley explains, the body is "the locus of unity" for a person; the mind is embodied and the body is ensouled.[58] Furthermore, the injustices and evils a person faces are often the result of the experiences and perceptions that others have of the person's body. Farley asserts that, in this way, the body can be understood as a cultural text with meanings that are socially constructed. This theoretical framework is based in lived realities. The meanings of the body are "forged in an ongoing social praxis" and, as such, the body can be a tool and object of social control.[59] In simple terms, Darren Wilson perceived Mike Brown as a threat because of his bodily presence and actions. He *was* his body, and he died because of that reality.

Although a requiem is spiritual, it is not escapist, and the body is crucial to its theological underpinnings. The traditional requiem mass of the Roman Catholic Church underwent changes after the Second Vatican Council, and although it is solemn, it is now also joyful, anticipating the hope in the resurrection to come.[60] The resurrection is a bodily event, not only a spiritual one, and thus the requiem potentially avoids escapist pitfalls. Although there is an otherworldly element in its appeals to an eternal world where the souls of the departed might find rest, this eternal world is not completely separate or distinct from our own. The eternal world on the other side shares with this one a coexistence of lightness and darkness, suffering and release, and grace in the face of evil. Mathewes asserts that a Christian, Augustinian conception of evil is paradoxically hopeful "by affirming that realities such as malice, suffering, and injustice do not tell the whole truth about reality, but are in some way partial, perhaps even accidental, to the ultimate nature of reality itself."[61] Can a requiem convey paradoxical hope? Consider these words from the Entrance Antiphon of the Catholic requiem that speak to eventual peace and joy:

> May the Lord open to [the dead] the gates of Paradise,
> that he [or she] may return to that homeland
> where there is no death, where eternal joy endures.[62]

There is an eschatological element to the hope of the requiem, which is also the hope of Christian engagement with public life. "Hope is our mode of recognizing our *distensio*, our experience of tantalizing incompleteness that we confess we exist in at present, yet proclaim will be healed in the eschaton."[63] Like solidarity, hope provokes us to see our world in its brokenness while maintaining a vision of something more. Acting in hopeful citizenship, Christians recognize their creaturely limitations but nevertheless participate in cultivating the world to make it fitting of the love God bestows upon it.[64] Judgment and perpetual light coexist in the world of the requiem, as they do in movements of social justice.

Finally, the change desired by hopeful citizenship requires "the cohesion and integration needed to cultivate the rich intellect."[65] Efforts to address the whole human project must connect to a whole human person. Aesthetic responses address a person who is more than a mind or a body who acts; they seek out the part of humanity that feels. They are intended to move us internally so that we might move externally, so that we might change and live transformed (or transfigured). The caution against artistic responses is that they too must not be used in isolation. Poems, images, choral works, and performances must accompany responses that seek to rectify the law and policy. Art cannot replace political advocacy for social change. But political advocacy in the form of lobbying or protests of marchers with placards can too easily become about strategy and expediency. The political rhetoric on television or radio is often too simplistic; it appeals to an audience presumed to have opinions already formed one way or another. Contemporary political discourse places an emphasis on effectively winning verbal skirmishes and votes rather than transforming hearts, and transformation must remain a part of Christian practice if it is to be based in love for the world.

Conclusion

Christianity at its best asserts that even those who are devalued as persons in this life are treasured by God, whose justice will ultimately triumph over the injustices present in the fallen world of human politics and legal frameworks. As Christians fulfill their call to love the world enough to work for its betterment, they must seek out means of advocacy and change that resonate within them affectively, not only intellectually. The modern requiem and other aesthetic responses to injustice have the ability to move us by expressing the voices that are too often silenced or devalued. The requiem seeks to connect our souls to those of the departed, and this holds the potential for true transformation. As we are transfigured by justice, we pray that those who die from injustice might be transfigured, too, and that their true value might be affirmed.

Notes

1. Alicia Garza to *The Feminist Wire*, October 7, 2014, http://thefeministwire.com/2014/10/blacklivesmatter-2/.

2. Ysaye M. Barnwell, "Biography: Dr. Ysaye M Barnwell, Barnwell's Notes, Inc & Barnwell's Notes Publishing," http://www.ymbarnwell.com/about.php. Sweet Honey in the Rock is a vocal ensemble that draws upon African American culture and traditions. Their music seeks to entertain and educate. Barnwell was a member of the group for thirty-four years.

3. In addition to two performances of the requiem, the Clarice Smith Performing Arts Center hosted several events in a series curated by Barnwell. The series had other musical events, such as a community sing and a "ring shout." A ring shout is a cultural and religious ritual first practiced by enslaved Africans. Participants sing, dance, clap, and call out as they move around in a circle or ring. The *Fortune's Bones* series also included discussions on campus and in local libraries about slavery, medical ethics, connections between Fortune's story and Henrietta Lacks's case, and issues like "Who Speaks for Fortune?" Karen Shih, "Fortune's Tellers: Clarice Smith Center, Community Honor a Slave," *Terp*, Spring 2012, 26–27.

4. Ibid., 26.

5. Here I am referring to the man's bones, which inspired these artistic works, not just the compositions and performances themselves.

6. Quoted in Shih, "Fortune's Tellers," 26.

7. "Fortune's Story: Who Was Fortune?" Mattatuck Historical Society, http://www.fortunestory.org/fortune/who.asp. Based on his skeleton, researchers were able to determine that Fortune had had several injuries during his lifetime, including injuries to his hands and feet and a broken lower back, all of which were typical of agricultural workers of his era. He died around sixty years of age, likely from a broken neck. The cause of the neck injury is unknown, but it was sudden and does not appear to be inflicted from hanging.

8. Ibid.

9. Marilyn Nelson, "Preface," in *Fortune's Bones: The Manumission Requiem* (Asheville, NC: Front Street, 2004), 13.

10. "Fortune's Story: Why Wasn't Fortune Buried?" Mattatuck Historical Society, http://www.fortunestory.org/fortune/why.asp.

11. Barnwell notes that this is what is "horrifying to so many people." Quoted in Shih, "Fortune's Tellers," 26.

12. Nelson, *Fortune's Bones*, 15.

13. Harriet A. Washington, *Medical Apartheid: The Dark History of Medical Experimentation on Black Americans from Colonial Times to the Present* (New York: Anchor Books, 2008), 121.

14. Ibid., 125.

15. Ibid., 134.

16. Ibid., 136.

17. "Fortune's Story: How Did the Skeleton Get to the Museum?" Mattatuck Historical Society, http://www.fortunestory.org/fortune/how.asp.

18. "Fortune's Story: The Future for Fortune," Mattatuck Historical Society, http://www.fortunestory.org/fortune/future.asp.

19. US Department of Justice, "Investigation of the Ferguson Police Department" (Washington, DC: USDOJ Civil Rights Division, March 4, 2015), 4.

20. On February 26, 2012, Trayvon Martin, a seventeen-year-old black male, was walking in Sanford, Florida, when he was confronted and killed by George Zimmerman, a neighborhood watch captain: "Trayvon Martin Shooting Fast Facts," *CNN Library*, http://www.cnn.com/2013/06/05/us/trayvon-martin-shooting-fast-facts/. Jordan Davis was a black teen killed by Michael Dunn on November 23, 2012, at a gas station in Jacksonville, Florida, after a dispute over loud music. Dunn's first trial for Davis's death ended in mistrial, but he was found guilty when the case was retried. Derek Kinner, "Michael Dunn Verdict: Florida Man Found Guilty of Attempted Murder in Loud-Music Trial," *Huffington Post*, February 15, 2014, http://www.huffingtonpost.com/2014/02/15/michael-dunn-verdict_n_4796068.html. Eric Garner, a forty-three-year-old African American man, died on July 17, 2014, when New York city police officer Daniel Pantaleo put him in a chokehold: Rebecca Davis O'Brien, Michael Howard Saul, and Pervaiz Shallwani, "New York City Police Officer Won't Face Criminal Charges in Eric Garner Death," *Wall Street Journal*, December 4, 2014, http://www.wsj.com/articles/new-york-city-police-officer-wont-face-criminal-charges-in-eric-garner-death-1417635275?mod=WSJ_hpp_LEFT-TopStories. Freddie Gray was a twenty-five-year-old African American man who died on April 19, 2015, from spinal cord injuries sustained while being transported in a Baltimore police van: "Timeline: Freddie Gray's Arrest, Death and the Aftermath," *Baltimore Sun*, http://data.baltimoresun.com/news/freddie-gray/.

21. Larry Buchanan et al., "Q &A: What Happened in Ferguson?" *New York Times*, November 25, 2014.

22. Ibid.

23. Holbrook Mohr and David A. Lieb, "Feds: Evidence Backs Ferguson Officer's Account in Shooting," *New York Times*, March 4, 2015.

24. Katherine Mangan, "How Professors in St. Louis Are Teaching the Lessons of Ferguson's Unrest," *Chronicle of Higher Education*, August 26, 2014, http://chronicle.com/article/How-Professors-in-St-Louis/148479/.

25. The scope of this essay limits discussion of topics taken up at length in other works, most notably Alexander's book about the racialized impact of criminal justice policies. Michelle Alexander, *The New Jim Crow: Mass Incarceration in the Age of Colorblindness*, rev. ed. (New York: New Press, 2010).

26. Human Rights Watch, *Punishment and Prejudice: Racial Disparities in the War on Drugs*, HRW Reports, vol. 12, no. 2 (May 2000), http://www.hrw.org/reports/2000/usa/Rcedrg00.htm. While these statistics concern drug arrests and convictions, racial disparities have also been documented in traffic stops and "stop-and-frisk" policies. Alexander writes, "The New York Police Department released statistics in February 2007 showing that during the prior year its officers stopped an astounding 508,540 people—an average of 1,393 per day—who were walking on the street. . . . The vast majority of those stopped and searched were racial minorities, and more than half were African American." Alexander, *The New Jim Crow*, 134–35.

27. Alexander, *The New Jim Crow*, 103.

28. Ibid.

29. Bill Chappell to The Two-Way, August 18, 2014, http://www.npr.org/blogs/thetwo-way/2014/08/18/341313667/ferguson-update-national-guard-deployed-school-postponed.

30. Buchanan et al., "Q &A: What Happened in Ferguson?"

31. At the time of this writing, similar images of protest about the death of Freddie Gray in Baltimore are being regularly televised.

32. Rebecca Rivas, "Demonstrators 'Disrupt' St. Louis Symphony Singing a 'Requiem for Mike Brown,'" *St. Louis American*, http://www.stlamerican.com/news/local_news/article_d3d4e0b0-4c48-11e4-bc55-275aa0a96f33.html.

33. Ibid. Griesbach explains her motivation: "It is my duty and desire to try to reach out and raise that awareness peacefully but also to disrupt the blind state of white St. Louis, particularly among the people who are secure in their blindness."

34. M. Shawn Copeland, *Enfleshing Freedom: Body Race, and Being*, ed. Anthony B. Pinn and Katie G. Cannon (Minneapolis, Minnesota: Fortress Press, 2010), 99–100.

35. Ibid., 99.

36. Ibid. Copeland, a womanist theologian, convincingly argues that Christians must stand against the oppression of poor women of color. Without minimizing the particularity of her claim, I employ her argument to black men, another group of "victims of history."

37. Ibid., 100.

38. David Jasper, *The Sacred Community: Art, Sacrament, and the People of God* (Waco, TX: Baylor University Press, 2012), 164.

39. There are many relevant concepts from Mathewes's work that apply to this discussion, but I have narrowed it to hopeful citizenship to focus my analysis.

40. Charles T. Mathewes, *A Theology of Public Life* (Cambridge: Cambridge University Press, 2007), 214.

41. Ibid., 216–17.

42. Bruce Ellis Benson, *Liturgy as a Way of Life: Embodying the Arts in Christian Worship*, ed. James K. A. Smith (Grand Rapids, MI: Baker Academic, 2013).

43. Ibid., 24.

44. Copeland, *Enfleshing Freedom*, 82.

45. Ibid., 83.

46. Ibid.

47. I want to credit and express my gratitude to Courtney Bryant, a PhD student at Vanderbilt University. In her paper from the Ethics Section at the 2014 AAR Annual Meetings, Bryant raised several points that are relevant to this essay. Her paper, "And the Burdens of Our Hearts Rolled Away: Black Film as Cultural Catharsis and the Simulation of Solidarity," skillfully applied critiques by Emilie Townes, Beverly Wildung Harrison, Rebecca Todd Peters, Mark Anthony Neal, and others against a simulated solidarity that viewers of black film might experience, letting them off the hook for engaging in real action. I have a similar concern, that someone could watch a performance of a requiem without responding in other ways to the devaluation of life presented in it. I am grateful to Bryant for raising these objections and providing me with her bibliography. I cite many of the sources that she used in the discussion that follows.

48. Rebecca Todd Peters, *Solidarity Ethics: Transformation in a Globalized World* (Minneapolis, Minnesota: Fortress Press, 2014), 36.

49. Ibid., 36–37. In the responsibility stage, moral agents take direct action but are often champions of individual liberties and opportunities as a solution to injustices and fail to recognize the realities of systemic oppression. The final category of mutuality, which focuses on building relationships and partnerships of engagement for both parties across social and economic differences, holds the most potential for addressing the causes of a problem.

50. Ibid., 42.

51. Beverly Wildung Harrison, "Theological Reflection in the Struggle for Liberation," in *Making the Connections: Essays in Feminist Social Ethics*, ed. Carol S. Robb (Boston: Beacon, 1985), 244. I am aware that phrasing the question in this way and describing the oppressed as "them" seems to presume that readers are not among the oppressed. I have chosen to

echo Harrison's tone and audience. She addresses academic theologians and criticizes the inadequacies of speaking about "solidarity with the oppressed" without welcoming the critique of the oppressed and being willing to alter "our" reality. I acknowledge that readers of this journal may be located at a nexus of overlapping or varied forms of oppression, but because of their connection to the academy, I presume nearly all have some level of class privilege. For this reason, I am retaining the us/them language of Harrison's assertion.

52. Mathewes, *A Theology of Public Life*, 216–17.

53. Nelson, *Fortune's Bones*, 27.

54. Ibid., 25.

55. Ibid., 27.

56. Ibid.

57. It is not uncommon to hear someone speak of a soul that has left the body and gone to a physical place to be with the Lord. From this perspective, a connection between body and soul has ceased to exist.

58. Margaret A. Farley, Preface to *Embodiment, Morality, and Medicine*, ed. Lisa Sowle Cahill and Margaret A. Farley (Dordrecht, The Netherlands: Kluwer Academic Publishers, 1995), vii.

59. Ibid., vii–viii.

60. "Requiem," in *The Columbia Encyclopedia* (New York: Columbia University Press, 2013), http://literati.credoreference.com.ezproxy.baylor.edu/content/entry/columency/requiem/0.

61. Mathewes, *A Theology of Public Life*, 230.

62. "Entrance Antiphon (Outside Easter Time)," in *The Roman Missal*, trans. The International Commission on English in the Liturgy, 3rd typical ed. (Washington DC: United States Catholic Conference of Bishops, 2011), 1371.

63. Mathewes, *A Theology of Public Life*, 257.

64. Ibid., 235.

65. Ibid., 236.

The Return of Neo-Scholasticism?
Recent Criticisms of Henri de Lubac on Nature and Grace and Their Significance for Moral Theology, Politics, and Law

Thomas J. Bushlack

Henri de Lubac's (1896–1991) treatment of the relationship between nature and grace helped the Catholic Church to move beyond the antagonisms that had defined its relationship with the modern nation-state. In critiquing de Lubac, some recent scholarship has presented an interpretation of Aquinas that is remarkably similar to the problems associated with the neo-Scholastic method. These approaches indicate that in order for late modern democratic states to achieve their connatural ends of justice and the common good, they must directly advert to revealed knowledge and Church teaching. This essay proposes an alternative correction to de Lubac that both maintains a distinction between nature and grace and facilitates a capacity for Christians to engage in a nuanced dialogue of affirmation and critique of the human goods sought by late modern political and legal institutions. In the conclusion, this nature-grace distinction is used to analyze the way the US Catholic Bishops have engaged in moral, political, and legal debates over the Patient Protection and Affordable Care Act.

Introduction

The influence of Henri de Lubac's construal of the relationship between nature and grace upon postconciliar Roman Catholic theology is so pervasive that it almost taken for granted. De Lubac argued that the ends of human nature and human culture are fully revealed in the light of the grace of Jesus Christ made visible by the gift of the Holy Spirit. For example, de Lubac's thesis undergirds the *communio* ecclesiology articulated by Pope John Paul II, Pope Benedict XVI, and Hans Urs von Balthasar, which has become the hallmark of much postconciliar Catholic social thought.[1] A recent wave of scholarship, however, indicates that some scholars are engaging in a critical reappraisal of the influence that de Lubac's thesis has had upon the Catholic Church's engagement in

Thomas J. Bushlack is an assistant professor of Christian Ethics at the University of St. Thomas in St. Paul, Minnesota. 2115 Summit Ave, JRC 153, St. Paul, MN 55105; tjbushlack@stthomas.edu, thomasjbushlack.com.

Journal of the Society of Christian Ethics, 35, 2 (2015): 83–100

the late modern world.[2] These scholars suggest that de Lubac's thesis may have had unfortunate—albeit unintended—consequences for Christian engagement in culture and politics. For example, the contributors to a recent volume on de Lubac's influential book *Surnaturel* (originally published in 1946) suggest that his construal of nature and grace may have inadvertently contributed to many of the problems of the post–Vatican II Church. These include "declining vocations, a confused moral theology, [and] a revitalized secular hostility to the Christian religion."[3] These scholars recommend reasserting a much stronger distinction between nature and grace than de Lubac and many postconciliar theologians tend to favor in order to address these challenges to Christian cultural engagement.

This essay considers some of these recent criticisms of de Lubac's thesis in light of central texts from Thomas Aquinas insofar as the way in which one construes the relationship between nature and grace bears directly upon a normative description of the role of Christian engagement in the political and legal structures of late modern democratic institutions. On the one hand, I agree that there is a need to posit a stronger distinction between nature and grace than de Lubac's work seems to allow. On the other hand, however, I believe that some of the proposed alternatives to de Lubac move too far in the opposite direction.

I will argue that scholars such as Steven A. Long and Reinhard Hütter combine a more radical distinction between nature and grace with a lack of attention to the historical context of the development of Aquinas's theology. They also tend to combine this more radical nature/grace distinction with a denigration of the moral capacities of human nature in precision from grace.[4] In general, the neo-Scholastics tended to practice an ahistorical method of speculative inquiry proceeding via deductive reasoning from timeless first principles. One of the reasons, however, that this method was abandoned was because it was unable to deal adequately with the political realities presented by the development of liberal-democratic regimes. More specifically, the neo-Scholastic affirmation of political authority was dependent upon the state's official recognition of and support for the authority of the Church, either through an officially recognized, state-endorsed Church or through some kind of official union between Church and state.

By paying closer attention to the historical context and development of Thomistic notions of nature and grace, this essay proposes a more nuanced critique of de Lubac's construal of nature and grace that preserves de Lubac's essential contributions and provides a necessary corrective to his project. I uphold a distinction between nature and grace in order to defend the moral normativity of nature as a theological concept. This requires us to navigate a middle ground between de Lubac and his more radical critics. One of the goals of this essay is to outline the contours of this middle ground without collapsing nature into grace (as de Lubac tends to do), and without defending a theory of nature drained of its positive normative moral content (as some of the more radical criticisms of de Lubac tend to foster). The conclusion considers how this nuanced approach might help us to reframe the US Conference of Catholic Bishops' (USCCB) concerns over religious freedom vis-à-vis the Patient Protection and Affordable Care Act (ACA) that was signed into law by President Barack Obama in 2010.

Avoiding Extremes: Dualism and Integralism

De Lubac was motivated in part by a desire to move away from both a neo-Scholastic dualism between nature and grace, and from what scholars have referred to as "integralism" in Catholic political thought.[5] Integralism refers to a normative theological vision that seeks a restoration of an intimate relationship between the Church and political institutions, or between altar and throne. At the same time, de Lubac wanted to distance himself from the total rejection of modern liberal forms of democratic political institutions that had characterized the more reactionary voices during the modernist controversy. The modernist controversy involved attempts by various Catholic leaders either to reject the developments in philosophy, theology, and politics that had occurred in the modern period or to incorporate them into theological reflection. Therefore, it was necessary for de Lubac to delineate a nuanced position.

The more vocal conservative Catholic voices amid the modernist controversy rejected the rise of modern liberal political institutions and sought a return to some form of integralism.[6] However, these reactions against modernity, when combined with a nostalgia for integralism, stifled the Catholic Church's engagement with the liberal and democratic political and legal structures that developed during the period between the late eighteenth and early twentieth centuries. This left Catholics with very few practical options for promoting the common good in secular democratic societies. One of the theological-practical problems, therefore, that motivated the work of de Lubac and others was the need to provide a theological framework in which Catholic political thought could move beyond its attachment to integralism and the stifling effects of the modernist controversy while also avoiding the opposite extreme that would entail falling back into a neo-Scholastic dualism between nature and grace. This was—and still is—no small task.

These debates over the relationship between nature and grace were not merely speculative abstractions. They had important implications for the manner in which the Church as a whole and individual Christians would conceive of their involvement in the political cultures of modern, liberal nation-states. Gerald McCool writes, for example, "The theological controversies of the nineteenth century cannot be divorced from the Church-state tensions of the period. The relations between faith and reason and the relations between Church and state after all were aspects of the one basic problem concerning the relation between grace and nature."[7] Those who defended the more integralist theological positions also tended to align themselves with the most right-wing forms of political engagement, such as Charles Maurras's *Action Française*, a movement that was eventually condemned by Pope Pius XI in 1926. McCool writes that such troubled political times "were forging an alliance between integralist theology and right-wing politics."[8]

Given his strong reaction against neo-Scholastic dualism, de Lubac tended more toward an integralist position. The main problem with the integralist approach is that the category of "nature" does almost no critical or descriptive work for defining the natural, human ends of political institutions. As Guy Mansini states it, "everything ends up on the theological bank of the divide," as "there is no divide, because there is nothing really and truly to divide the supernatural from."[9] Integralist claims lead to the conclusions that the true nature of human culture and politics can only be known in the Church. David Schindler writes, for example, that "to cure the world, to liberate any human or nonhuman entity or any aspect thereof to be what it truly is, we must look to the Church."[10] Within an integralist account, the natural ends of the political community seem to have no intrinsic intelligibility or normativity outside of the completion of the state by grace via the Church. This raises a question posed by Russell Hittinger when he asks "whether there is an ontological landscape internal to social forms."[11] For Schindler and others who follow de Lubac's construal of nature and grace, it seems that there is not an ontological landscape intrinsic to human social and political institutions. The problems that arise within an integralist approach draw attention back to the importance of how one construes the relationship between nature and grace as the foundation for Christian engagement in democratic institutions.

Natural Desire and Natural Ends

Some of de Lubac's recent critics, such as Steven A. Long, Lawrence Feingold, and Reinhard Hütter, suggest that his construal of the relationship between nature and grace downplays the integrity of nature in Catholic theology and ethics. For example, Long accuses both de Lubac, Schindler, and others who follow de Lubac of overlooking the true "ontological density" of nature as a category on its own terms.[12] By referring to nature's "ontological density," he seems to mean that the nature of each species of existents remains morally intelligible within its own natural endowments and capacities. He believes that this loss of the ontological density and integrity of nature makes natural law reasoning both theoretically unintelligible and practically ineffective. He draws upon recent critical scholarship on de Lubac in order to argue for a stronger emphasis upon the role of nature, natural ends, natural teleology, and a metaphysics of nature in Roman Catholic natural law as a foundation for moral and political thought.[13]

Many of these discussions and disagreements revolve around the role of the natural desire for God in Aquinas's work. Aquinas proposes two sets of seemingly contradictory texts. On the one hand, Aquinas states clearly that "every intellect by nature desires the vision of the divine substance" (*Summa contra Gentiles* [*ScG*] III 57), and that "final and perfect happiness can consist in nothing else than the vision of the Divine Essence . . . [since] for perfect happiness the intellect needs to reach the very Essence of the First Cause" (*Summa Theologiae* [*ST*] I-II 3.8). Thus, the human intellect and will remain unsatisfied until coming to rest in the contemplation of God's Trinitarian essence in the beatific vision. Furthermore, Aquinas claims that "a natural desire cannot be in vain" (*Compendium Theologiae*, I 104).[14] Thus it appears that humans have one, final end—direct contemplation of the divine essence in the beatific vision—along with a correlative natural desire for that end. If this were the whole picture, then this end must be understood to be implanted within the ontological contours of created human nature, and it would seem that all humans are naturally capable of achieving this end.

In a second set of texts, however, Aquinas states that no person can achieve this ultimate end by her natural faculties or capacities alone. He writes, "Every knowledge that is according to the mode of created substance falls short of the vision of the Divine Essence, which infinitely surpasses all created substance. Consequently, neither the human person, nor any creature, can attain final happiness by his natural powers" (*ST* I-II 5.5). Thus, the human person is in need of additional help—that is, grace—in order to achieve his final end. Following Aquinas's logic, every rational creature naturally desires to see the divine essence, no natural desire can be in vain, and yet human nature itself is insufficient to attain its own end. These claims seem prima facie incompatible, and here one encounters the paradox and challenge of interpreting Aquinas on these points. If human nature is incapable of reaching its final end by its own natural powers, in what sense can the desire for God be *natural*?

The picture is further complicated by the fact that Aquinas posits one end of happiness for the human person—which is the beatific vision—but he also qualifies this by stating consistently that the single end of the human person can be analyzed under a "twofold aspect" (*duplex est*).[15] For Aquinas, there is an imperfect, natural happiness that can be had in this life through the exercise of the person's natural faculties and in particular through the acquisition and perfection of the cardinal virtues. At the same time there is the perfect, ultimate happiness that can only be found in the next life, in the end that transcends all human powers.

Unfortunately, Aquinas never directly considers the question of the relationship between nature and grace in a manner that would provide definitive solution to the paradox inherent in his treatment of the twofold end of human nature.[16] He simply leaves us with a paradox, albeit one that he felt was rationally defensible in the light of faith and his theological method.

In his commentary on Aquinas regarding the natural desire for God, de Lubac relies heavily on the notion of paradox to describe the condition of the created rational creature called to an end that transcends her natural capacities. "The desire to see [God] is in us, it constitutes us, and yet it comes to us as a completely free gift. Such paradoxes should not surprise us, for they arise in every mystery; they are the hallmark of a truth that is beyond our depth."[17] This depth, he concludes, can only be understood in the light of faith. For de Lubac, only with faith does a person understand the paradox that undergirds her true spiritual nature and the destiny to which she is called.

While I agree with de Lubac that the transcendent end of the human person presents a paradox that can only be comprehended in the light of faith, he seems to resolve this paradox too heavily in favor of seeing a direct desire for God implanted within the ontological structure of human nature. In his attempt to refute later commentators on Aquinas such as Cardinal Tommaso Cajetan (1469–1534) who posit a pure nature within Aquinas's thought, he resolves the paradox by collapsing everything up toward the supernatural. It seems that everything is so naturally ordered by grace that there is nothing to delineate the natural from the supernatural. As a consequence, de Lubac's solution leaves few tools that could enable Christians to think about the pursuit of the temporal common good as a penultimate, created, natural good that has inherent worth for the human community, even as each person is paradoxically called to an ultimate end that transcends the terrestrial good.

According to de Lubac, the late medieval commentators—in particular Cajetan—tended to interpret Aquinas as if he believed there were such a thing as a "pure nature" divorced from the supernatural economy of grace, and they did so precisely in order to defend the total gratuity of God's gift of grace. In doing so, according to de Lubac, they began to posit a "modern theory of a spiritual nature . . . with a 'purely natural' finality, [that] was born and developed in the intellectual context of a watered-down idea of what finality is."[18] This kind of natural finality he believes "to be verbal and irrelevant" for Aquinas himself.[19] He continues by claiming that a supernatural finality thus comes to be "considered as something fairly extrinsic: not a destiny inscribed in a man's very nature, directing him from within, and which he could not ontologically escape, but a mere destination given him from outside when he was already in existence."[20] In other words, nature and grace become seen as a two-tiered, dualistic system where grace does not seem to touch the essential nature of the human being but rather becomes a superstructure added onto an already self-sufficient human nature.

Once taken to the extreme of positing a pure nature, de Lubac believes that the desire for God is no longer natural and innate but is a foreign desire that must be superimposed upon an already self-sufficient intellect and will. In short, grace and all that comes with it become unnecessary for the satisfaction of human desires. For de Lubac, what began as a necessary and carefully nuanced philosophical and theological *distinction* in Aquinas between nature and grace becomes for the later commentators "a complete divorce."[21]

Three Responses to de Lubac

A recent wave of critical scholarship has begun to reevaluate de Lubac's thesis.[22] Some of these scholars question whether de Lubac's correctives to the neo-Scholastic interpretation of Aquinas's corpus may elide a necessary distinction between nature and grace. They claim that by subsuming nature into grace, or supernaturalizing the natural, de Lubac's solution to the paradox of the human person seems to indicate that grace will flow naturally out of a spiritualized human nature. According to this logic, the character of grace as unmerited gift is lost if it seems to emerge naturally from within the contours of an already-graced human nature. As David Braine states the problem, this makes it seem that "grace is an inevitable development of nature and therefore not gratuitous."[23] Or, as Lawrence Feingold articulates the problem, de Lubac's position would "divinize the nature of the creature, or make grace inscribed in nature."[24] Even though de Lubac himself consistently defends the gratuity of grace, these scholars are correct in noting that if supernatural grace is tethered too closely to the essential and intrinsic qualities of human nature, then the doctrine of grace as an unmerited gift of God is obscured. This position, however, leads de Lubac and his followers into another form of integralism. In de Lubac's form of theological integralism, the free gift of grace may come to be seen as equally unnecessary as de Lubac thinks it is for those who uphold the theory of a pure nature since it already appears to be "given"—or at least inevitably will be given—in the natural created order itself.

On the face of it, Aquinas affirms clearly that human persons have a natural desire for the vision of God's glory, which lends weight to de Lubac's thesis. The previous quote from *ScG* III 57 affirms the natural desire of every created intellect for the divine essence. What Aquinas does not make entirely clear is just how far this natural desire can carry the human intellect in pursuit of the contemplation of God as pure essence—that is, toward the beatific vision. Is it a natural desire for knowledge of God only insofar as God can be known as the first cause of all that exists, an inchoate conclusion reached on the basis of analogical inference and natural human reasoning? Or is it an implicit desire for the vision of God in God's essence (*ipsum esse*)—that is, a desire to know the

Trinitarian God revealed in the person of Jesus Christ and attested to by the scriptures? While de Lubac's position is carefully researched and nuanced, on the whole he seems to prefer the latter interpretation.[25]

Three schools of thought emerge among those who want to reconsider de Lubac's thesis. Among recent scholars, Denis Bradley defends the natural desire for God's innermost being in Aquinas as *implicitly* contained within the innate, natural human desire for perfect happiness.[26] Among those who uphold the strongest criticisms of de Lubac are Stephen A. Long, Lawrence Feingold, and Reinhold Hütter, each of whom claims that Aquinas speaks of two types of desire, one innate (or natural) and the other that must be "elicited" by grace and revealed knowledge.[27] For Long, Feingold, and Hütter the desire for God as *ipsum esse* is made natural only to the person in the state of sanctifying grace and in possession of faith. In a third group, a number of other scholars express reservations about de Lubac's thesis while defending a more nuanced position on the status of the natural desire for God, including Jean-Pierre Torrell, Guy Mansini, David Braine, Edward Oakes, Nicholas Healy, and Christopher Malloy. These scholars want to provide a corrective to de Lubac's supernaturalizing of the natural without going so far as those who seem to move too far back toward the neo-Scholastic preference for Cajetan's language of "pure nature" and the concept of "elicited desire," first used by the Spanish Jesuit theologian Francisco Suárez (1548–1617).

Those in this third group speak of a qualified natural desire for God, insofar as within the natural dynamism of the intellect there is an innate desire for truth and goodness. For Aquinas, this natural desire expresses itself in a dynamic curiosity that is activated by wonder, leads into philosophical inquiry, and proceeds toward metaphysical truths by way of analogical inference and logic (*ST* I 12.1, I-II 3.8). This natural desire, however, for Aquinas is not yet an *implicit* desire for the fullness of the beatific vision as it seems to be for de Lubac. Indeed, even in order for this natural desire to become the more particular desire to know God as first cause of all that is (and here one is still within the capacities of unaided reason), this desire must be further extended by the intellect's innate desire to know the causes of the observable phenomena within creation.

For example, in Question 14 of the *De Veritate*, Aquinas comments on the desire for the beatific vision by citing St. Paul's comment that "no eye has seen, nor ear heard, nor the human heart conceived, what God has prepared for those who love him" (1 Cor 2:9). Aquinas describes the natural desire as sufficient for pursuing the natural end of the kind of knowledge "of which the philosophers speak" (*De Veritate*, 14.2). The infusion of faith in the intellect, however, also activates a desire in the will that "is made to exist inchoately within the human being" (ibid). It is inchoate because the intellect needs to be moved from potency to act by some object external to it through the will's affection. This suggests that Aquinas's argument for the natural desire to see God is intended to establish the *possibility* that the blessed will truly come to see God's essence. He does not therefore conclude that every person implicitly desires to come to such a particular end in the absence of additional revealed or infused knowledge and virtue.

In Aquinas's analysis of the relationship between intellect and will, the paradox of the natural desire for God is again displayed, but this paradox does not imply a collapsing of the distinction between nature and grace as de Lubac seems to do. Rather, the possibility of knowing God through revealed knowledge presupposes just such a distinction. The natural desire for God as a capacity remains inscribed within the contours of human nature because human persons are made in the image and likeness of God and as rational creatures possess a capacity to see and know God—either as first cause or more specifically as the Trinitarian communion of persons. Thus, when explicit knowledge of God as Trinity is revealed through scripture or via infused grace, this is not something imposed over and above human nature (as de Lubac feared). Rather, infused grace activates and extends the capacity for God that naturally resides in the intellect and will.

Two Clarifications of de Lubac's Thesis

Two further steps toward clarifying the paradoxical status of the natural desire for God are provided in articles by Jean-Pierre Torrell and David Braine. Torrell notes that Aquinas always considers the human person within the actual order of providence that humans experience in this world as it has been revealed in the biblical narrative and the person of Jesus Christ. According to Torrell, some scholastics prior to Aquinas had debated whether the first created human being was endowed with sanctifying grace from the first moment of existence. Aquinas takes the position that human nature from the very moment of creation was endowed with the gift of sanctifying grace.[28] What this signifies, according to Torrell, is that Aquinas is primarily concerned with articulating the natural desire for God as it exists in all human persons who have been irrevocably influenced by the gift of sanctifying grace at the moment of creation and its subsequent loss due to original sin.

Prior to the Fall, human beings created in a state of grace would have had a qualified "natural" desire to see God's essence not because of the inherent principles of human nature per se but because of the gratuity of grace from the first moment of creation. This gift of habitual grace in the moment of creation conferred an explicit desire for God upon the first human beings. After the Fall, this natural desire is in need of further aid and specification through faith (and the other theological virtues) in order that the intellect and the will may be elevated, healed, and directed toward God's innermost being, as it had originally been at the moment of creation. This subtle but important distinction between *nature-as-such* and *nature-from-the-very-moment-of-creation* enables humankind to appreciate that the desire for God as an original imprint within human nature is felt on an existential level without it being inscribed within the contours of human *nature-as-such*. Thus, de Lubac is correct to note that this desire for a supernatural finality is experienced by those persons who exist in this order of creation and providence. This does not entail, however, that it is fully inscribed within of the natural capacities of the human intellect and will themselves.

David Braine's observations build upon this point from Torrell as he identifies a tendency for de Lubac to conflate human *nature-as-such* with human *persons* existing after the Fall. For Braine, "[de Lubac] should have said that supernatural finality is something given to *persons* in virtue of a relation, rather than that it gives them a *distinct nature*."[29] De Lubac's thesis provides an existentially correct description of human *persons* after the Fall, but it fails to distinguish between human persons *qua* beings existing in this providential order of God's creation and the intrinsic principles of human *nature-as-such*. This subtle philosophical oversight leads de Lubac to conclude that the supernatural end must be imprinted upon human nature itself. A more historically and hermeneutically precise manner of interpreting Aquinas on this point enables us to view the desire for God via the beatific vision as something that was (1) given at the moment of creation, (2) subsequently lost after the Fall, (3) experienced by all persons in human history as something missing, and, therefore, (4) naturally desired.

Taken together, these insights from Torrell and Braine provide important qualifiers that enable a more nuanced appreciation of de Lubac's contribution to the nature/grace discussion. They facilitate a recognition that human *nature-as-such* is defined first and foremost in relation to its connatural end rather than its supernatural end but that *persons* nonetheless experience an incipient desire for the beatific vision that has been lost. This provides an important insight into why a proper understanding of the relationship between nature and grace enables Christians to recognize and pursue the natural ends of the political community without requiring political institutions to make direct advertence to revelation or the Church.

Thus, even as God created human beings with sanctifying grace in this order of providence with the sole end of eternal felicity with God, the nature of the human species remains normatively distinguished by its natural capacities and powers. Reading Aquinas's comments on the desire for God through these historical (Torrell) and philosophical (Braine) corrections to de Lubac's thesis preserves Aquinas's insistence upon a distinction between nature and grace. At the same time, these insights lend further weight to de Lubac's rejection of the theory of pure nature. It helps to explain why Aquinas never speaks of a "pure nature" in the way the sixteenth-century commentators would later speak of it (and as Long, Feingold, and others now seek to rehabilitate). The concept of pure nature belies a further level of speculative abstraction that Aquinas himself was not primarily concerned with exploring or defending. Unlike Cajetan's later speculative preoccupations, Aquinas's primary concern is to present a philosophically and historically accurate analysis of the conditions of human persons in this order of creation once touched by grace but longing for its loss. Indeed, Aquinas never used the term *natura pura* in any of his writings.[30] On this point de Lubac was correct to criticize later commentators in their eisegesis of a putative pure nature in Aquinas's discussion of nature and grace. However, Aquinas does consider it a worthwhile theological enterprise to consider what is essential to human nature in precision from grace and in relation to its own natural endowments and powers. This latter point tends to be overlooked by de Lubac and is of central importance for Christian engagement in modern political institutions and the pursuit of the common good.

Epistemological Superiority

Among those scholars who critique de Lubac's thesis, Stephen A. Long and Reinhard Hütter consistently follow these criticisms to their logical implications for natural law and the Church's moral and political forms of witness in liberal-democratic cultures.[31] For Long, the global consensus that has emerged in public discourse and international law on the existence of human rights in the latter half of the twentieth century and continues to develop in the twenty-first is not a witness to the cogency of natural rights based upon natural law. Rather than providing a foundation for upholding human dignity and justice, he believes that such practical agreement—devoid of speculative agreement on the metaphysical principles of natural law—will instead foster "incessant political and social conflict."[32] Hütter similarly claims that only "a theologically enlightened, genuine liberalism" can attain to truly good ends for the human community.[33] For both Hütter and Long, liberal political institutions can only attain to their true, connatural ends if they appeal to the guidance of the Church.

In Long's view, true social cohesion will only be practically possible when all persons can agree upon the speculative foundations of natural law, the teleological ordering of ends, direct and intentional "advertence to revelation," and the privileged location of the Catholic Church as "our tutor in natural law."[34] Whereas Catholic neo-Thomists in the mid-twentieth century such as John Courtney Murray and Jacques Maritain had claimed that because of particular historical circumstances and intellectual commitments within the Church, natural law had survived in Catholic intellectual tradition, Long seems to claim that natural law is *only* intelligible within Catholic tradition.[35] He rejects natural law as the proper inheritance of all humankind or as a foundation for a universal humanism and affirmation of universal human dignity (as it was recently defended in the introduction to the International Theological Commission's "In Search of a Universal Ethic: A New Look at the Natural Law").[36]

Both Long and Hütter believe that all forms of natural law reasoning will be intrinsically flawed if they are not subsumed into revelation and the Church's magisterial authority. They also concur that democratic institutions are unable to achieve their connatural ends of securing justice, protecting human rights, and pursuing the common good in the absence of guidance from the Church. For Hütter, the wounding of human nature is so deep, and the healing effects of grace so profound, that forms of natural law reasoning that do not *explicitly* advert to divine law (revelation), tether human reason to eternal law, or defer to the Church's magisterial authority will *always* be incapable of providing any effectively normative order to human morality and civil law. Hütter writes, for example, that "the natural love of God above all that orders a society to the common good *is no longer efficaciously operative in the state of wounded human nature*."[37] Because of this, "genuine, theologically enlightened liberalism" is only possible when liberal thought submits to official teachings of the Church regarding natural law.[38]

Long's and Hütter's analyses of natural law reasoning implicitly reject Murray's claim regarding natural law that it "has no Roman Catholic presuppositions," that its antecedents are in Greco-Roman philosophy and jurisprudence and its potential analogues may be found in other non-Western traditions.[39] For them, natural law *is* Roman Catholic philosophical reasoning, and this reasoning is superior to all other modalities of moral reason. Long writes, for example, that "the condition of philosophy in the life of the Christian is superior both because (1) subjectively, there is the aid of the superior illumination of grace, and (2) objectively, revelation both *medicinally* reveals certain truths nonetheless properly natural and available to reason, while it also provides negative and positive norms that help to inspire and guide [moral] inquiry."[40] By denigrating the moral significance of human nature and its teleologically ordered inclinations to virtue after the Fall, and by upholding the Church as *the* privileged location of grace-infused reasoning, he proclaims an epistemic superiority to Christian moral discourse.

Ironically, Long's and Hütter's proposals end up overlapping with integralist positions such as de Lubac's and Schindler's insofar as both groups share a similar rejection of what Hittinger has called the ontological landscape of natural social institutions. On the one hand, I have claimed that the proposals offered by Feingold, Long, and Hütter uncritically appropriate a nature/grace dualism that was perpetuated in neo-Scholastic thought. I have also argued that they have combined this dualism with a denigration of the moral normativity of nature itself. Moral reasoning based upon natural law in the neo-Scholastic perspective is ineffective either for individuals or as a guide to the formation, creation, and sustaining of just social institutions in civic life. On the other hand, the integralist perspective overlooks the integrity of nature in precision from grace, moving too quickly into the full perfection of nature via grace. The integralist position therefore ends up with very similar conclusions about the natural intelligibility of moral reasoning and the natural ends of the political institutions of the political community, as do those who advocate for a more radical nature/grace distinction. Although they do so for very different reasons, both the integralist and the neo-Scholastic solutions to the question of how best to construe the nature/grace relationship leave little room for moral reasoning about the natural, penultimate goods that are to be pursued in human society.

Conclusion: Christian Public Witness and the ACA

In the current debate in the United States over health care reform, the USCCB Committee on Domestic Justice and Human Development has established the following four criteria to guide a fair and just reform of health care in America:

- a truly universal health policy with respect for human life and dignity;

- access for all with a special concern for the poor and inclusion of legal immigrants;

- pursuing the common good and preserving pluralism including freedom of conscience and variety of options; and

- restraining costs and applying them equitably across the spectrum of payers.[41]

These goals provide an excellent example of the Catholic moral tradition at work in a pluralistic and democratic society. They reflect a balanced perspective of the Catholic tradition's emphasis upon universal human rights, the preferential option for the poor and vulnerable, a positive role for government in pursuit of the common good, and the principles of distributive justice. While these principles are derived from particular religious commitments, they are understood to be a reflection of natural law as a universal capacity of human reason. In principle, therefore, persons from a wide array of backgrounds could come to a reasonable public consensus on these points. As such, they implicitly reflect an underlying distinction between nature and grace as well as a correlative appreciation for the manner in which distinctively religious arguments function to inform public policy in pursuit of the common good in a pluralistic, democratic society.

When it comes to a moral assessment of the particulars of the ACA however, the bishops' analysis focuses almost exclusively on the right to freedom of conscience. Despite occasional references to the good achieved by extending health care to millions of Americans, in multiple public statements the USCCB has consistently repeated its rejection of the law. In their estimation it does not provide sufficient conscience protection for those who wish to be exempted from health care plans that pay for elective abortions or for ensuring that no federal tax funds will be used to pay for abortions.[42]

There is an inherent tension between a moral analysis rooted in a nature/grace distinction and a more integralist position in these public pronouncements. On the one hand, the four principles of reform are congruent with an understanding of the natural goods of persons and the natural ends of the state as a guide to promoting the common good and the genuine flourishing of its citizens. On the other hand, a more integralist argument is used to reject the law *tout court* on the basis of insufficient conscience protection rights. The USCCB's responses to the law suggest that the rights claims for conscience protection function as a trump card over and above the moral urgency to create a health care policy that meets the needs of uninsured Americans. The bishops seem to be demanding that the government of the United States allow the Church to become "our tutor in natural law" (Long) in order to achieve a "genuine, theologically enlightened liberalism" (Hütter). The statements of the USCCB seek to uphold both a commitment to the common good amid pluralism while also reverting to integralist arguments when they are unsatisfied with the consensus reached in the passing of a law intended to extend health care to all Americans.

The public witness provided by this kind of moral reasoning appears to many citizens—including many Catholics, even those troubled by current abortion laws—to be overly focused on one particular aspect of a law that provides much-needed reform and relief to uninsured Americans. From an integralist perspective, the ACA—or any law for that matter—would need to meet the full moral vision provided by the Catholic tradition in order to be acceptable to Catholic citizens. One could also focus upon the law's inadequate attention to providing health care for immigrant populations, or to engage in a moral analysis regarding whether it adequately restrains costs or applies them equitably among a wide array of payers. In the USCCB's moral analysis of the law, no attention is given to how one might weigh the proportionate importance of the aim of extending health care as a universal right with the practicalities of protecting conscience rights vis-à-vis abortion funding.

In light of this, it behooves Catholics and others to recall the lessons of history in which the more reactionary Catholic responses to liberal governments who failed to meet certain standards of congruence with Catholic moral tradition tended to align themselves with right-wing political movements that sought to impose an integralist theology upon a pluralistic culture. Ultimately, these tendencies were either condemned or simply abandoned by the majority of Catholics because of the detriment such a stance caused to human rights and to the political stability necessary to uphold the common good. Neither a neo-Scholastic dualistic paradigm nor an integralist model has proven capable of providing Catholics or others with practical options for promoting the common good in secular democratic societies. The goal of this essay has been to defend a more nuanced distinction between nature and grace than the one provided by either de Lubac or contemporary integralist political theologies, and to claim that this distinction provides a necessary middle ground for leveraging religious arguments on behalf of the common good. In some cases that may mean that we as Christians are unable to demand the full legal implementation of our particular religious ideals. But such is the price of committing ourselves to the pursuit of the common good in a pluralistic society. If Christians wish to maintain an influence upon the political and legal structures of late modern democratic societies in ways that do not demand total adherence to our particular moral vision, then this kind of middle ground is required for securing the common good now and into the future.

Notes

1. See David Schindler, *Heart of the World, Center of the Church: Communio Ecclesiology, Liberalism, and Liberation* (Grand Rapids, MI: Eerdmans, 1996), 51–52n9.

2. See, for example, the following, nonexhaustive list: Bernard Mulcahy, OP, *Aquinas's Notion of Pure Nature and the Christian Integralism of Henri de Lubac: Not Everything Is Grace* (New York: Peter Lang, 2011); Stephen A. Long, "On the Possibility of a Purely Natural End for Man," *Thomist* 64 (2000): 211–37; Stephen A. Long, "On the Loss, and the Recovery, of Nature as a Theonomic Principle: Reflections on the Nature/Grace Controversy," *Nova et Vetera* 5, no. 1 (2007): 133–84; Stephen A. Long, *Natura Pura: On the Recovery of Nature in the Doctrine of Grace* (New York: Fordham University Press, 2010); Reinhard Hütter, *Dust Bound for Heaven: Explorations in the Theology of Thomas Aquinas* (Grand Rapids, MI: Eerdmans, 2012); Reinhard Hütter, "Aquinas on the Natural Desire for the Vision of God: A Relecture of Summa contra Gentiles III, c. 25 apres Henri de Lubac," Thomist 73 (2009): 573–79; Reinhard Hütter, "Desiderium Naturale Visionis Dei—Est Autem Duplex Hominis Beatitudo Sive Felicitas: Some Observations about Lawrence Feingold's and John Milbank's Recent Interventions in the Debate over the Natural Desire to See God," *Nova et Vetera* 5, no. 1 (2007): 81–131; the collection of essays edited by Serge-Thomas Bonino, OP, in *Surnaturel: A Controversy at the Heart of Twentieth-Century Thomistic Thought*, trans. Robert Williams (Ave Maria, FL: Sapientia Press of Ave Maria University, 2009); Nicholas Healy, "Henri de Lubac on Nature and Grace: A Note on Some Recent Contributions to the Debate," *Communio* 35 (2008): 535–64; Peter A. Pagan-Aguiar, "St. Thomas Aquinas and Human Finality: Paradox or Mysterium Fidei?" *Thomist* 64 (2000): 375–99; Guy Mansini, OSB, "Henri de Lubac, the Natural Desire to See God, and Pure Nature," *Gregorianum* 83, no. 1 (2002): 89–109; David Braine, "The Debate between Henri de Lubac and His Critics," *Nova et Vetera* 6, no. 3 (2008): 543–90; Edward T. Oakes, SJ, "The Surnaturel Controversy: A Survey and a Response," *Nova et Vetera* 9, no. 3 (2011): 625–56; and Christopher J. Malloy, "De Lubac on Natural Desire: Difficulties and Antitheses," *Nova et Vetera* 9, no. 3 (2011): 567–624.

3. See the publisher's annotation of Bonino, *Surnatural*.

4. Such claims are reminiscent of the positions defended by Hans Urs von Balthasar that the "theological concept of nature is primarily a negative one" that provides an empty vacuole for sanctifying grace. Hans Urs von Balthasar, *The Theology of Karl Barth: Exposition and Interpretation*, trans. Edward T. Oakes (San Francisco: Ignatius Press, 1992), 282; and Karl Rahner's claim that nature is simply a "residual" or "remainder concept" abstracted from the graced horizon of the supernatural existential in Karl Rahner, "Concerning the Relationship between Nature and Grace," *Theological Investigations*, vol. 1, trans. Cornelius Ernst (London: Darton, Longman, & Todd, 1974), 301–3.

5. See, for example, Russell Hittinger's reference to "l'integrisme" in "Introduction to Modern Catholicism," in *The Teachings of Modern Roman Catholicism on Law, Politics, and Human Nature*, ed. John Wittee Jr. and Frank Alexandar (New York: Columbia University Press, 2007), 30; and Louis Bouyer's comments on integralism in *The Church of God: Body of Christ and Temple of the Holy Spirit*, trans. Charles Underhill Quinn (San Francisco: Ignatius Press, 2011), 158.

6. See Pope Pius IX's *Syllabus of Errors* (1864) and Pope Pius X's *Pascendi dominici gregis* (1907).

7. Gerald McCool, *Nineteenth-Century Scholasticism: The Search for a Unitary Method* (New York: Fordham University Press, 1989), 27.

8. Ibid., 246.

9. Mansini, "Henri de Lubac," 97.

10. Schindler, *Heart of the World*, 29.

11. Hittinger, "Introduction," 14.

12. Long writes that "the negation of the ontological density of nature is thus liable to introduce dialectical distortions into our contemplation of God." Long, *Natura Pura*, 95; and later he adds that "the ontological density of nature and its proximate teleology is essential to the overcoming of secularism" (155).

13. Lawrence Feingold's *The Natural Desire to See God According to St. Thomas Aquinas and His Interpreters*, 2nd ed. (Ave Maria, FL: Sapientia Press, 2010), is frequently cited and seems to have motivated many of these recent criticisms.

14. See also *ScG* III 51: "it is impossible for a natural desire to be incapable of fulfillment."

15. See *ST* I 23.1, 62.1; I-II 62.1; and *De Veritate*, 14.2.

16. Jean-Pierre Torrell, OP, writes that "Thomas never wrote a monograph on nature and grace. . . . Right away he considers them in their relations, as though, at least when dealing with man, the one could not be defined without the other." Torrell, "Nature and Grace in Thomas Aquinas," in *Surnaturel: A Controversy at the Heart of Twentieth-Century Thomistic Thought*, trans. Robert Williams, 155–88 (Ave Maria, FL: Sapientia Press of Ave Maria University, 2009), 155.

17. Henri de Lubac, *The Mystery of the Supernatural*, trans. Rosemary Sheed (New York: Crossroad, 1998), 167.

18. Ibid., 68.

19. Ibid., 67.

20. Ibid., 68–69.

21. Ibid., 35.

22. See note 2 above.

23. Braine, "The Debate," 574.

24. Feingold, *Natural Desire*, 442. Torrell also writes that Aquinas's discussion of "integral nature" helps to safeguard the autonomy of the natural order of creation and demonstrates that "grace does not enter into the definition of nature" (Torrell, "Nature and Grace," 171). Such claims are reminiscent of Pope Pius XII's comment in *Humani generis* that "others destroy the gratuity of the supernatural order, since God, they say, cannot create intellectual beings without ordering and calling them to the beatific vision" (§ 26). Many scholars assumed this encyclical was written as a direct critique of de Lubac's thesis. However, Pius XII later wrote to de Lubac to personally thank him for his theological contributions to the life of the Church (see David Schindler's "Introduction to the 1998 Edition" in *Mystery*, xxxiii).

25. The general contours of de Lubac's position can be found in his appendix to *Surnaturel: Etudes Historiques* (Paris: Desclée de Brouwer, 1991), 431–38; *Mystery*, 207—21; and *Augustinianism and Modern Theology*, trans. Lancelot Sheppard (New York: Crossroad, 2000), 147–83.

26. "The desire to see God, then, is implicit in the desire for perfect beatitude." Denis J. M. Bradley, *Aquinas on the Twofold Human Good: Reason and Human Happiness in Aquinas's Moral Science* (Washington, DC: Catholic University of America Press, 1997), 459, emphasis in original.

27. Long, "On the Possibility," 221; and Feingold, *Natural Desire*, 15–16, 44, and 397. Reinhold Hütter concurs with Feingold's reading of Aquinas on elicited desire (*Dust Bound for Heaven*, 225–27). It should be noted that Feingold correctly notes that this language of innate and elicited desire is not used by Aquinas himself, and that it is attributable to Suarez's later commentary on Aquinas (*Natural Desire*, 15–16, 44).

28. Torrell notes the ways in which Aquinas's commitment to this point becomes stronger through the course of his career. For example, in *In II Sent.*, d.29, q.1, a.2, he writes that "since man was created in the integrity of his natural faculties (*in naturalibus integris*) and they could not stay inactive, *it is more probable* that, turned toward God in the first instant of his creation, he received grace" (emphasis added). However, by the time of writing the *De Malo*, he is much more forceful in his assertion where he writes that "original justice includes sanctifying grace and I do not believe that it is true that the first man was created with purely natural endowments" (*De Malo*, q.4, a.2, *ad* 1; also cited in Torrell).

29. Braine, "The Debate," 553, emphasis added.

30. Torrell notes that the term "natura pura" never occurs in the Index Thomisticus ("Nature and Grace," 168).

31. See Long, *Natura Pura*, 140–99; and Hütter, *Dust Bound for Heaven*, 102–28.

32. Long, *Natura Pura*, 153.

33. Hütter, *Dust Bound for Heaven*, 11. Later he writes that "When liberalism embraces such a catechesis [from the Church] it becomes explicitly genuine, theologically enlightened liberalism" (108).

34. Long, *Natura Pura*, 178.

35. Maritain writes, for example, that "the idea of natural law is a heritage of Christian and classical thought." It belongs to the heritage that leads back "to Grotius, and before him to Suarez and Francisco de Victoria; and further back to St. Thomas Aquinas; and still further back to St. Augustine and the Church Fathers and St. Paul; and even further back to Cicero, to the Stoics, to the great moralists of antiquity and its great poets." Jacques Maritain, *Christianity and Democracy and the Rights of Man and Natural Law*, trans. Doris C. Anson (San Francisco: Ignatius Press, 2011), 103.

36. International Theological Commission, "In Search of a Universal Ethics: A New Look at the Natural Law," Vatican (2009), accessed November 5, 2014, http://www.vatican

.va/roman_curia/congregations/cfaith/cti_documents/rc_con_cfaith_doc_20090520_legge-naturale_en.html.

37. Hütter, *Dust Bound for Heaven*, 108; italics added.

38. Ibid., 108.

39. John Courtney Murray, *We Hold These Truths: Catholic Reflections on the American Proposition* (Lanham, MD: Sheed & Ward, 2005), 109. Stephen J. Pope also provides an historical and thematic survey of the ways in which the concept of natural law has developed from classical antiquity, into medieval theology, and finally into the modern era. See Pope, "Natural Law and Christian Ethics" in *The Cambridge Companion to Christian Ethics*, 2nd ed., ed. Robin Gill (New York: Cambridge University Press, 2012), 67–87.

40. Long, *Natura Pura*, 187.

41. These goals are articulated in "USCCB Health Care Reform Summary and Timeline of Events." USCCB, August 26, 2010, http://www.usccb.org/issues-and-action/human-life-and-dignity/health-care/.

42. The USCCB Office of General Counsel released a legal analysis of the ways in which President Obama's executive orders fail to meet the standard for conscience protection set by the Hyde Amendment, which has prohibited the use of federal funds to pay for elective abortions since 1976. Anthony Picarello and Michael Moses, "Legal Analysis of the Provisions of the Patient Protection and Affordable Care Act and Corresponding Executive Order Regarding Abortion Funding and Conscience Protection," USCCB, March 25, 2010, http://www.usccb.org/issues-and-action/human-life-and-dignity/health-care/.

The Protectionist Purpose of Law: A Moral Case from the Biblical Covenant with Noah

David VanDrunen

Political and legal theorists sometimes assign attempts to define the purpose of law and government into one of two categories: *protectionism* indicates that law and government should protect people from the violation of their rights while *perfectionism* indicates that law and government should also actively promote virtue in the human community. In this essay I draw primarily from the biblical covenant with Noah (Gn 8:21–9:17), supplemented with other biblical and moral-theological considerations. I argue that protectionism, contrary to common assumptions, need not be individualist, subjectivist, or indifferent to the broader well-being of society. Furthermore, and chiefly, I argue that a strong (yet rebuttable) protectionist presumption ought to govern Christian ethical reflection upon the purpose of law and government.

WHAT IS THE PURPOSE OF CIVIL LAW AND OF GOVERNMENTS that operate according to the rule of law? Political and legal theorists sometimes assign attempts to answer this question into one of two categories: *perfectionism* or *protectionism*. As Nicholas Wolterstorff puts it, perfectionism claims that the "task of the state is to promote virtue in the citizens" while protectionism holds that the "task of the state is to protect citizens from being wronged."[1] Cathleen Kaveny frames the debate more colloquially, contrasting two approaches, law-as-moral-teacher and law-as-police-officer.[2] Should the law and the governments that implement it strive actively to promote the moral excellence of the political community, or should they limit their function to defending the community's members against harm?

Framing questions about the purpose of law under these categories has several limitations. For one thing, many laws arguably have purposes other than protecting from wrong or promoting virtue; laws regulating state-administered goods and services (such as infrastructure, education, or health care) are prominent

David VanDrunen, JD, PhD, is the Robert B. Strimple Professor of Systematic Theology and Christian Ethics at Westminster Seminary California, 1725 Bear Valley Parkway, Escondido, CA 92027; dvandrunen@wscal.edu.

Journal of the Society of Christian Ethics, 35, 2 (2015): 101–117

examples. Thus, the perfectionist/protectionist debate can likely only be one part of a larger discussion about the purpose of law. For another thing, neither perfectionism nor protectionism represents a monolithic political perspective. Perfectionists disagree among themselves about what vision of virtue law ought to promote while protectionists disagree about which rights law ought to protect.[3] Finally, perfectionist/protectionist disputes sometimes proceed by way of caricature, which obscures rather than illumines. A recent moral-theological defense of perfectionism, for example, portrays protectionism in terms of a society of lone individualist cowboys in which the only morality is the freedom to create one's own morality.[4] A protectionist may well retort by characterizing perfectionism in terms of a stifling puritanical society. Protectionism and perfectionism can indeed take extreme forms—and presumably Christian ethicists would reject both—but many protectionists do not advocate cowboy individualism, just as many perfectionists do not advocate a fundamentalist utopia.

Despite such limitations, these categories provide one way to facilitate debates about whether law should ever aim—primarily and for its own sake, without need for further justification—at promoting individual and community virtue, or whether its purpose should focus more narrowly on doing justice through the protection of rights.[5] Setting aside the (important) issue of state-supplied goods and services in order to keep this essay within reasonable bounds, I offer a case for a nonperfectionist protectionism. I argue specifically that a strong yet rebuttable protectionist presumption ought to govern Christian moral reflection about law and government. By making my argument primarily through the lens of the biblical covenant with Noah (Gn 8:21–9:17), I present a new way of approaching this debate and promote a version of protectionism that incorporates some of perfectionism's legitimate moral concerns and does not fall prey to its key critiques. I will first explain why I approach the perfectionist-protectionist debate by means of the Noahic covenant and then present my case for a protectionist presumption.

The Importance of the Noahic Covenant

Some readers may wonder: if we are going to consider what light scripture might shed on the perfectionist/protectionist debate, why not just investigate Romans 13:1–7? This text provides the New Testament's most extensive teaching on civil authority and would thus seem to be much more important for our subject than the Noahic covenant. Wolterstorff centers his defense of protectionism in Romans 13:1–7. What is the benefit of turning to an account from Old Testament primeval history?

Wolterstorff's handling of Romans 13 actually provides the answer. Although I concur in his protectionist conclusion, I am not convinced that he ultimately succeeds in making his case. Wolterstorff helpfully shows how Paul describes government as authorized by God to redress wrongs as a matter of justice and thus to function as a *"rights-protecting* institution."[6] Whether government ought to redress wrongs as a matter of justice, however, is not the point of dispute between perfectionists and protectionists. Both agree that government should take this responsibility. The point of dispute is whether government has *only* this responsibility or should also promote a virtuous community. The question to ask of Romans 13, therefore, is this: did Paul mean to describe the sole legitimate function of government, or did he simply mention its most prominent duty without meaning to exclude others? Wolterstorff does not ignore this issue. He notes Paul's silence on whether government has other legitimate functions not strictly required in justice; he mentions infrastructure as an example. Wolterstorff does not think Paul would have a problem with this sort of thing but concludes that Paul's silence with respect to perfectionist functions is significant: "The God-given task of government is not to pressure citizens into becoming virtuous and pious; its God-given task is instead to pressure citizens into not perpetrating injustice."[7]

Wolterstorff's case from Romans 13 seems underargued. Why exactly should we conclude that Paul's silence about some nonprotectionist government activities (infrastructure) is not significant but is significant for others (promoting virtue among citizens)? Does Paul's silence have any significance at all?

I believe it does, but to understand what insight Romans 13 contributes to the perfectionist/protectionist debate, we need to appreciate this text's place in the larger biblical canon rather than come to it directly as an isolated proof text.[8] Here is where the Noahic covenant becomes important. This covenant has a foundational place in the biblical canon, especially concerning matters of social-political life. Several considerations demonstrate why this is the case.

The most basic reason is that the Noahic covenant is a charter for the world as it now exists. Genesis 6–7 describes the great flood and Genesis 8:1–19 recounts God's re-formation of the earth. Although this story occurs so early in biblical history, scripture presents the great flood as a decisive, history-dividing event such that the period before the flood is viewed as an entirely different era from that which follows: 2 Peter calls that prior era "the world that then was" (2 Pt 3:6). This explains why the great flood becomes the preeminent harbinger of the final judgment in many later biblical texts (e.g., Isa 24:18, 26:20; Lk 17:26–27; 2 Pt 3:5–7) and why the description of the waters receding in Genesis 8:1–19 reads like a new creation account that in many ways echoes the original creation account in Genesis 1.[9] Immediately after this new creation account, God instituted the covenant with Noah as a charter decreeing the preservation of the entire natural order—cosmic, animal, and human—until this present earth is no more.[10]

Several items in the previous sentence are worth highlighting. First, this Noahic covenant promised the *preservation* of the world through maintenance of proper boundaries—between water and land (Gn 9:11, 15) and between human and animal (9:2)—but did not promise *redemption:* that is, no promise of a Messiah, the destruction of evil, forgiveness of sins, or eschatological life. Second, God extended this promised preservation to the entire natural order, encompassing the cosmic bodies (8:22), the earth (8:21), the animal kingdom (9:12, 15–17), and human society (8:21–9:17). This is a *universal* covenant. Third, God put this covenant into effect for as long as the earth endures (8:22). Thus God's governance of the world through the Noahic covenant continues to the present day. Even Christ's death and resurrection did not alter its normative status.

Since scripture presents this covenant as a charter instituted by God in order to govern the world in its various realms, this covenant evidently ought to be foundational for Christian thinking about the topics it addresses. Among such topics are law and civil authority: "As for your lifeblood I will require a reckoning: from every beast I will require it and from man. From his fellow man I will require a reckoning for the life of man. Whoever sheds the blood of man, by man shall his blood be shed, for God made man in his own image" (Gn 9:5–6).[11] With most contemporary Jewish and Christian commentators, I take this latter statement to be prescriptive and not merely descriptive.[12] God is the ultimate judge of those who shed human blood, but delegates a penultimate judicial authority to human beings. Thus, given the foundational place of the Noahic covenant in the biblical canon, I begin my investigation of the perfectionist/ protectionist debate here and will revisit Romans 13 at a later point.[13]

The Noahic Protectionist Presumption

In this section I argue that the Noahic covenant establishes for Christian ethics a presumption for a protectionist view of law and civil authority. The following argument makes two assumptions. I assume, first, that the use or threat of coercion against fellow human beings—concerning their person or property—is illegitimate unless justified.[14] In other words, coercion must be authorized.[15] Human beings may presume to have a right not to be coerced by another unless that other can justify his or her authority to coerce.[16] A theological reason for this assumption is that human beings are created in the image of God. As such, all people are morally responsible for how they use their gifts in God's service, and therefore attempts to interfere forcibly with a human being's body, actions, or resources constitute an implicit claim of authority over someone else's servant—i.e., God's. And since the creation of humans in the image of God also means that every person is ontologically equal to all other people, no one may arbitrarily claim authority over another. Thus the use or threat of coercion must be justified.

I also assume that all government actions, even those authorized by the law, are either overtly coercive or operate under threat of coercion. This includes government-provided benefits and services as well as government proclamations and exhortations. These actions themselves may not be coercive, but they depend upon taxation collected under threat of coercion. Thus, if all use or threat of coercion must be justified to be legitimate (my first assumption), then all government action must be justified. Governments may well be able to justify many of their actions, but justified they must be.

In the Noahic covenant, Genesis 9:5–6 provides such justification, under certain conditions, for one person to use coercion against another. God grants human beings authority to shed the blood of another human being as just punishment for an act of bloodshed by the latter. This authorization of coercion has more in view than simply capital punishment for murder; in fact, capital punishment is not really the point at all.

In short, Genesis 9:5–6 authorizes coercion against person A that is proportionate to the (unauthorized) coercion perpetrated by A against another person B. The blood-for-blood idea in Genesis 9:6 is an expression of the lex talionis, better known under the formula "eye for an eye, tooth for a tooth" (see Ex 21:23–25; Lev 24:18–21; Dt 19:21). The point of the lex talionis is not that hacking off body parts is the essence of justice. The point is that *proportionality* is key to justice. The punishment must fit the crime. The reason why the lex talionis was a staple of Old Testament Mosaic jurisprudence, and a staple of many other legal systems through history, is because it captures the principle of proportionality so perfectly and simply. Nothing is more equivalent to blood than blood, or to an eye than an eye. As scholars have argued, ancient legal systems that codified the lex talionis did not expect it always, or even ordinarily, to be applied literally (that is, by physical mutilation). The point was to establish the principle of proportionality as a loadstar for keeping punishments from being either too lax or too severe, and thus to deescalate cycles of violence.[17]

Genesis 9:5–6 seems to have government and civil law in view, as explained further below. Thus the Noahic covenant indicates that law and civil officials are authorized to carry out protectionist functions.

Since all coercive actions require justification, that is no insignificant conclusion. Nevertheless, it does not settle the point at issue. Both perfectionists and protectionists believe that law and civil officials have legitimate protectionist functions. The question is whether they *only* have such functions or also rightly pursue the perfectionist goal of promoting the virtue of citizens and society. The fact that the Noahic covenant only speaks about protectionist purposes does not necessarily imply that it forecloses other purposes. So the main question is whether there is a good reason to conclude that the Noahic covenant rules out perfectionism by authorizing an exclusively protectionist purpose for law and government.

Answering this question requires consideration of Genesis 9:5–6 in context. To begin, I reflect upon Genesis 9:5–6 in the context of the Noahic covenant as a whole and identify three considerations that, at least cumulatively, make a nonperfectionist protectionist interpretation plausible.

First, the Noahic covenant takes a sober view of human sin. This sobriety is evident at the outset of God's covenantal words: "every inclination of the human heart is evil from childhood" (Gn 8:21, NIV).[18] The Noahic covenant regards *every* human being as inherently corrupt. This means that any person who happens to hold a position of civil authority suffers from exactly the same corruption of sin as everybody else. To make matters worse, history and experience show that possessing political power over other people often has a deleterious moral effect on otherwise upstanding people. As Lord Acton memorably put it, "power tends to corrupt, and absolute power corrupts absolutely."[19] Thus, it seems considerably more likely that the Noahic covenant would aim to limit the authority of law and government than to grant them expansive authority. Thus, insofar as perfectionism tends to envision a greater scope for law's reach than does protectionism, a protectionist interpretation of Genesis 9:5–6 becomes initially plausible.

Second, the purposes of the Noahic covenant are important but narrow. For one thing, God promises merely to preserve the world and human society within it, not to redeem it or bring it to eschatological consummation. Those latter promises occur elsewhere in scripture, but not here. Corresponding to this, the Noahic covenant prescribes human social obligations of a minimalist character: be fruitful and multiply (9:1, 7), eat plants and animals responsibly (9:3–4), and administer proportionate justice (9:5–6). This is not an insubstantial social morality, but it is thin. Thus, insofar as perfectionism depends upon a thicker moral vision than does protectionism, this adds additional plausibility to a protectionist interpretation of Genesis 9:5–6.

Third, the Noahic covenant legitimizes a pluralistic society. By a "pluralistic society" I mean a society whose members hold a variety of different views about religion and the deepest issues of life. The Noahic covenant does not *authorize* a pluralistic society, in the sense of commanding it, but it does *legitimize* it, because God establishes this covenant with all living creatures (9:10, 12, 15, 16, 17), including all human beings for the rest of history (9:9, 12). In striking contrast to the Mosaic covenant, the Noahic covenant provides no religious or worldview qualification for membership. And if God has instituted human judicial authority for all human beings regardless of religion or worldview, then no human community may rightfully exclude people because they hold minority views on religion, philosophy, or lifestyle.[20] For pluralistic societies to survive, however, law must keep their members from unjustly coercing one another, which describes law's protectionist function. But the compatibility of perfectionism with a pluralistic society is more tenuous. Insofar as perfectionism's thick vision of the virtuous person or virtuous community must be explicitly rooted in a substantive theology or worldview, it seems odd that the Noahic covenant, on the one hand, would legitimize societies that are pluralistic in terms of its members' worldviews and yet also, on the other hand, leave open the possibility that governments might craft the law to pressure members to become virtuous according to the terms of a particular worldview. This adds still further plausibility to a protectionist interpretation of Genesis 9:5–6.[21]

The preceding considerations, internal to the Noahic covenant, make a protectionist interpretation of Genesis 9:5–6 plausible. An important point arising from the broader context of the narrative about Noah strengthens this plausibility.

Prior to the Noahic covenant (Gn 8:21–9:17), Genesis recounts the story of Noah's ark and the great flood (6:14–8:20). Before this, Genesis 6:1–13 describes the wickedness of the world and explains that God would destroy the earth because of it. In fact, these verses state God's rationale twice. The second time, God sees that the earth is "corrupt" and "filled with violence" (6:11–12), and thus he says to Noah: "I have determined to make an end of all flesh, for the earth is filled with violence through them" (6:13). These verses do not identify the nature of this corruption and violence that provoke such a terrible judgment. But the prior verses, 6:1–4, explain why God grieved that he had created human beings and resolved to blot them out (6:5–7).

The text states simply: "The sons of God saw that the daughters of man were attractive. And they took as their wives any they chose" (6:2). Shortly thereafter it adds: "The Nephilim were on the earth in those days, and also afterward, when the sons of God came in to the daughters of man and they bore children to them. These were the mighty men who were of old, the men of renown" (6:4). Biblical interpreters have often taken these mysterious statements to refer to angelic beings copulating with human women and producing unusually prodigious offspring. While the phrase "sons of God" does refer to angels in some other biblical texts, it is unlikely here. Calling attention to angelic sin serves little point in a text meant to establish why God would destroy the *human race*, and scripture nowhere else mentions the strange idea of angel–human procreation.[22] More likely is that the "sons of God" are royal figures. Kings, in other words, promiscuously took wives from the community. Perhaps they were amassing harems. Others have effectively defended this view, and I simply note that it reflects both the ancient Near Eastern background in which kings were often regarded as divine sons and the common biblical association of divine sonship with the exercise of royal authority.[23] The bottom line for present purposes is this: the violence and corruption that God saw on the earth, which provoked the great flood, was at least in large part *political* in nature. Kings were abusing their positions of power by taking whichever women they wanted. David Novak describes it bluntly: it was "politically sanctioned rape."[24]

The statement in Genesis 6:4 about the "Nephilim" seems to confirm this conclusion. The text does not say that these enigmatic Nephilim were the offspring of the sons of God and daughters of man but notes that they were on the earth in those days—and later as well (cf. Nm 13:33).[25] Therefore, kings were illicitly taking whichever women they wanted for wives at the same time that the Nephilim were roaming the earth. By describing the Nephilim as "mighty men" and as (literally) "men of name," the biblical text seems to indicate that they were arrogant military warriors.[26] We see again that the violence upon earth was political in nature—the violence was *state-sponsored*, to use anachronistic but appropriate terminology.

These considerations provide important canonical context for answering the main question before us: does Genesis 9:5–6 ascribe *only* a protectionist purpose to law and government? The preflood narrative suggests that the answer is affirmative. As just discussed, Genesis 6 explains that the problem of violence was what triggered the great flood. After the flood, the Noahic covenant addressed this problem of violence by authorizing the punishment of those who shed human blood. But it is important to note that the chief perpetrators of violence before the flood were kings and military warriors—officers of the state. For the Noahic covenant to constrain human violence effectively, its first concern had to be to limit political power. It is therefore compelling to read Genesis 9:6 not as illustrating one among many possible uses of political power but as prescribing boundaries for its exercise: that is, political power may be wielded to defend against those who violate others' rights, and for this purpose only. Thus, the broader biblical context of the Noahic covenant strengthens the plausibility of a protectionist interpretation of Genesis 9:5–6.

The Noahic covenant therefore provides a protectionist presumption for Christian ethical reflection. This covenant obviously does not provide a full-orbed political or legal theory, but Genesis 9:5–6 is most plausibly interpreted as presenting a nonperfectionist protectionist authorization for coercive civil authority. And given this covenant's foundational place in the biblical canon, I suggest that Christian advocates of perfectionism bear a burden of proof to show why this Noahic protectionist framework should not regulate our reflection about law and government.

The Broader Biblical Context

With respect to broader biblical considerations, the first and most obvious candidates for rebutting the protectionist presumption are the perfectionist provisions pervading the Mosaic law. However, while the protectionism of Genesis

9:5–6 is part of the Noahic covenant instituted to govern all human societies generally, thus including our own, the Mosaic law was promulgated as part of the covenant made exclusively with Israel to constitute it as a theocratic nation with a unique mission in the unfolding of God's redemptive purposes in history. The presence of perfectionist provisions in the Mosaic law that were evidently appropriate for Israel in its unique redemptive-historical circumstances does not in itself provide evidence for the appropriateness of perfectionist law for ordinary human societies existing under the much narrower purposes of the Noahic covenant. Thus they do not rebut the Noahic protectionist presumption.

Old Testament texts concerning Israel's Gentile neighbors, however, are relevant for present purposes in a way the Mosaic law is not because these nations, like our own, were in relationship to God merely through the Noahic covenant. Several Israelite prophets indicate that the rulers of these nations were God's servants and, as such, possessed legitimate authority, and the prophets often condemn these nations, and their rulers especially, for exhibitions of hubris and unjust violence.[27] Yet no prophet judges them for the failure of their laws to have perfectionist functions. Insofar as these texts indicate the proper nature of their governmental authority, therefore, it is the kind of protectionist authority reflected in Genesis 9:5–6. Thus the Old Testament prophets, if anything, confirm rather than rebut the Noahic protectionist presumption.

New Testament evidence points to a similar conclusion: a number of texts ascribe lawful authority to civil magistrates, as servants of God, and instruct Christians to honor and submit to them, at least in most circumstances (e.g., Mt 22:15–22; Rom 13:1–7; 1 Tm 2:1–2; Ti 3:1; 1 Pt 2:13–17). But the New Testament never teaches that these magistrates ought to pursue a perfectionist project.

It may help to look again at Romans 13:1–7 since this not only is the lengthiest New Testament discussion of civil authority but also presents as positive a picture of civil authority as the New Testament affords. If the New Testament has a perfectionist streak, this would be the most likely place to find it. Yet the number of remarkable similarities between Romans 13:1–7 and Genesis 9:5–6 is noteworthy. Both present their instructions as universally obligatory, neither associates civil authority with promises of salvation, both recognize authority to bring justice through coercion, both characterize justice in retributive terms, and both describe civil authority as delegated by God.[28] Oliver O'Donovan may be correct to believe that Romans 13 presents the state's sole authority as the rendering of judgment, but if so he seems to be incorrect to say that this is a *new* characteristic, following upon Christ's exaltation.[29] It is in fact as old as the Noahic covenant.

The only possible argument I can see that Paul adds a perfectionist element to what was already established in Genesis 9 is that, when Paul speaks of government praising those who do "good" and punishing those who do "evil"

(Rom 13:3–4), he uses general terms that envision civil officials with a broad authority to promote virtue and suppress vice.

But this conclusion is unlikely. Paul's reference to government praising those who do "good" is somewhat enigmatic, but evidence suggests that Paul referred to Roman officials rendering honor to wealthy public benefactors, not to the general promotion of community virtue.[30] Likewise, Paul's statement about government punishing the one who does "evil" does not refer to the general suppression of vice. Paul's precise claim is that the magistrate is an "*avenger*" unto *wrath* for the one who does *evil*" (my translation of Rom 13:4, emphasis added). With this terminology, Paul alludes back to the verses immediately preceding chapter 13, Romans 12:17–21, where he instructs Christians not to pay back "evil for evil" or to "avenge" themselves, but to leave a place for God's "wrath," because "vengeance" is his.[31] In short, what Christians (at least in their private capacity) ought not to do, civil magistrates should do.[32] This is important for the present question because what Paul tells Christians not to do is administer the lex talionis: "paying back evil for evil" (12:17). What Paul is saying in Romans 13:3–4, therefore, is that civil officials ought to administer the lex talionis, in the sense of enforcing proportionate justice. To be an avenger of wrath toward evildoers, therefore, is to carry out precisely what Genesis 9:5–6 prescribes.

Rather than add something to the protectionist responsibilities described in the Noahic covenant, Romans 13:1–7 echoes them. To bolster this conclusion, we might step back for a moment and ask: would Paul, given all his knowledge and experience with Roman government, *really* have envisioned them as nurses of virtue, even nurses of *Christians*' virtue? I find it difficult to disagree with Wolterstorff's conclusion: "Not a chance."[33] Thus I conclude, as I did with the Old Testament prophets, that the New Testament never overcomes the Noahic protectionist presumption. If anything, it confirms it.

Additional Moral-Theological Considerations

The previous section concluded that the Noahic protectionist presumption can be considered a broader biblical protectionist presumption. That should be a weighty matter for Christian ethics, but it is still merely a presumption. Perhaps broader moral-theological considerations should overturn it.

A recent moral-theological defense of perfectionism, Kaveny's *Law's Virtues*, provides a good test case. I focus on several of her key critiques of protectionism, which she believes display the strength of her modest perfectionism. Generally speaking, I concur with the moral concerns underlying these critiques. Christian ethicists have good reason to reject any protectionist theory unable to account for them. A cowboy individualist protectionism—against which Kaveny polemicizes[34]—indeed cannot account for these moral concerns. The theory of Joel Feinberg, Kaveny's chief protectionist interlocutor, probably cannot account for all of them either.[35] But a protectionist perspective grounded in the Noahic covenant does account for the moral concerns Kaveny raises. Therefore, the validity of these moral concerns does not demand overturning the protectionist presumption for which I argued above. On the contrary, these moral concerns further confirm its strength.

One of Kaveny's objections against protectionism is that its view of freedom is individualistic.[36] This charge is possibly true of Feinberg's position—although he goes out of his way to dispel this suspicion[37]—but it is not *necessarily* true of every protectionist theory. The Noahic covenant does not deal with human beings merely as individuals, although it does imply that every human bears God's image equally.[38] God established the covenant with the human race corporately and the covenant's first and last requirement is to be fruitful and multiply.[39] The protectionist purpose of law expressed in this covenant surely implies protection not only of individuals but also of families and other human associations. Human beings, as social animals, seem to have a natural proclivity to form associations to accomplish a variety of tasks. If a protectionist theory calls for government to protect such associations, it is no more inherently individualistic than perfectionism.

Kaveny also critiques protectionism for resting upon a subjectivist view of value.[40] This may well be a fair critique of Feinberg's protectionism, but it is clearly not true of a Noahic protectionism. In Noahic perspective, law is meant to protect human beings, made in the image of God. God has entrusted image-bearers with responsibility to serve God and their fellow creatures. Protection from unjust coercion is ultimately to protect people from those who would hinder them from using their skills and resources to fulfill that calling. Of course, offering such protection often means protecting people in their poor pursuit of this calling, but it is not fair to assume that the law's permission of evil conduct entails endorsement.[41] Broadly speaking, in Noahic perspective law should be embedded in a high view of human life, a high view of family and child-rearing, and a respect for animals and the broader creation order. This does not represent a subjectivist view of value.

A third concern of Kaveny is that human law inevitably communicates a moral vision. It "communicates something to its subjects about the ways in which they should and should not go about living their lives," and perfectionism "recognizes, emphasizes and takes responsibility" for this fact.[42] Protectionism, however, fails to take this seriously since it wants law to function only negatively and fails to inculcate a positive vision.[43] I suspect Kaveny is correct to say that law inevitably communicates something about how people ought to live. But it is not fair to suggest that protectionism, because it defines law's function negatively, fails to point to any positive social vision. As protectionist law focuses upon the defense of justice, it communicates that those living under the law ought to uphold justice in their mutual relations and, thus, that human beings should live together and collaborate peacefully, as far as possible, whatever their religion, ethnicity, or geographic origin.[44] That is a positive moral vision that can hardly be taken for granted in most of the world today. If protectionist law communicates a positive moral vision, it can also serve as a moral teacher, one of Kaveny's central concerns.

These conclusions suggest that some forms of protectionism and some forms of perfectionism may not be as far apart as one might suspect. What seems to divide them is not whether law may promote virtue in any sense but whether it may do so directly or only indirectly. My Noahic protectionist proposal suggests that law can and should promote certain virtues, but indirectly, as a consequence of its pursuit of justice and protection of rights. The virtues that law properly (and indirectly) promotes are thus those that orient people toward honoring the rights that law properly protects.[45]

When discussing the Noahic covenant above, I claimed that its internal context suggests the plausibility of a protectionist reading of Genesis 9:5–6, insofar as its perfectionist alternative envisions a greater scope for law's reach, depends upon a thicker moral vision, and must be rooted in a more deeply substantive theology or worldview. Yet these qualifications are contestable, for some protectionist theories have an expansive understanding of rights that may in fact envision a greater scope for law, depend upon a thicker moral vision, and be rooted in a more deeply substantive worldview than some modest perfectionist theories.[46] This leads to two further observations. First, the protectionist purpose of law suggested by the Noahic covenant seems to point to a version of protectionism with a relatively less expansive view of rights.[47] Second, a modest perfectionism consistent with the limited purposes of law suggested by the Noahic covenant may be imaginable. This is because the virtues such a modest perfectionism envisions law promoting are precisely those that orient people toward honoring the (relatively less expansive) rights that law aims to protect, as mentioned above. These versions of protectionism and perfectionism would thus tend to converge practically, although they would presumably understand the relative priority of rights and virtues differently in the legal context.

Conclusion

In this essay I have tried to avoid the caricatures sometimes present in perfectionist/protectionist debates and have presented a modest case for protectionism that is grounded in scripture and shares the perfectionist rejection of individualism, subjectivism, and indifference to the broader well-being of society. Christian moral theologians may agree about these general concerns while disagreeing whether the proper task of law and government extends beyond the protection of justice to the direct promotion of virtue. If nothing else, I hope this essay establishes that point.

But I conclude with a cordial challenge to Christian advocates of perfectionism. I have argued that the Noahic covenant, interpreted in context and in light of its foundational place in the biblical canon, provides not a dogmatic or definitive case for protectionism but a presumption in its favor. A presumption may be overcome, but I have argued that neither subsequent biblical teaching nor weighty moral-theological considerations succeed in overcoming this protectionist presumption. I do not foreclose the possibility that other arguments might succeed, but I conclude that any case for perfectionism must meet this serious Noahic challenge in order to be persuasive.

Notes

I wish to thank Nico Vorster, Manfred Svensson and his political philosophy group at the University of the Andes (Chile), and one of the anonymous SCE referees for helpful feedback on an earlier version of this article.

1. Nicholas Wolterstorff, *The Mighty and the Almighty: An Essay in Political Theology* (Cambridge: Cambridge University Press, 2012), 101.

2. Cathleen Kaveny, *Law's Virtues: Fostering Autonomy and Solidarity in American Society* (Washington, DC: Georgetown University Press, 2012), chap. 1.

3. Thus, perfectionist theories and protectionist theories span the political spectrum. For illustration of the range of possible perfectionist visions, see, e.g., Robert P. George, *Making Men Moral: Civil Liberties and Public Morality* (Oxford: Clarendon, 1993); Kaveny, *Law's Virtues;* and Joseph Raz, *The Morality of Law* (Oxford: Clarendon, 1986). For illustration of the range of possible protectionist theories, see, e.g., Randy Barnett, *The Structure of Liberty: Justice and the Rule of Law*, 2nd ed. (Oxford: Oxford University Press, 2014); Wolterstorff, *Mighty and the Almighty;* and Ronald Dworkin, *Justice for Hedgehogs* (Cambridge, MA: Belknap Press of Harvard University Press, 2011).

4. Kaveny, *Law's Virtues*, 74–75.

5. I share Kaveny's basic approach: "I mean the two labels of 'law as police officer' and 'law as teacher' to function as heuristic devices, not as comprehensive and exhaustive analytical categories. They are designed to focus the reader's attention on the question of the fundamental purpose of human law." *Law's Virtues*, 18.

6. Wolterstorff, *Mighty and the Almighty*, 87–90 (italics his).

7. Ibid., 98–99.

8. In what follows, I interpret scripture as a completed canon. Thus, my use of scripture may reflect the spirit of "a canonical biblical theology" that "is not based on historical reconstructions, but on the Bible in its completed form." Charles H. H. Scobie, *The Ways of Our God: An Approach to Biblical Theology* (Grand Rapids, MI: Eerdmans, 2003), 183.

9. See, e.g., Nahum Sarna, *Genesis* (Philadelphia: Jewish Publication Society, 1989), 49–50.

10. For arguments that the whole of Genesis 8:21–9:17 recounts the Noahic covenant, see Stephen D. Mason, "Another Flood? Genesis 9 and Isaiah's Broken Eternal Covenant,"

Journal for the Society of the Old Testament 32, no. 2 (2007): 184–86; and David VanDrunen, *Divine Covenants and Moral Order: A Biblical Theology of Natural Law* (Grand Rapids, MI: Eerdmans, 2014), 101–2.

11. Unless otherwise indicated, translations of scripture are taken from The Holy Bible, English Standard Version ® (ESV®), copyright © 2001 by Crossway Bibles, a publishing ministry of Good News Publishers. Used by permission. All rights reserved.

12. This follows the approach of many prominent Old Testament scholars. E.g., see Sarna, *Genesis*, 61; Gerhard von Rad, *Genesis: A Commentary*, rev. ed. (Philadelphia: Westminster, 1972), 132; Claus Westermann, *Genesis 1–11: A Commentary*, trans. John J. Scullion, SJ (Minneapolis: Augsburg, 1984), 468–69; Gordon J. Wenham, *Word Biblical Commentary*, vol. 1, *Genesis 1–15* (Waco, TX: Word, 1987), 193–94; Victor P. Hamilton, *The Book of Genesis Chapters 1–17* (Grand Rapids, MI: Eerdmans, 1990), 315; and Bruce K. Waltke, *Genesis: A Commentary* (Grand Rapids, MI: Zondervan, 2001), 145.

13. The Noahic covenant is relevant not only because of its foundational place in the biblical canon but also because it provides a theological foundation for a Christian theory of natural law, as argued in detail in VanDrunen, *Divine Covenants and Moral Order*; cf. Jonathan P. Burnside, *God, Justice, and Society: Aspects of Law and Legality in the Bible* (Oxford: Oxford University Press, 2011), 79. I mention this to make clear that the argument that follows, which is largely biblical in nature, is not meant to be biblicist. I believe that the things made known in the Noahic covenant are not obscure but in accord with human nature as designed by God to live in a good but fallen world. That idea is worth keeping in the background, even though it is not my focus at present.

14. I use the term "coercion" purposefully. I might have spoken instead of "harm," in light of debates about the so-called harm principle in modern political theory. "Coercion" is not entirely free from ambiguity, but it is better for present purposes than using the term "harm." For one thing, sometimes we speak intelligibly about "harm" when no one has done anything coercive. For example, my business may be harmed by another business across town that has come to offer better goods and services than mine, but this other business has done nothing coercive simply by achieving a greater degree of excellence. Genesis 9:6 clearly does not authorize punishment for this kind of harm. In addition, we can also speak intelligibly of "coercion" when we do not think an action was harmful. For example, all government actions involve the use or threat of coercion, but some government actions bring benefit rather than harm. So again, insofar as Genesis 9:6 seems to be authorizing governmental action, it is better to speak of "coercion," not "harm." Kaveny does not speak quite accurately when she states: "The 'law as police officer' [i.e., protectionist] approach does not contend with the fact that there is substantial disagreement about what constitutes a harm that justifies legal intervention." *Law's Virtues*, 47. Advocates of this approach indeed *contend* with it, although their conclusions lead them in different directions from Kaveny's theory. Joel Feinberg, Kaveny's chief protectionist interlocutor, acknowledges the importance of developing a nuanced understanding of "harm"; see Feinberg, *The Moral Limits of the Criminal Law*, 4 vols. (New York: Oxford University Press, 1984–88), 1:12, 36, 214, 245.

15. I am sensitive to the objection that I have linked authority and coercion too closely. Authority presupposes the power of coercion, but authority is not simply the right to coerce. A property of authority does not necessarily define the essence of authority. At present I simply presume that where coercion is rightfully exercised, the coercer has some sort of authority to coerce under the circumstances.

16. A number of writers already cited—including Kaveny, Raz, and Feinberg—acknowledge some sort of similar right, but under the category of "autonomy." In the context of Christian ethics, I believe that considering this matter in terms of responsibilities for image-bearers of God is more theologically helpful and less liable to misunderstanding.

17. See William Ian Miller, *Eye for an Eye* (Cambridge: Cambridge University Press, 2006). For an argument that the lex talionis allows consideration of restorative as well as retributive justice, see VanDrunen, *Divine Covenants and Moral Order*, 501–5.

18. Even more sobering is that God's description of the human heart after the flood sounds essentially identical to his evaluation of the heart before the flood—an evaluation that prompted God's decision to send the flood in the first place: God saw "that every inclination of the thoughts of the human heart was only evil all the time" (Gen 6:5, NIV). Translations of scripture denoted by "NIV" are taken from The Holy Bible, New International Version® NIV®. Copyright © 1973, 1978, 1984, 2011 by Biblica, Inc. Used by permission. All rights reserved worldwide.

19. Acton penned this famous line in a letter to Mandell Creighton in 1887. See John Emerich Edward Dalberg-Acton, *Essays on Freedom and Power* (New York: Meridian, 1955), 335.

20. For further argument of this point, see David VanDrunen, "A Natural Law Right to Religious Freedom: A Reformed Perspective," *International Journal for Religious Freedom* 5, no. 2 (2012): 140–44.

21. See Wolterstorff, *Mighty and the Almighty*, 123, for observations that helpfully reinforce this point.

22. Rita F. Cefalu summarizes objections to this view in "Royal Priestly Heirs to the Restoration Promise of Genesis 3:15: A Biblical Theological Perspective on the Sons of God in Genesis 6," *Westminster Theological Journal* 76 (2014): 354–56. For a recent defense of the angelic view, see Jeffrey J. Niehaus, *Biblical Theology*, vol. 1, *The Common Grace Covenants* (Wooster, OH: Weaver, 2014), 164–73.

23. For further argument, see Cefalu, "Royal Priestly Heirs," 356–67; David Novak, *Natural Law in Judaism* (Cambridge: Cambridge University Press, 1997), 36–37; and Meredith G. Kline, "Divine Kingship and Genesis 6:1–4," *Westminster Theological Journal* 24 (1962): 187–204.

24. Novak, *Natural Law in Judaism*, 36.

25. As argued in Cefalu, "Royal Priestly Heirs," 359–60.

26. Elsewhere in the Old Testament the Hebrew term here translated "mighty men" often indicates strength and heroism in battle. Being "men of name" suggests *arrogance*, especially in light of the subsequent description of the tower-builders in Babel as those hubristically wishing to "make a name" for themselves (Gn 11:4). Genesis 10:8–12 identifies Nimrod as a "mighty man" and the founder of many cities, including Babel in the land of Shinar. Scripture describes Babylon, the great city later to rise up in Shinar, as brimming with arrogance (e.g., Is 13:19; 14:12–17; Dn 4:28–30). All of this confirms the link I am claiming between arrogance and political-military might.

27. For detailed discussion of such texts, see VanDrunen, *Divine Covenants and Moral Order*, chap. 4.

28. a) God institutes the Noahic covenant with *all* human beings (Gn 9:9, 12, 16–17) and Paul commands "every person" to be subject to the governing authorities (Rom 13:1). For further explanation and defense, see David VanDrunen, "Power to the People: Revisiting Civil Resistance in Romans 13:1–7 in Light of the Noahic Covenant" (forthcoming, *Journal of Law and Religion*). b) As noted, the Noahic covenant promises only preservation of earthly life, for a time. With respect to Romans 13:1–7, many commentators mention the striking absence of any reference to Christ or salvation in him; e.g., see James D. G. Dunn, *Word Biblical Commentary*, vol. 38B, *Romans 9–16* (Dallas: Word, 1988), 771; Arland J. Hultgren, *Paul's Letter to the Romans: A Commentary* (Grand Rapids: Eerdmans, 2011), 467; N. T. Wright, "The Letter to the Romans: Introduction, Commentary, and Reflections," in *The New Interpreter's Bible*, vol. 10 (Nashville: Abingdon, 2002), 717; and

Thomas H. Tobin, SJ, *Paul's Rhetoric in Its Contexts: The Argument of Romans* (Peabody, MA: Hendrickson, 2004), 396. c) The Noahic covenant prescribes "blood" for "blood." Romans 13:4 speaks of civil officials bearing "the sword." d) The Noahic covenant speaks of justice in terms of the retributive lex talionis (Gen. 9:6). I explain below how Romans 13:3–4 reflects the lex talionis. As noted, the lex talionis does not necessarily have an exclusively retributivist character but is also capable of accounting for restorative concerns; see VanDrunen, *Divine Covenants and Moral Order*, 501–5. e) Genesis 9:5 states that God will require a reckoning from all who shed human blood, and then 9:6 indicates that God ordains human acts of justice to accomplish this on his behalf. Romans 13:1–2 states that civil authorities are instituted by God, and subsequent verses declare them God's "servants" (13:4) and "ministers" (13:6).

29. E.g., see Oliver O'Donovan, *The Ways of Judgment* (Grand Rapids, MI: Eerdmans, 2005), 4.

30. See Bruce W. Winter, "The Public Honouring of Christian Benefactors: Romans 13.3–4 and 1 Peter 2.14–15," *Journal for the Study of the New Testament* 34 (1988): 87–103.

31. Among New Testament scholars who see a similar connection between Romans 13:3–4 and these earlier verses in Romans 12, see Dunn, *Romans 9–16*, 759; Douglas J. Moo, *The Epistle to the Romans* (Grand Rapids, MI: Eerdmans, 1996), 792, 802; Wright, "The Letter to the Romans," 717–18; and Robert Jewett, *Romans: A Commentary* (Minneapolis: Fortress, 2007), 796.

32. At this point I disagree sharply with Wolterstorff's understanding of Romans 13:1–7 since he argues that Paul recognizes no retributive function for government. See Wolterstorff, *Mighty and the Almighty*, 85–87; and Nicholas Wolterstorff, *Justice in Love* (Grand Rapids, MI: Eerdmans, 2011), 198.

33. Wolterstorff, *Mighty and the Almighty*, 118.

34. See Kaveny, *Law's Virtues*, 74–75.

35. Feinberg presents his theory comprehensively in *The Moral Limits of the Criminal Law*. I note below some areas in which Feinberg may not be as vulnerable to Kaveny's critiques as she suggests.

36. Kaveny, *Laws Virtues*, 22. Cf. Raz, *Morality of Freedom*, 18.

37. Kaveny mentions Feinberg's alleged individualism in *Law's Virtues*, 27. Yet Feinberg says that "the most significant truth about ourselves" is "that we are social animals"; see *The Moral Limits of the Criminal Law*, 3.46. Later he speaks of "the central and indispensable importance of community in human lives"; see 4.81; cf. 4.84. And see all of chap. 29A. Another protectionist mentioned above also tries to dispel the anticipated accusation of individualism; see Barnett, *Structure of Liberty*, 349.

38. In Genesis 9:6, which speaks in general of human beings as created in God's image, the blood of one person is an equivalent exchange for the blood of another person, implying that each human being's blood is of the same value as everyone else's, whether pauper or prince.

39. The Noahic covenant not only portrays human beings as living in community with each other but also portrays them in (a somewhat uneasy) community with the broader animal kingdom (9:2–4). David L. Clough thus understandably makes considerable use of the Noahic covenant in *On Animals*, vol. 1, *Systematic Theology* (New York: Bloomsbury T&T Clark, 2012).

40. Kaveny, *Law's Virtues*, 19.

41. Kaveny draws often upon Thomas Aquinas's claim in *Summa Theologiae* 1a2ae 95.3, following Isidore of Seville, that law should be "virtuous, just, possible to nature, according to the custom of the country, suitable to place and time, necessary, useful," and so on. This

translation is from *Summa Theologica*, 5 vols., trans. Fathers of the English Dominican Province (Allen, TX: Christian Classics, 1981). Thomas thus thought that law should not punish many things that are sinful. But Thomas clearly did not think that permission entailed endorsement. Also relevant here is his discussion of why all vices are not subject to repression by human law; see *Summa Theologiae* 1a2ae 96.2.

42. Kaveny, *Law's Virtues*, 28; cf. 17, 77. As noted, she uses the terms "law as moral teacher" and "law as police officer" to represent, respectively, perfectionist and protectionist approaches.

43. Ibid., 19, 77.

44. Among protectionist writers mentioned above, see some relevant comments in Feinberg, *Moral Limits of the Criminal Law*, 4.100; and Barnett, *Structure of Liberty*, 303–4.

45. Space limitations unfortunately do not permit interaction with Kaveny's claim that law ought to focus upon violations of justice but also ought to promote the other three cardinal virtues; see *Law's Virtues*, 33.

46. For example, the protectionist theories of Wolterstorff and Dworkin, cited earlier.

47. For further discussion of this topic, see David VanDrunen, "Natural Rights in Noahic Perspective," *Faulkner Law Review* 6 (Fall 2014): 103–34.

Doing Justice to the Complex Legacy of John Howard Yoder: Restorative Justice Resources in Witness and Feminist Ethics

Karen V. Guth

John Howard Yoder's reclamation of Christ's law of love as normative for Christian ethics makes important contributions to the field, but this pacifist legacy is tainted by his sexual violence against women. Prominent "witness" and "feminist" ethicists either defend or condemn Yoder, reflecting retributive approaches to wrongdoing. Restorative justice models—with their emphasis on truth-telling, particularity, and communal responses to violence—illuminate common ground between these often antagonistic groups of ethicists, whose specific resources are needed to "do justice" to Yoder's legacy. Yoder claimed that "Christian identity itself calls for feminist engagement," but he failed to fully develop this claim in his theology or embody it in his life. By collaborating in such a truly feminist pacifist politics, witness and feminist ethicists not only strengthen their own internal projects with respect to the church's mission and the promotion of women's flourishing but also more effectively address sexual violence.

IN MARCH 2007 I PRESENTED MY FIRST ACADEMIC CONFERence paper. Still in coursework as a second-year doctoral student at the University of Virginia, I had submitted a seminar paper comparing Dietrich Bonhoeffer's and John Howard Yoder's accounts of the relationship between Christian discipleship and violence. Before giving the paper, I experienced what I suspect was a normal level of nervousness. But I had done my best to prepare, anticipating potential questions, considering possible responses, even practicing the presentation aloud. After I delivered the paper, an audience member raised her hand and asked: "How can you give a paper on Yoder's account of Christian pacifism without acknowledging his violence against women?"

I was stunned: I knew nothing of Yoder's violence against women. Although Yoder's behavior and the church disciplinary process it prompted were publicly known since 1992 when reporter Tom Price's five-part series on Yoder's case appeared in the *Elkhart Truth*, I was not aware of these articles or the brief

Karen V. Guth, PhD, is an assistant professor in the Department of Theology at Saint Catherine University, 209 Whitby, 2004 Randolph Ave., St. Paul, MN 55105; kvguth@stkate.edu.

Journal of the Society of Christian Ethics, 35, 2 (2015): 119–139

news notice in the *Christian Century* about the suspension of Yoder's ministerial credentials.[1] The Yoder I knew was the one I had met through his theology in graduate seminars and study of the secondary scholarship. It was to this literature that I returned after the conference, intent on locating the critical information that I had somehow missed in my original research. But my subsequent search uncovered little to nothing in the way of public acknowledgment of Yoder's behavior.[2] Is this just?

This is just one of many questions that Yoder's complex legacy raises. Those directly impacted by Yoder's behavior—most importantly, the women he violated—have long grappled with his actions.[3] The Indiana-Michigan Mennonite Conference suspended Yoder's ministerial credentials and initiated a four-year disciplinary process in 1992. Yoder's local congregation, Prairie Street Mennonite Church, also formed a task force that year. More recently, Herald Press announced that it will include a disclaimer about Yoder's behavior in future publications of his work.[4] Anabaptist Mennonite Biblical Seminary (AMBS) released a statement addressing teaching and scholarship related to Yoder and held "a service of lament, confession and commitment" to "acknowledge the experiences of women who were sexually violated" by Yoder.[5] And the Mennonite Church USA initiated the fact-finding mission and discernment group that culminated in historian Rachel Waltner Goossen's comprehensive account of Yoder's sexual abuse and institutional responses. She indicates that beginning at least in the 1970s, Yoder violated as many as one hundred women by "making suggestive comments, sending sexually explicit correspondence, and surprising women with physical coercion . . . [and] more rarely, sexual intercourse."[6] As Goossen notes, although Yoder served as president of the Society of Christian Ethics (SCE) from 1987 to 1988, he was "never formally disciplined by the broader academic and religious peers with whom he was closely affiliated," including the SCE.[7] What are Christian ethicists' responsibilities to the women Yoder violated, to Yoder's theology, to our students, to the church, to the public, to our field? How are we to relate to this "traumatic past?"[8]

Consideration of how best to respond to wrongdoing arises in many contexts. One might think, for example, of the judicial system and legal responses to wrongdoing that end in either exoneration or condemnation. Responses to Yoder's legacy from Christian ethicists often seem characteristic of retributive approaches. On one hand, "witness ethicists" emphasize Yoder's submission to his church's disciplinary proceedings, arguing that his theology remains valuable despite his egregious actions.[9] While condemning Yoder's behavior, this move defends, vindicates, and even exonerates his theology, paying inadequate attention to the claims of Yoder's victims that the problem is not only the abuse they suffered but also the perpetuation of this trauma through the acclaim Yoder's theology continues to receive.[10]

Feminists, on the other hand, tend to ignore Yoder.[11] Women in the Mennonite Church, including Carolyn Holderread Heggen, Ruth Elizabeth Krall, Barbra Graber, and AMBS president Sara Wenger Shenk, have been pivotal in demanding accountability.[12] Feminist Mennonite scholars including Gayle Gerber Koontz, Elizabeth G. Yoder, and Lydia Harder have been raising important issues vis-à-vis Yoder's theology and peace church theology more broadly for years.[13] But to my knowledge, there are no prominent non-Mennonite feminists engaged in discussions of Yoder's legacy.[14] Apart from criticism of Yoder's discussion of "revolutionary subordination," there is and has always been very little feminist engagement with Yoder's theology itself.[15] This dismissal of Yoder's work expresses appropriate degrees of condemnation (or disinterest) but fails to reckon with the importance of Yoder's theology. In short, neither the witness nor the feminist approach gets us far in "doing justice."[16]

Is there a better way to think about "what it means to 'do justice' when living with [Yoder's] past wrongs?"[17] Feminist theologian Rachel Muers argues that restorative justice models offer resources beyond the criminal and political contexts in which they are often employed. Her use of restorative justice themes to explore approaches to sexist texts is suggestive. Might restorative justice models provide a useful interpretive lens for approaching Yoder's legacy?

Yoder's legacy presents particular difficulties. We are not dealing with Yoder himself. The women he violated, his church, and some of his academic institutions have begun that work. Nor are we dealing with problematic aspects of his texts.[18] We are dealing with his legacy—which is different territory altogether. The problem for us is not so much how to deal with the person who violated other persons or how to read problematic texts but the complicated intersection of the two: the continuing trauma of Yoder's violations in the acclaim of his theology. Mark Oppenheimer puts it well: the problem is that Yoder's "influence and stained past . . . live on."[19] How are we to handle Yoder's legacy given that the continued authority of his texts—texts central to Christian ethics—may perpetuate the trauma he inflicted? What would it mean to "restore justice" in this situation?

I argue that restorative justice provides a particularly salient model for reflecting on Yoder's legacy. Its emphasis on communal responses to wrongdoing enables the naming of stakeholders in Yoder's case and clarifies the role Christian ethicists may play in repairing harm caused by Yoder's legacy. Indeed, the central features of restorative justice illuminate common ground between witness and feminist ethicists—the very ethicists whose insights are especially needed to respond to Yoder's case yet rarely engage each other. Several features of restorative justice—the importance of truth-telling, emphasis on particularity, and communal responses to violence in its various forms—also figure centrally in witness and feminist ethics. I show not only how these features of restorative justice highlight structural similarities between these seemingly disparate ethical stances but also how embracing these aspects with respect to Yoder's case actually enables witness and feminist ethicists to better embody their own professed commitments.

More specifically, I argue that witness and feminist theologians can collaborate in doing justice to Yoder's theological legacy by developing a feminist pacifist politics. As the primary heirs to Yoder's theology, witness theologians have a moral obligation to develop in their work Yoder's own claim that "Christian identity itself calls for feminist engagement."[20] In particular, witness ethicists need to connect their emphasis on ecclesiology and the church's peaceable mission to the problem of sexual violence.[21] Feminists are also indispensable in handling Yoder's legacy because their particular resources, including sustained analysis of the systemic violence of sexism and promotion of women's flourishing, are desperately needed to combat sexual violence. Moreover, both sets of ethicists are particularly well-situated to analyze the contributions to peace theology made by the women who demanded justice in the wake of Yoder's wrongdoing.[22] My use of restorative justice themes to reflect on Yoder's legacy thus facilitates needed dialogue between witness and feminist ethicists, showing how their collaboration not only strengthens their own internal projects with respect to the church's mission and the promotion of women's flourishing but also more effectively addresses sexual violence.

Restorative Justice as a Model for Responding to Wrongdoing

Restorative justice approaches to wrongdoing provide productive complements or alternatives to punitive justice. Used in a variety of settings from criminal justice to national truth and reconciliation commissions and implementing a variety of processes from family-group conferences to victim-offender dialogue, restorative justice looks beyond retribution to repair harm and restore relationships. Rather than an exclusive focus on the punishment of perpetrators without regard to particular situations or to victims' suffering, it attends to wrongdoing within the context of community and in some contexts involves concerns normally relegated to the religious world—healing and reconciliation.[23] Among its numerous virtues, advocates emphasize its ability to uncover, acknowledge, and repair harms; to empower victims and address their needs; to further justice, responsibility, and accountability for individuals and institutions; to ascertain and recommend needed reforms or reparations; to maximize reintegration and reduce revictimization and recidivism; and to enable the possibility of apology, forgiveness, healing, and reconciliation.[24]

Restorative justice is not without its drawbacks. Critics argue that if it does not include retributive elements, restorative justice potentially short-circuits justice in the name of forgiveness. Others question its benefits for victims.[25]

Still others argue that, despite its religious aspects, restorative justice empha-sizes process at the expense of religious substance.[26] Feminist critics also iden-tify problems, including significant limits in contexts of domestic or sexual violence that are often marked by "gendered or other asymmetrical forms of social relations."[27]

Restorative justice is relevant to Yoder's case in various ways. The account-ability and disciplinary process conducted by the Indiana-Michigan Menno-nite Conference and the censure of Yoder's local congregation were based on the Christian practice of binding and loosing described Matthew 18.[28] This practice resembles restorative justice in its emphasis on reproval, repentance, forgiveness, and reconciliation. Although witness theologians have been quick to point to this process as evidence of Yoder's commitment to the convictions of his theology, there were limits to the process. Yoder demanded that his victims meet him alone, face to face—a stipulation many deemed unreasonable—and, despite the process's emphasis on repentance and forgiveness, Yoder did not publicly apologize.[29] Many doubt his repentance was genuine.[30] While this process and discussion of its merits is important, Yoder's legacy—not his actual behavior—is my focus here.

Difficulties with Yoder's Case

One of the benefits of restorative justice as an interpretive lens for approaching Yoder's legacy is that it enables the identification of the various stakeholders and harms involved while also illuminating the difficulties of responding to the particular wrongdoing represented by a legacy. The women Yoder violated are of course the primary victims of Yoder's wrongdoing. Their views of how to repair the harm—in this case, of whether and how Yoder's theology might be read and taught in ways that do not further the trauma he inflicted—are critical and merit a much larger role in current discussions.[31] But, as in other restorative justice contexts, the harm here extends beyond that of the primary victims and must be named in order to repair the full range of harm.[32] Yoder's family and his local and larger Mennonite ecclesial and academic communities are also harmed by his wrongdoing. At the same time, many of Yoder's ecclesial and academic communities are also complicit in his wrongdoing. Similarly, members of the SCE, while certainly not the primary victims of Yoder's wrong-doing, are also impacted. Gerald Schlabach's insightful reflections in "Only Those We Need Can Betray Us" voice this important insight: while not the primary victims of Yoder's violations, we Christian ethicists—especially those who are students of Yoder or his theology—are also betrayed.[33] Given that Yoder served as president of the SCE, it is also important to consider how the SCE is both harmed and carries responsibility to repair harm.[34]

The question of responsibility is particularly acute for those Christian ethicists who teach his work or are dedicated to his theological vision. If we continue to teach and write about Yoder's work as though it does not carry painful reminders of his wrongdoing, we not only risk reinforcing this traumatic past for his primary victims—of becoming perpetrators rather than merely stakeholders—we also risk extending the harm to our students and our wider communities by perpetuating a culture that condones sexual injustice and fails to confront abuses of power. What, then, are our obligations as teachers and scholars? Can we both acknowledge Yoder's theological contributions and repair the harms of his legacy?

"Witness" Responses: The Attempt to Salvage Yoder's Legacy

Yoder's behavior is certainly egregious enough to consider whether we should continue to read and teach his work. We may choose—again using the legal language of the courtroom—to condemn his theology. Many concerned parties suggest just this.[35] Although feminist ethicists have not explicitly made such calls, their lack of engagement with Yoder may be tantamount to this approach. But even if we tried this response, it would be difficult. As Muers notes, doing Christian theology necessarily entails being in a relationship of responsibility to the dead, eliminating the possibility of outright condemnation.[36] We cannot erase the past or pretend Yoder's theology never existed. Nor would this be desirable. Yoder's work is important. We simply cannot and should not write him out of our history.

Recognizing this fact, "witness" ethicists aim to salvage Yoder's theology. Some emphasize Yoder's submission to the disciplinary proceedings of the Indiana-Michigan Mennonite Conference as an example of his commitment to repentance. Glen Stassen, for example, argued that "John's humbling himself to participate in the [church task force's] process . . . is a remarkable witness to the very themes of the church as an alternative community, peace-making, reconciliation, Christian discipleship, and servanthood that his writings have taught so many of us."[37] Stanley Hauerwas echoed Stassen's assessment and predicted that rather than detracting from it, Yoder's submission to the process would likely enhance his standing in the field.[38] Others contextualize Yoder's behavior. Mark Thiessen Nation, for example, argues that Yoder's relationships with women were not wholly marked by abuse; he in fact had healthy relationships with many women in his life.[39] Still others reconcile the discrepancy between Yoder's behavior and the ideals of his theology with theological claims about God's power to use flawed human instruments for God's purposes.[40] These approaches all clearly condemn Yoder's actions but nevertheless focus on redeeming Yoder's theology. They neglect healing for the women Yoder violated, the problem of sexual violence, and how Christian ethicists might repair the harm caused by Yoder's legacy.

Problems with the Witness Response

The first oversight in witness response is the failure to reckon with the difficulties that Yoder's legacy presents for the women he abused—namely, Yoder's abuse and the trauma he inflicted live on through his influence. No matter how often Yoder's behavior is condemned, reiterating the importance of Yoder's theology only exacerbates the problem. As Barbra Graber points out, "There is no peace for many women who lost, along with their families, years of normal, healthy, joyous living for having been sexually abused by male leaders of the Mennonite Church. And [Yoder] remains a symbol of those widespread wounds like no other churchman."[41] The problem Graber identifies is not "Can a bad person be a good theologian?"[42]—which witness theologians answer by emphasizing Yoder's repentance, contextualizing his wrongdoing, and maintaining the importance of his theology—but "How do we repair harm that outlives the wrongdoer and prevent it from happening again?" Or, as Stephanie Krehbiel puts it, "What changes if we make respect for the humanity of survivors our first priority?"[43] In their desire to ensure that Yoder's theological contributions remain influential, witness theologians move too quickly to forgiveness and reconciliation without first repairing the harm.[44]

A second problem with witness approaches is that they do not deal satisfactorily with Christian ethicists' responsibilities to address sexual violence. If we approach the dilemma focused on questions of how to reconcile Yoder's theological contributions with his abusive behavior, we lose sight of other important questions. Some of these questions are indeed about Yoder's legacy: How do we teach Yoder? How do we write about him? What do we need to do as members of the SCE to publicly acknowledge Yoder's abuse?[45] But Yoder's case begs other pressing questions about the systemic violence of sexism, misogyny, sexual abuse, and abuses of power, including consideration of the ways academic and ecclesial structures and practices may facilitate these problems.[46] It is striking how rarely witness responses identify the need to address sexual abuse as one of the clear mandates of Yoder's case.[47]

Feminism as Christian Politics: A New Agenda for Witness Theologians

A third problem is that witness theologians' questions about the "irreconcilability" of Yoder's theology and his actions have not yet fully identified the problem: we are dealing not merely with an apparent contradiction between the violence of Yoder's life and the pacifism extolled in his theology—we are dealing with a theologian who identified feminism as a central component of the church's pacifist politics and yet who abused women.[48] Much has been made of Yoder's unpublished memos on sexual ethics, but his unpublished memos on feminist theology have gone completely unmentioned. Although Yoder neither identified as a feminist theologian nor substantially engaged feminist theologies, "feminism" is a concern of his work.[49] He describes as "feminist" a major component of what he regards as the church's political identity: the social egalitarianism of the early church.[50] He mentions "feminism" along with hospitals, service of the poor, generalized education, egalitarianism, and abolitionism as examples of cultures that Christians created.[51] And his "feminist theology" memos identify Jesus as a feminist and argue for the centrality of social egalitarianism to Jesus's ministry, the content of which looks something like "mothering," a way of life marked by certain "feminine" qualities of relating to others.[52] In short, for Yoder, feminism and Christianity are "intrinsically interlocked rather than merely mutually compatible."[53]

I am not arguing that Yoder's "feminist" theological reflections and references to feminism are needed to legitimate feminist scholarship or that Yoder himself was a champion of women's empowerment; clearly, he was not.[54] But these references do suggest an important relationship between feminist theologies and his radical reformation vision. At the very least, they provide a fuller description of Yoder's account of Christian politics. Although he did not fully develop it in his theology or live it out in his life, these memos clearly place feminism at the heart of Christian identity and the church's political witness. Dealing with Yoder's claims about feminism renders the conflict between his life and his theology more acute. It also suggests a way forward for witness theologians whose work is indebted to Yoder's theology and who are committed to repairing the harm his legacy causes.

"Doing Justice" to Yoder's Legacy

Restorative justice provides a particularly helpful resource for the SCE to move forward in doing justice to Yoder's legacy not only because its purpose is to respond to wrongdoing but also because its central features are shared by witness and feminist ethicists whose stances are often seen as being at cross purposes. These shared features include the importance of truth-telling, emphasis on particularity, and reconciling practices that shape peaceable communities. In exploring these shared emphases, I also identify specific opportunities for witness and feminist theologians to collaborate in doing justice to Yoder's legacy with the hope of initiating dialogue between them.

Truth-Telling

Restorative justice's emphasis on truth-telling is paramount in doing justice to Yoder's legacy. This element of restorative justice is central in both witness and feminist theological reflection. Witness theologians emphasize the importance of narrative and storytelling to their projects, often describing their stance as being centrally about the truth of Christian convictions and how to form communities whose members' lives witness to those truths. As Stanley Hauerwas puts it, "The only reason for being Christian . . . is because Christian convictions are true; and the only reason for participation in the church is that it is the community that pledges to form its life by that truth. . . . I am convinced that the intelligibility and truthfulness of Christian convictions reside in their practical force."[55] Similarly, feminist theologians emphasize the power of truth-telling through their efforts to identify, critique, and dismantle sexism in the tradition. In Muers's words, "Theology has a properly critical function as anti-idolatry—the uncovering and condemnation of any God-talk that is unworthy of God; and feminist theology has been, and remains, engaged in an ongoing critique of the idolatry of male power."[56] Much of this critique is informed by first-person narrative and other forms of storytelling.

Restorative justice places a premium on truth-telling for enabling victims to name the wrong done to them and for its healing potential. The clear and perceptive calls for this kind of truth-telling by Graber, Heggen, Krall, and other Mennonite women have been tremendously significant in pursuing transparency.[57] How might we as Christian ethicists follow suit?

First, we can speak truthfully about Yoder's wrongdoing. Despite the use of the term "abuse" by the Mennonite Church USA and AMBS, many witness theologians avoid this language. Nation uses the language of "sexual misconduct," arguing that most of Yoder's behavior did not constitute abuse.[58] Similarly, Hauerwas describes Yoder's behavior variously as "a pattern of behavior with women that was, to say the least, problematic"; "experimenting"; "seductions"; "misuse"; and "inappropriate relations."[59] These terms fall short of accurately naming the behavior documented by the Mennonite Church USA. One hopes that these descriptions are merely indicative of a previous lack of knowledge about the magnitude and scope of Yoder's abuse.[60]

It may well be the case—as in other contexts in which restorative justice is used, such as with the South African Truth and Reconciliation Commission—that it is not possible to uncover and name everything that happened. But, as Michael Ignatieff notes, despite its limits, the truth-telling process "narrowed the range of impermissible lies that one can tell in public . . . [and] rendered some lies about the past simply impossible to repeat."[61] We may not be able to undo or uncover all of the harm Yoder caused, but we can strive to speak truthfully so as to limit untruths and half-truths. We can also acknowledge Yoder's violations in scholarship on his work, offering the women Yoder abused "recognition of their suffering . . . recognition [that] in itself is a component of justice."[62] Perhaps more importantly, we can produce scholarship that analyzes the contributions made to the field by the women who demanded justice in the wake of Yoder's wrongdoing.

Second, we can be transparent with students and colleagues about the difficulties of Yoder's case. We cannot continue teaching Yoder's theology without addressing the ethical questions it raises about gender, sexuality, and power; about the relationship between author and text, theory and practice. Many are already asking these questions: "Can a bad person be a good theologian?"[63] Can we detect signs of Yoder's abuse in his theology?[64] Does his behavior suggest fundamental flaws in witness theology?[65] When I teach Yoder's work, I disclose his complex legacy and invite my students to think about its implications.

The Importance of Particularity

Another important element of restorative justice featured prominently in witness and feminist ethics is attention to particularity. Witness theologians often emphasize the particularity of Christian language, doctrine, and practices over against modern liberal forms of reasoning. Indeed, this emphasis on particularity both grounds witness claims that the communication of Christian truth requires an embodied "witness" and often funds witness critiques of feminist theology. Although feminists do not champion the particularity of Christian truth claims in this way, they nevertheless share this emphasis on particularity. Feminist attention to the particular historical, social, cultural, and political context of Christian beliefs and practices enables the naming of idolatry so central to feminist projects. Feminists are also attentive to particularity because of their recognition that paying attention to specific, concrete persons and contexts is required to determine what constitutes justice in a given situation. This attention to the concrete allowed pioneering feminists to challenge the normativity of male identity and experience in the tradition and also funds the significant womanist, *mujerista*, Latina, and Asian critiques of white feminism as well as poststructural analysis of the complexities of identity and power.

In restorative justice, the emphasis on particular contexts helps identify fitting responses to particular cases of wrongdoing. In many contexts—like postapartheid South Africa—retributive approaches simply do not work. In that situation the magnitude of violations rendered it logistically impossible to prosecute all of the perpetrators and difficult to enable a shared future. This emphasis on context helps us identify the nature of our specific problem—namely, we are not dealing with an existing perpetrator who can participate in mediation and potentially apologize for wrongdoing but a legacy that both perpetuates trauma and depends upon our engagement for its continued existence. Discussions of limits to restorative justice in gendered violence, specifically domestic abuse, are particularly illuminating here. As in those situations, we are dealing with a context in which the offenses are not "past event[s] for which reparation can be made readily."[66] We are dealing with ongoing trauma—not because, as in domestic abuse, one is married to the responsible party but because Yoder's offenses live on in his influence.

The emphasis on context within restorative justice also enables the identification of Yoder's sexual abuse as part of larger societal structures that enable gendered violence. Restorative justice clarifies that Yoder's wrongdoing extends beyond the women he violated to the Mennonite Church USA, AMBS, the University of Notre Dame, and the SCE. Also important, it shows his abuse to be connected to larger structural problems. As Julie Stubbs notes, "Theorizing crime primarily as a conflict between individuals fails to engage with questions of structural disadvantage and with raced, classed and gendered patterns of crime."[67] Consequently, restorative justice places responsibility for wrongdoing (and "the justice-making process") with the community.[68] "'We are all to blame' is the 'restoration of a common ground' that 'opens a new footing of co-responsibility to the erstwhile enemy.'"[69] To treat Yoder's wrongs more systematically we need to acknowledge that his actions are underwritten by a culture—and academic, ecclesial, and other institutional practices and structures—that often demean women.[70] Emphasizing a communal response to wrongdoing not only identifies all relevant stakeholders and the larger social problems of relevance, it also identifies the multiple resources available for repairing the harm. Restorative justice emphasizes the need for the "community from which victims and perpetrators have come" to be involved in the "justice-making process."[71] Although we as Christian ethicists are not the primary responsible party, we are part of the community and need to be part of "the resolution of the conflict and appropriate reparations."[72] What might reparations look like in this case?

Communal Moral Responses: Resisting Violence

Answering the question of what reparations might look like requires attention to the communal resources available; here again both witness and feminist ethicists emphasize the centrality of practices of ethical formation and the role of the church in providing countercultural resistance to violence. For witness theologians, this often means an emphasis on the priority of the church and its witness over against the violence of the modern state. One of the richest contributions of witness theologians to Christian ethics has been their emphasis on the church, its liturgy, and concrete practices of moral formation in shaping a peaceable community. Although witness theologians often perceive feminists to be hostile to the church and its traditions, feminist critique of patriarchy, sexism, and other forms of injustice and oppression in the life of the church is grounded in this same recognition of the significance and morally formative power of ecclesial identity and practices. Their attention to the role of power in the construction of tradition as well as the ways theology is informed by a multiplicity of cultural identities, subjectivities, and social locations may affirm the significance of ecclesiology in a different way from that of witness theologians, but the undergirding convictions are the same. Important work being done on Christian practices by feminists like Rebecca S. Chopp and Mary McClintock Fulkerson shares with witness ethicists an emphasis on ecclesial practices.[73]

Although witness theologians tend to cast their emphasis on the church and its communal practices of moral formation in terms of the church's mission to provide a countercultural witness of peace, feminist ethicists promote their own version of this mission: their focus on the preferential option for the poor and marginalized—specifically women—has led them to emphasize the church as a countercultural witness over against systems of gender injustice and violence. For example, Rosemary Radford Ruether's pioneering feminist work advocating for "feminist base communities" as places where Christians committed to Jesus's emancipatory vision embody that vision and bring it "to bear on the institutionalized Church" and the wider world anticipates witness accounts of the church as countercultural witness.[74] Similarly, more recent feminist work like Fulkerson's studies the role of Christian homemaking practices in creating "a place to appear."[75] Although these practices "are the everyday, lived world activities of average people," they "are redemptive and political" because they "brought people together in a variety of settings that contravened many of their inherited racialized enculturations."[76] Marie M. Fortune's work on ecclesial responses to the sin of sexual violence provides another prime example.[77] While feminist theologians often focus on the systemic violence of sexism and racism, they nevertheless share the witness conviction that the church should provide alternatives to violence. This shared emphasis on ecclesial practices of moral formation and resistance to violence—especially given witness and feminist ethicists' divergent conceptions of violence—will be indispensable in crafting fitting forms of restitution for the injuries caused by Yoder's legacy.[78] Given these shared convictions, how might we as Christian ethicists approach reparations with respect to Yoder's legacy? Or, to put it in Hauerwas's and Fulkerson's respective terms, how might we as Christian ethicists be "second chance people" with respect to Yoder's legacy, using it as an opportunity to create theologies that respond to the "wound" of sexual violence?[79]

Addressing Sexual Abuse as a Moral Problem

Our first response should be to address sexual violence. We need to continue and extend the important work that many Christian ethicists, and particularly SCE members, are already doing in the areas of sexual justice.[80] We should take advantage of the opportunity Yoder's case provides to address this pressing problem, especially since sexual abuses—particularly by religious figures—are not limited to Yoder's case. Recent public attention to sexual violence, especially in religious communities and on college campuses, makes clear that sexual violence is facilitated not only by cultural attitudes toward women and structural gender injustices but also by the failed policies and practices of law enforcement and ecclesial and academic institutions.

Feminism as the Church's Pacifist Politics

Witness and feminist ethicists can also—and this is the heart of my argument—do justice to Yoder's legacy by collaborating in the development of a feminist pacifist politics. As primary heirs to Yoder's theology, witness theologians cannot appropriate Yoder's work without incorporating feminist insights about structural and internal forms of violence that demand resistance. Simply put: Witness theologians need to end their refusal to engage feminist theologies. If for no other reason than that Yoder himself identified feminism as both indispensable to Christian identity and central to the church's pacifist politics, witness theologians devoted to Yoder's legacy need to engage feminist work. Yet, as I have argued elsewhere, witness theologians devoted to Yoder's legacy continue to dismiss feminist theologies as versions of liberalism.[81] As Hauerwas, a prominent witness theologian, puts it, "My difficulty with much feminist theology is, in short, not that it is feminist, but that it is so often liberal Protestant theology in a different key."[82] Such claims underappreciate both the diversity of feminist approaches and Yoder's own identification of feminism as part and parcel of Christian identity.

Prominent witness accounts of the church as pacifist witness offer rich developments of Yoder's pacifist vision, but they follow Yoder in focusing on the Christian counterwitness to the violence of the state.[83] Feminist theologians have long been suggesting that an overly narrow focus on the violence of war obscures other types of violence that demand attention. Gloria Albrecht has called for the church to address systemic violence related to race, gender, and class.[84] Recent work on the internal violence of trauma by Serene Jones and Cynthia Hess broadens our conceptions of the forms violence takes in the everyday lives of many.[85] Womanist work, such as that of Emilie M. Townes, offers powerful analyses of "the cultural production of evil" that demands resistance.[86] Such work makes clear that a Christian witness of peace cannot be limited to resisting war.

Witness theologians cannot do justice either to Yoder's own theological vision or their own without incorporating these feminist analyses of the expansive forms violence takes. Only then can we think well about ecclesial resources for shaping communities that can prevent sexual violence. They might start by considering what Christian ethicists can learn about Christian nonviolence from "those courageous and principled women who have stood up, decried the abuse, and insisted on setting wrongs right."[87] In short, incorporating analyses of these women's nonviolent practice as well as feminist work on sexism, racism, classism and other forms of structural and internal violence would enable witness theologians to strengthen their own accounts of the church as pacifist witness.

There are also practical ways that witness theologians could advance their own convictions about the church as a peaceable community. Witness theologians might dedicate themselves to the feminism of Yoder's pacifist politics by advocating for women—perhaps especially those committed to the peace tradition's theological vision—in the academy. As Graber notes, one of the damaging aspects of Yoder's legacy is that there is a missing generation of female Mennonite theologians.[88] Witness theologians can be in solidarity with their feminist colleagues in promoting women's presence and flourishing in the academy. What a profound way to "do justice" to Yoder's legacy—to repair this particular institutional harm.

Why Should Feminists Care?

Feminist theologians do not need Yoder's imprimatur to do their important work on feminism and issues related to sexual violence. Nevertheless, feminist ethicists can enhance the constructive reach of their own theological insights by dialoguing with their witness colleagues. While it is important to preserve academic boundaries that separate feminist approaches from others to guarantee feminists and others of "marginal" positions the space to do their theological work, it is paramount that feminist theologians seek in some sense to render redundant the "feminist" modifier in front of "theology" and "ethics." As Yoder argued, all Christian theology should be "feminist." Feminists should make strategic use of this claim to convince witness theologians of the need to engage their work. Collaborating with witness theologians to address the church's role in resisting sexual violence better ensures that feminist insights will be incorporated as widely as possible in the field. It holds out the possibility that rather than merely preaching to the choir, feminist ethicists might gain witness converts to their cause who can join them in combating sexual violence.

Conclusion

These proposals can only function as symbolic reparations for the harm Yoder caused. The fact that he died before publicly apologizing means that many of those hurt by Yoder may continue to struggle for healing. As Christian ethicists, we certainly cannot stand in for Yoder and make good on his failures. But as those who inherit his legacy, we can relate to it in ways that acknowledge the very real past (and present) wrongs it represents.

Better addressing sexual violence and appropriating Yoder's emphasis on the centrality of feminism to Christian identity may not undo past wrongs, but it may go some way toward what restorative justice practitioners identify as the purpose of reparations: to "help to repair damage, vindicate the innocent, locate responsibility and restore equilibrium."[89] There are limits to what reparations by a third-party can accomplish, but "symbolic reparations can . . . help redress harms that cannot be repaired . . . [and] go to a layer underneath specific harms, redressing the injury of injustice itself."[90] Dedicating an annual SCE meeting to issues related to sexual violence could be one important step toward addressing this significant problem. Christian ethicists might also develop accounts of feminist pacifist politics that combat sexual violence. Doing so is particularly important given that Yoder's case is hardly unique. In fact, many speculate that Yoder's case continues to be revisited because of the pervasiveness of sexual violence, especially that perpetrated by religious figures.[91]

Indeed, one of the best ways that witness theologians can respond to the harm caused by Yoder's legacy is to develop in their work Yoder's own claim that feminism is integral to Christian identity. This would allow witness theologians to make good on an insight of Yoder's theology that he himself failed to develop in his theology or honor in his life. It would also enable them to articulate more robust accounts of the church as pacifist witness, which is direly needed, given that it is precisely those witness theologians devoted to pacifism and Yoder's legacy who have most often neglected feminist theologies.[92] Feminists provide indispensable insights for witness theologians truly dedicated to their vision of the church as a countercultural witness to peace. Feminist theologians need equally, though, to engage the questions that Yoder's legacy raises. Yoder's case affords feminists the opportunity to expand the constructive reach of their insights, better advancing women's flourishing in the church, academy, and wider world.

"Doing justice" to Yoder's legacy thus enables opportunities for productive dialogue between witness and feminist ethicists who, although they have good reason to engage each other's work, rarely do so in nonantagonistic ways. As Christian ethicists, we should use Yoder's case as a direly needed occasion to think together about how we, in our teaching and scholarship, in our theological reflection on the church and our Christian practice, might best address sexual violence. It is time to move past the academic hostilities that prevent witness and feminist ethicists from embodying their own best insights to develop a truly pacifist ecclesial politics—that is, a feminist pacifist politics.

Notes

I thank the SCE audience and anonymous reviewers for their thoughtful engagement with these ideas. Special thanks to Marvin Ellison, Janna Hunter-Bowman, Amy Levad, Margaret Mohrmann, Mark Thiessen Nation, and Kathryn Getek Soltis for extended conversation. Thanks also to Stanley Hauerwas for his gracious response to my presentation.

This essay includes portions of revised material from Karen V. Guth, "The Feminist-Christian Schism Revisited," *Journal of Scriptural Reasoning* 13, no. 2 (November 2014).

1. See Tom Price, "Theologian Cited in Sex Inquiry," *Elkhart Truth*, June 29, 1992, B1; Tom Price, "Theologian's Future Faces a 'Litmus Test': Yoder's Response to Allegations Could Determine Standing in the Field," *Elkhart Truth*, July 12, 1992, B1; Tom Price, "Theologian Accused: Women Report Instances of Inappropriate Conduct," *Elkhart Truth*, July 13, 1992, B1; Tom Price, "A Known Secret: Church Slow to Explore Rumors against Leader," *Elkhart Truth*, July 14, 1992, B1; Tom Price, "Yoder Actions Framed in Writings," *Elkhart Truth*, July 15, 1992, B1; and Tom Price, "Teachings Tested: Forgiveness, Reconciliation in Discipline," *Elkhart Truth*, July 16, 1992, B1. See also "Yoder Suspended," *Christian Century* 109, no. 24 (August 12, 1992): 737–38.

2. In the preface to *The Wisdom of the Cross: Essays in Honor of John Howard Yoder* edited by Stanley Hauerwas, Chris K. Huebner, Harry J. Huebner, and Mark Thiessen Nation (Grand Rapids, MI: Eerdmans, 1999), Hauerwas makes a vague reference to the postponement of the book's publication "because of matters between John and the church which needed to be processed" (x). In *John Howard Yoder: Mennonite Patience, Evangelical Witness, Catholic Convictions* (Grand Rapids, MI: Eerdmans, 2006), Mark Thiessen Nation refers in a footnote to "allegations regarding inappropriate sexual activity" (25). A more recent volume on Yoder's work addresses his sexual violence in a foreword by Marva J. Dawn and an afterword by Lisa Schirch. See J. Denny Weaver, ed. *John Howard Yoder: Radical Theologian* (Eugene, OR: Cascade, 2014).

3. Carolyn Holderread Heggen, for example, lobbied for a meeting between women violated by Yoder and Mennonite Church officials. See her *Sexual Abuse in Christian Homes and Churches* (Scottdale, PA: Herald Press, 1993).

4. Kate Tracy, "Christian Publisher: All of Top Theologian's Books Will Now Have Abuse Disclaimer," *Christianity Today*, December 18, 2013, http://www.christianitytoday.com/gleanings/2013/december/publisher-john-howard-yoder-books-abuse-women-mennonite.html?paging=off.

5. "AMBS Statement on Teaching and Scholarship related to John Howard Yoder," February 27, 2012; approved April 30, 2012, http://www.ambs.edu/about/documents/AMBS-statement-on-JHY.pdf. See also Sara Wenger Shenk, "Revisiting the Legacy of John Howard Yoder," *Practicing Reconciliation* (blog), July 25, 2013, http://www.ambs.edu/publishing/2013/07/Revisiting-the-Legacy-of-John-Howard-Yoder.cfm; and Rich Preheim, "AMBS Holds Lament Service for Yoder Victims," *Mennonite*, March 23, 2015, http://themennonite.org/daily-news/ambs-holds-lament-service-for-yoder-victims.

6. Rachel Waltner Goossen, "'Defanging the Beast': Mennonite Responses to John Howard Yoder's Sexual Abuse," *Mennonite Quarterly Review* 89, no. 1 (January 2015): 11.

7. See ibid., 18.

8. Rachel Muers, "Doing Traditions Justice," in *Gendering Christian Ethics*, ed. Jenny Daggers (Newcastle: Cambridge Scholars Publishing, 2012), 7–22.

9. Witness ethicists are characterized in part by their concern about the accommodation of the church and its particularistic language and practices to non-Christian cultural forms. They emphasize the distinctive resources of the tradition, including the primacy of revelation, the role of the biblical narrative and church practices for the moral formation of Christian disciples, and the church as a distinctive polis that witnesses to the world. Stanley Hauerwas is currently the most prominent witness ethicist in the Society of Christian Ethics. Both Stanley Hauerwas and Glen Stassen take the approach that Yoder's theology remains valuable. See Price, "Teachings Tested." See also Hauerwas, *Hannah's Child: A Theologian's Memoir* (Grand Rapids, MI: Eerdmans, 2010).

10. I recognize that "victim" language potentially neglects the agency of those harmed. While the term "survivor/victim" avoids the problem of denying agency, it also runs the risk of assigning recovery to those who would not claim it for themselves. When possible, I refer to "the women Yoder violated" to acknowledge their right to name themselves.

11. This broad category neglects the diversity of feminist, womanist, *mujerista*, Latina, and Asian approaches but includes all those whose work emphasizes God's preferential option for the marginalized—especially women.

12. An indispensable resource on Yoder's case is Ruth Elizabeth Krall, *The Elephants in God's Living Room*, vol. 3, *The Mennonite Church and John Howard Yoder, Collected Essays*, http://ruthkrall.com/downloadable-books/volume-three-the-mennonite-church-and-john-howard-yoder-collected-essays/. See also Barbra Graber, "What's to Be Done about John Howard Yoder?" *Our Stories Untold* (blog), http://www.ourstoriesuntold.com/whats-to-be-done-about-john-howard-yoder/; and Shenk, "Revisiting the Legacy."

13. See, for example, Gerber Koontz, "Peace Theology and Patriarchy: The Trajectory of Scripture and Feminist Conviction," in *Essays on Peace Theology and Witness*, ed. Willard M. Swartley (Elkhart, IN: Institute of Mennonite Studies, 1988). Both Gerber Koontz and Harder have made efforts over the years to include discussion of Yoder's sexual abuse at conferences devoted to his legacy (Krall, *Elephants*, 83–84). See also Elizabeth G. Yoder, ed., *Peace Theology and Violence against Women* (Elkhart, IN: Institute of Mennonite Studies, 1992); and Lydia Harder, "Power and Authority in Mennonite Theological Development," in *Power, Authority, and the Anabaptist Tradition*, ed. Benjamin W. Redekop and Calvin W. Redekop, 73–94 (Baltimore: Johns Hopkins University Press, 2001).

14. There are also several self-identified feminist Mennonite graduate students writing on these issues. See Susie Guenther Loewen, "Remembering Yoder Honestly," *Canadian Mennonite Young Voices*, http://youngvoices.canadianmennonite.org/articles/rememberingyoderhonestly; and Hannah Heinzekehr, "Can Subordination Ever Be Revolutionary? Reflections on John Howard Yoder," *The Femonite* (blog), August 9, 2013, http://www.femonite.com/2013/08/09/can-subordination-ever-be-revolutionary-reflections-on-john-howard-yoder/.

15. Several feminists and womanists identify Yoder's discussion of "revolutionary subordination" as a stumbling block for feminist and womanist theologies. See Elisabeth Schüssler Fiorenza, *Bread Not Stone: The Challenge of Feminist Biblical Interpretation* (Boston: Beacon Press, 1984). For a womanist analysis of revolutionary subordination, see Rosetta Ross, "John Howard Yoder on Pacifism," in *Beyond the Pale: Reading Ethics from the Margins*, eds. Stacey M. Floyd-Thomas and Miguel A. De La Torre (Louisville, KY: Westminster John Knox Press, 2011), 199–207.

16. Muers, "Doing Traditions Justice," 10.

17. Ibid.

18. Further consideration is warranted of whether the very categories and methods of Yoder's theology itself need to be interrogated, corrected, and revised. I owe this formulation of the problem to Janna Hunter-Bowman.

19. Mark Oppenheimer, "A Theologian's Influence, and Stained Past, Live On," *New York Times*, October 11, 2013, http://www.nytimes.com/2013/10/12/us/john-howard-yoders-dark-past-and-influence-lives-on-for-mennonites.html?_r=0.

20. John H. Yoder, "Feminist Theology Miscellany #1: Salvation through Mothering?" Unpublished manuscript (October 1990), 5. Thanks to Mark Thiessen Nation, Gayle Gerber Koontz, and Eileen K. Saner for helping me locate these unpublished memos before they were digitized.

21. See Stanley Hauerwas, *The Peaceable Kingdom: A Primer in Christian Ethics* (Notre Dame, IN: University of Notre Dame Press, 1983).

22. I am deeply grateful to Marvin Ellison for raising the question of how to best honor the women who courageously condemned Yoder's abuse and advocated for justice. In his words, "What can we learn from their legacy (and not only his)? . . . Is Yoder the 'expert' about Christian nonviolence, or might it not be the women who have exemplified how to organize resistance to violence in a way that challenges, but does not replicate the violation?" Email correspondence, January 15, 2015.

23. See, for example, Daniel W. Van Ness and Gerry Johnston, "The Meaning of Restorative Justice," in *Handbook of Restorative Justice* (Portland, OR: Willan Publishing, 2007), 5–23. The purposes of restorative justice vary depending on the context. There is less emphasis on forgiveness and reconciliation in criminal justice versions. See also Howard Zehr, *The Little Book of Restorative Justice* (Intercourse, PA: Good Books, 2002).

24. The basic elements often span various contexts, including truth and reconciliation commissions, sexual violence, and criminal justice.

25. Annalise Acorn, *Compulsory Compassion: A Critique of Restorative Justice* (Vancouver: University of British Columbia Press, 2004), 161.

26. Geoff Broughton, "Restorative Justice: Opportunities for Christian Engagement." *International Journal of Public Theology* 3 (2009): 299–318.

27. See, for example, Kathleen Daly and Julie Stubbs, "Feminist Engagement with Restorative Justice," *Theoretical Criminology* 10, no. 1 (2006): 9–28. See also Julie Stubbs, "Beyond Apology? Domestic Violence and Critical Questions for Restorative Justice," *Criminology & Criminal Justice* 7, no. 2 (2007): 169–87. Stubbs notes, for example, that those who perpetrate domestic abuse often use apology to control the situation, undermining claims about the benefits of apology for victims in restorative justice.

28. See Yoder's discussion in "Binding and Loosing," in *The Royal Priesthood: Essays Ecclesiastical and Ecumenical*, ed. Michael G. Cartwright, 323–58 (Scottdale, PA: Herald Press, 1998); and John Howard Yoder, *Body Politics: Five Practices of the Christian Community before the Watching World* (Scottdale, PA: Herald Press, 1992).

29. Graber, "What's to Be Done?"

30. See Krall, *Elephants in God's Living Room*, 359–60.

31. This may be a limitation of the restorative justice paradigm for approaching Yoder's legacy. Ethicists who deem Yoder's theology indispensable may not be able to satisfy the concerns of those who would argue that Yoder's theology should be abandoned. Despite efforts to adopt a restorative paradigm, we may not be able to repair harm for all, much less reach reconciliation.

32. Thanks to Kathryn Getek Soltis for her helpful caution against naming the harm too narrowly in terms of continuing harm to Yoder's primary victims.

33. Gerald W. Schlabach, "Only Those We Need Can Betray Us: My Relationship with John Howard Yoder and His Legacy," *GeraldSchlabach.net* (blog), July 14, 2014, http://www .geraldschlabach.net/2014/07/10/only-those-we-need-can-betray-us-my-relationship-with-john-howard-yoder-and-his-legacy/.

34. The idea of participating as a guild in an externally facilitated restorative justice process surfaced in the conversation following my presentation at the 2015 annual meeting of the SCE. That discussion explored the potential merits and limitations of such a process, including concerns around the potential participation of women Yoder violated.

35. For example, in response to Schlabach's reflections, Mary Jane Breneman Eby writes, "I propose that all the writings by J. H. Yoder be taken off the market—no published materials!! . . . This is painful BUT very important for those many persons who have been so badly abused!!!" Similarly, one of the eight women who originally reported their abuse, "Clara," said, "I cannot use his writings at the point. (I) feel that they're not at all credible. He does not live up to what he writes and what he speaks." See Price, "Teachings Tested."

36. Muers, "Doing Justice," 11.

37. Quoted in Price, "Teachings Tested."

38. Quoted in ibid.

39. See Mark Thiessen Nation, with Marva Dawn, "On Contextualizing Two Failures of John Howard Yoder," *EMU Anabaptist Nation* (blog), September 23, 2013, http://emu.edu/now/anabaptist-nation/2013/09/23/on-contextualizing-two-failures-of-john-howard-yoder/.

40. See David Cramer, Jenny Howell, Jonathan Tran, and Paul Martens, "Scandalizing John Howard Yoder," *Other Journal*, July 7, 2014, http://theotherjournal.com/2014/07/07/scandalizing-john-howard-yoder/; and David Cramer, Jenny Howell, Paul Martens, and Jonathan Tran, "Theology and Misconduct: The Case of John Howard Yoder," *Christian Century* 131, no. 17 (August 20, 2014): 20–23.

41. Graber, "What's to Be Done?"

42. Oppenheimer, "A Theologian's Influence."

43. Stephanie Krehbiel, "The Woody Allen Problem: How Do We Read Pacifist Theologian (and Sexual Abuser) John Howard Yoder?" *Religion Dispatches*, February 11, 2014, http://religiondispatches.org/the-woody-allen-problem-how-do-we-read-pacifist-theologian-and-sexual-abuser-john-howard-yoder/.

44. Thanks to Jennifer Harvey and Amy Levad for discussion of the problems with restorative justice when a focus on reconciliation supersedes reparations.

45. Schlabach argues that "whatever else the SCE does, we should name and ritualize and use our best gifts as ethicists to reflect on such a legacy in such a way that we go deeper into the tragedy not around it, and resist every temptation to avoid its pain—either by minimizing the way the traumatic violation he has inflicted on some or by denying in any way the positive contributions he had made for others." See "Only Those We Need."

46. For a feminist theology of nonviolence grounded in the Mennonite tradition, see Elizabeth Soto Albrecht, *Family Violence: Reclaiming a Theology of Nonviolence* (Maryknoll, NY: Orbis, 2008).

47. One exception is Mennonite theologian Ted Grimsrud, "Reflections from a Chagrined 'Yoderian' in Face of His Sexual Violence," in *John Howard Yoder: Radical Theologian*, ed. J. Denny Weaver, 334–50 (Eugene, OR: Cascade, 2014). This failure mirrors the way Mennonite institutions focused their energies toward Yoder's rehabilitation rather than healing for the women he abused. See Goossen, "'Defanging the Beast,'" 65.

48. For my full account of "feminism as Christian politics" as a new agenda for witness theologians, see Karen V. Guth, *Christian Ethics at the Boundary: Feminism and Theologies of Public Life* (Minneapolis, MN: Fortress Press, 2015).

49. To my knowledge, the only major feminist theologians Yoder engages are Elisabeth Schüssler Fiorenza, *The Politics of Jesus: Behold the Man! Our Victorious Lamb* (Grand Rapids, MI: Eerdmans, 1972); Rosemary Radford Ruether, in *For the Nations: Essays Evangelical and Public* (Eugene, OR: Wipf and Stock Publishers, 1997); and Rosemary Radford Ruether, *The Jewish-Christian Schism Revisited*, eds. Michael G. Cartwright and Peter Ochs (Scottdale, PA: Herald Press, 2008).

50. John Howard Yoder, *The Priestly Kingdom: Social Ethics as Gospel* (Notre Dame, IN: University of Notre Dame Press, 1984), 73.

51. John Howard Yoder, "How H. Richard Niebuhr Reasoned: A Critique of *Christ and Culture*," in *Authentic Transformation: A New Vision of Christ and Culture*, Glen H. Stassen, D. M. Yeager, and John Howard Yoder (Nashville: Abingdon Press, 1996), 69.

52. Yoder, "Feminist Theology Miscellany #1," 6.

53. John Howard Yoder, "Feminist Theology Miscellany #2: What Kind of Feminist Was Jesus?" Unpublished manuscript (October 1990), 5.

54. Thanks to Marvin Ellison for challenging me to clarify my stance here.

55. Stanley Hauerwas, *A Community of Character: Toward a Constructive Christian Social Ethic* (Notre Dame, IN: Notre Dame University Press, 1981), 1.

56. Muers, "Doing Justice," 7.

57. Truth-telling is the first of nine "practical suggestions for moving us toward justice, peace, and healing" that Graber offers in "What's to Be Done?"; Heggen recently noted the continued use of inaccurate terms like "allegations" and "alleged victims" in discussion of Yoder's sexual abuse. See "Opinion: Misconceptions and Victim Blaming in Yoder Coverage," *Mennonite*, July 1, 2014, https://themennonite.org/opinion/misconceptions-victim-blaming-yoder-coverage/; Krall also discusses the importance of truth-telling. See, *Elephants in God's Living Room*, 5.

58. Email correspondence with Mark Thiessen Nation, July 18, 2014. While this caution honors the importance of speaking truthfully with respect to every separate case, the language of "sexual misconduct" conceals Yoder's nonconsensual abuse of power.

59. Hauerwas, *Hannah's Child*, 242–47.

60. Hauerwas acknowledged at our SCE discussion that he was not aware of the extent of Yoder's behavior and was wrong to have encouraged the conclusion of the 1992 disciplinary proceedings. See also "Report Reveals Full History of Theologian's Abuse, Institutions' Response," *Christian Century* 132, no. 5 (March 4, 2015): 13–14.

61. Michael Ignatieff, Introduction to *Truth & Lies: Stories from the Truth and Reconciliation Commission in South Africa*, ed. Jillian Edelstein (New York: New Press, 2002), 20–21.

62. Alan Cairns, "Coming to Terms with the Past," in *Politics and the Past: On Repairing Historical Injustices*, ed. John Torpey (Lanham, MD: Rowman & Littlefield, 2003), 83–84.

63. Oppenheimer, "A Theologian's Influence."

64. Ted Grimsrud, "Word and Deed: The Strange Case of John Howard Yoder," *Thinking Pacifism* (blog), December 20, 2010, http://thinkingpacifism.net/2010/12/30/word-and-deed-the-strange-case-of-john-howard-yoder/.

65. Stephen H. Webb, "John Howard Yoder and the Violent Power of Pacifism," *First Things*, October 15, 2013.

66. Stubbs, "Beyond Apology?" 171.

67. Ibid.

68. Heather Thomson, "Satisfying Justice," *International Journal of Public Theology* 3 (2009): 322, 325.

69. Broughton, "Restorative Justice," 304, citing Charles Taylor, *A Secular Age* (Cambridge, MA: Belkap Press of Harvard University Press, 2007), 709–10.

70. Ibid., 305. Failure to acknowledge the systemic nature of Yoder's sexual abuse is one flaw inherent to attempts to contextualize Yoder's behavior.

71. Thomson, "Satisfying Justice," 325.

72. Ibid.

73. Rebecca S. Chopp, *Saving Work: Feminist Practices of Theological Education* (Louisville, KY: Westminster John Knox Press, 1995); and Mary McClintock Fulkerson, *Places of Redemption: Theology for a Worldly Church* (New York: Oxford University Press, 2007).

74. Rosemary Radford Ruether, *Sexism and God-Talk: Toward a Feminist Theology* (Boston, MA: Beacon, 1983), 205.

75. Fulkerson, *Places of Redemption*, 21.

76. Ibid., 23, 154.

77. See, for example, Marie M. Fortune, *Sexual Violence: The Sin Revisited* (Cleveland, OH: Pilgrim Press, 2005).

78. Restitution "should be as closely related to the particular injury as possible." See Daniel W. Van Ness, "New Wine and Old Wineskins: Four Challenges of Restorative Justice." *Criminal Law Forum* 4, no. 2 (1993): 269.

79. Stanley Hauerwas, *The Hauerwas Reader*, ed. John Berkman and Michael Cartwright (Durham, NC: Duke University Press, 2001), 317; and Fulkerson, *Places of Redemption*, 13–14.

80. The *Journal of the Society of Christian Ethics* has featured articles on various issues related to sexual justice. For example: Karen Peterson-Iyer, "Mobile Porn? Teenage Sexting and Justice for Women," *Journal of the Society of Christian Ethics* 33, no. 2 (Fall–Winter 2013): 93–110; Kathryn D. Blanchard, "Who's Afraid of the Vagina Monologues? Christian Responses and Responsibility to Women on Campus and the Global Community," *Journal of the Society of Christian Ethics* 30, no. 2 (Fall–Winter 2010): 99–122; and Cristina L. H. Traina, "Captivating Illusions: Sexual Abuse and the Ordering of Love," *Journal of the Society of Christian Ethics* 28, no. 1 (Spring–Summer 2008): 183–208.

81. See Guth, "The Feminist-Christian Schism Revisited."

82. Stanley Hauerwas, "Failure of Communication *or* a Case of Uncomprehending Feminism," *Scottish Journal of Theology* 50, no. 2 (1997): 234. Hauerwas has since acknowledged that he can be "rightly criticized for not writing about the challenges raised by feminism." See Stanley Hauerwas, "Remembering How and What I Think: A Response to the *JRE* Articles on Hauerwas," *Journal of Religious Ethics* 40, no. 2 (2012): 302.

83. Several feminists make this claim about Stanley Hauerwas, arguably the most prominent advocate for Yoder's legacy. See, for example, Debra Dean Murphy, "Community, Character, and Gender: Women and the Work of Stanley Hauerwas," *Scottish Journal of Theology* 55, no. 3 (2002): 341.

84. Gloria Albrecht, *The Character of Our Communities: Toward an Ethic of Liberation for the Church* (Nashville: Abingdon, 1995), 117.

85. Serene Jones, *Trauma and Grace: Theology in a Ruptured World* (Louisville, KY: Westminster John Knox, 2009); and Cynthia Hess, *Sites of Violence, Sites of Grace: Christian Nonviolence and the Traumatized Self* (Lanham, MD: Lexington Books), 2009.

86. Emilie M. Townes, *Womanist Ethics and the Cultural Production of Evil* (New York: Palgrave Macmillan, 2006).

87. Email correspondence with Marvin Ellison, January 15, 2015.

88. Graber, "What's to Be Done?"

89. Susan Sharpe, "The Idea of Reparation," in *Handbook of Restorative Justice*, ed. Gerry Johnstone and Daniel W. Van Ness (Portland, OR: Willan Publishing, 2007), 28.

90. Ibid., 31–32.

91. See "The Decision to Disinvite John Howard Yoder to Speak: An Interview with James C. Juhnke, former history professor at Bethel College," *Mennonite*, June 2014, 46.

92. Krehbiel notes, "Pacifist theologians . . . who have built their careers as Yoder apologists seem particularly unable to assimilate or even acknowledge feminist critique," in "The Woody Allen Problem."

Reconciling Evangelical Christianity with Our Sexual Minorities: Reframing the Biblical Discussion

David P. Gushee

Most evangelical Christians have understood their faith, rooted in a high view of biblical authority, to be irreconcilable with "homosexuality." This has meant that devoted LGBT people raised as evangelical Christians must choose between their sexuality and their faith/religious community. This creates enormous psychic distress, turns LGBT Christians and their allies away from (evangelical) Christianity, and contributes to intense alienation between the gay community and evangelicals all over the world. But traditional evangelical attitudes on LGBT people and their relationships are beginning to change. This paper offers a description of the state of the conversation in the North American evangelical community on this issue, and summarizes my own normative proposal.

ARGUMENTS IN THE WESTERN CHRISTIAN WORLD OVER lesbian, gay, bisexual, and transgender persons (LGBT) have now leaped the gap between mainline Protestantism and evangelicalism.[1] Evangelicals largely looked on from a distance over the past four decades as the gay rights movement advanced in Western and US culture and as mainliners began writing their scholarship and undertaking their long, often stalemated denominational debates. In evangelical circles, however, until the past few years, everyone who raised a challenge to "traditionalist" views immediately experienced some form of exclusion.

The space for conversation in evangelicalism is still very fragile and almost exclusively confined to the Western/Northern Christian world.[2] However, a number of new books have been written and organizations founded by avowed evangelicals attempting to open up conversational space, plead for better treatment, reframe the issues, or revise the traditionalist posture. The landscape is changing dramatically. And if even part of the vast evangelical community softens its stance, it could presage (even more) dramatic cultural and legal changes in the United States and other lands where evangelicals are a large part of the population.

David P. Gushee, PhD, is Distinguished University Professor of Christian Ethics at Mercer University, 3001 Mercer University Drive, Atlanta, GA 30341; gushee_dp@mercer.edu.

Journal of the Society of Christian Ethics, 35, 2 (2015): 141–158

Pro-LGBT evangelical forerunners go back decades, such as Ralph Blair and his group, Evangelicals Concerned.[3] The first blockbuster memoir from within the evangelical world was by Mel White, a gay man who once served in the Christian Right.[4] In the late 1990s Fuller Seminary ethicist Lewis Smedes suggested a more accepting posture toward gay couples in a well-known essay and video.[5] Evangelical psychologist David Myers, alone and working with others, has been making his faith- and science-grounded plea for full LGBT acceptance for over a decade.[6] Andrew Marin shocked many in 2009 when he called for dialogue rooted in well-informed love in a book triggered by his three best friends coming out as gay (*Love Is an Orientation*).[7]

But now the call for "generous spaciousness" has been expanded.[8] Senior evangelical pastor and ex-Vineyard Church leader Ken Wilson has called for a full "embrace" of LGBT Christians "in the company of Jesus," though he attempts to frame his approach as a "third way," emphasizing Christian unity rather than moral approval.[9] No such distinctions, though, have been accepted by the Vineyard Church, as Wilson has suffered rejection and the loss of the church he founded decades ago. In December 2014 he launched a new evangelical congregation.

Memoirs are surfacing in increasing numbers, including by gay evangelicals. These have considerably increased evangelical understanding of the gay Christian experience.[10] The first memoir by a (formerly) evangelical lesbian has appeared—musician Jennifer Knapp's *Facing the Music*.[11] The transgender issue, meanwhile, is just beginning to surface.[12]

The six most widely cited purportedly antigay Bible passages—I will call them the Big Six here—and the scholarship undergirding their traditional interpretation are being challenged directly by some evangelical scholars. In 2014, for example, biblical scholar James Brownson published a significant treatment of the relevant textual issues in his book *Bible, Gender, Sexuality*.[13] It is a rigorous work of scholarship.

Most visibly, also in 2014, young prodigy Matthew Vines, a Harvard dropout of great intelligence and vision, came out with a memoir-plus-biblical-excavation called *God and the Gay Christian*.[14] Vines has also launched a national evangelical movement called the Reformation Project.[15] This effort began as a training seminar and is growing into the most prominent LGBT activist platform in evangelicalism.

Full disclosure: I now know almost all of these people and have made my own contribution in my recent book *Changing Our Mind*.[16] I have realized over the last few years that this issue demands my attention—and my repentance, because what little I had said about LGBT-related issues until recently had been inadequate, and because evangelical churches and families are still doing an awful lot of harm to gay people, beginning with their own children.

This essay offers a description of the state of the conversation in the North American evangelical community, summarizes my own normative proposal, and reflects on the broader significance of this conversation for Christian ethics.

The State of the Evangelical Conversation

For purposes of this essay I distinguish between the US evangelical community as a *discrete, self-conscious subculture of theologically conservative white Protestants* over against evangelicalism as naming certain theological tendencies and convictions, much as one might name neo-orthodoxy or postliberalism. This distinction draws on earlier work I have done that describes US evangelicalism beginning as a Protestant renewal movement but settling into a religious community with its own ethos, leaders, and institutions that are self-consciously distinct from mainline Protestant, Catholic, and other religious communities.[17] This is true even though some members of the latter groups share what might be described as evangelical methodological, theological, or ethical commitments.

Sociologists of religion further distinguish white evangelicals from black Protestants and Latino/a Protestants as distinctive religious communities, even though many black and Latino/a Protestants are also "evangelical" in theology.[18] Therefore, although the LGBT/conservative Protestant interaction carries similarities across racial lines, the differences are sufficient to dissuade me from straying outside the white evangelical situation with this essay.[19] I will further focus on the US setting.

Mainline Protestantism has had an LGBT debate for decades, and often the traditionalist side of these debates self-identifies as evangelical.[20] But mainline Protestants live in a different religious subculture than evangelical counterparts. It is one thing for Wesley Seminary, the Presbyterian Church (USA), and Fortress Press to discuss LGBT issues; it is something else for Fuller Seminary, the National Association of Evangelicals, and Baker Books to do so. There has not been—until now—a full-fledged LGBT conversation in the evangelical world. That is because "everyone knew" that evangelical Christianity ruled out any acceptance of nonheterosexual sexual relationships—and everyone knew that accepting or not accepting such relationships was the sum total of the LGBT controversy. This is now changing.

How Evangelicals Think: Sola Scriptura

Despite centuries of historical-critical methodology and more recent challenges to the way evangelicals tend to read and use the Bible, a majority of my religious tribe still tend to narrow the (explicit) grounds for their religious knowledge claims to the Bible as the premier, if not the sole, authority.[21] This is sometimes called evangelical biblicism.[22] With variations, most evangelicals still believe that the (Protestant) Bible is divinely inspired, the truthful and authoritative Word of God to humans, and the only sure guide for Christian faith and practice. Most evangelicals have been deeply shaped by a sometimes productive, sometimes destructive biblical populism in which it is believed that any literate, reasonably devout Christian can read an English translation of the Bible and receive a clear understanding of God's Word and will.[23] This creates a chronic authority problem because there is no universally recognized authority to adjudicate competing evangelical interpretations of the Bible.[24] Every religious tradition has its own epistemological and authority repertoire, with its own limits and problems, and this has been ours.

Evangelical biblicism means that rarely if ever will an evangelical claim that a biblical text or writer is inaccurate, erroneous, or harmful. More often they will subtly move problematic texts into the background, where they gradually recede from view along with thousands of other ignored texts. Evangelicals will rarely if ever allow a claim from science, experience, or tradition to challenge what they believe to be a claim from the "plain sense" of scripture (often with little or no reference to social context), though they sometimes will cite other sources to buttress or supplement their "biblical" claims.[25] Claims to "what the Bible says" must generally be met within evangelicalism by stronger counterclaims to what the Bible (really) says, not to externally grounded claims.

Evangelicals also tend to be suspicious of intrascriptural moves that would offer any kind of explicit trumping or relativizing of specific scriptural texts to resolve disputed issues. For example, a common move of Christian reformists on issues as diverse as slavery, women's roles, and sexuality has been to appeal to broader biblical themes, motifs, or threads as trumping problematic specific passages, which are often set aside as culture-bound or erroneous. Conservative evangelicals, at least, have tended to resist this move vigorously, especially if the trumped texts offer clear moral rules and the trumping move is seen as weakening them.[26]

In general, those evangelicals who define the texts that are to be viewed as most relevant to an issue dominate the discussion of that issue. This is true especially because evangelicals are rarely self-conscious about interpretive traditions in relation to scripture; no one has suggested that the very texts we treat as relevant to an issue are themselves a product of earlier choices and their transmission through some kind of ecclesial tradition.

Evangelicalism has fragmented in recent decades, and what I am saying about evangelical knowledge claims applies more to conservative evangelicals than to progressive evangelicals, who are methodologically more open to liberal or postliberal approaches. Progressive evangelicals are also much more open to hearing criticisms about the difficulties inherent in our particular way of grounding normative knowledge claims; sometimes they are so open that they abandon evangelicalism altogether.

Especially as a result of brutal disputes in evangelical life in recent decades, the conservative side has tended to heighten its claims about biblical inspiration, truth, and authority. It is hard to question the authority of a book treated as God-breathed, completely inerrant, and utterly supreme in its authority.[27] Such claims tend to rule out conversation other than in the form of a heavily cognitive exchange of exegetical claims.[28]

The Traditionalist LGBT and Scripture Paradigm

The essentials of the traditionalist (often but not exclusively evangelical) reading of scripture in relation to what might generically be called the LGBT issue can be rendered by this formula:

Genesis 1–2 +
Genesis 19 (cf. Judges 19) +
Leviticus 18:22/20:13 +
Matthew 19:1–12/Mark 10:2–12 +
Romans 1:26–27 +
1 Corinthians 6:9 (cf. 1 Timothy 1:10) +
All biblical references to sex and marriage that assume male + female
= A clear biblical ban on same-sex relationships.

Sometimes traditionalists simply assemble some or all of the words, phrases, and sentences in these texts into a cumulative condemnation of gay people and their relationships. Other times they attempt something like a broader theological-ethical rendering of the issue, rooted in these biblical texts.

Here I summarize these references:

Genesis 1–2 offers creation accounts in which (1) God makes humanity in the divine image as male and female and commands (blesses) that they be fruitful and multiply and have dominion, and (2) God responds to the man's loneliness by creating a suitable helper-partner, woman, then giving her to the man, with the narrator connecting this primal divine act to marriage. These stories have been understood traditionally by Christians as establishing an exclusively male–female gender and marital sexual-ethical paradigm. The most coherent broader theological-ethical rendering of a traditionalist position argues that the Bible's message on sexuality is consistently gendered, complementarian, procreative, and marital, with all of these dimensions grounded in God's design in primeval creation and all ruling out same-sex relations for all time.

Genesis 19 and Judges 19 tell stories of perverse local city men seeking to sexually assault male guests receiving hospitality in local households but instead being offered defenseless women. This long has been understood as a condemnation of "homosexuality."

Leviticus 18:22 commands men not to lie with men as with women, presumably sexually; *Leviticus 20:13* prescribes the death penalty for this offense. The Hebrew word "*toevah*" used in these passages has generally been translated "abomination" to describe God's abhorrence. These passages still are cited in evangelical circles, even where Leviticus has otherwise disappeared from use.

Matthew 19:1–12 / Mark 10:2–12 depict Jesus responding to questions about the morality of divorce. He appeals to Genesis 1–2 to ground his rigorous response setting strict limits on initiating divorce. These texts are often read as Jesus's implicit affirmation of an exclusively male–female creation design for sex and marriage and thus the broader theme in Genesis 1–2.

Romans 1:26–27 is part of an argument Paul is making about why everyone needs the salvation offered in Jesus Christ. In an apparent effort to illustrate the idolatry and sinfulness of the Gentile part of the human community, Paul makes a harshly negative reference to "degrading" passions and "unnatural, shameless" same-sex acts on the part of men and perhaps also women; later he condemns twenty-one other debased behaviors or vices. This passage continues to function as the most important text cited for condemnation of same-sex acts and relationships.

1 Corinthians 6 and 1 Timothy 1 offer vice lists as part of moral exhortations. The Corinthians text excludes unrepentant practitioners of the vices in the list from the kingdom of God. The rare Greek words "*malakoi*" and especially Paul's neologism "*arsenokoitai*" used in these passages have recently been translated into English as "homosexuals" or related terms. These English terms have been formative for many Christians who have not been informed about the significant translation challenges involved.

If we take the most commonly cited texts on the issue from the traditionalist side, they derive from 11 of the 1,189 chapters in the Bible. This body of biblical citations is seen as settling "the LGBT issue."

Engagement with this issue and with traditionalists has led me to notice four problems:

(1) The texts offer language so harsh about the perverse character and ungodly posture of those desirous of or participating in same-sex acts that they continue to fund an attitude of contempt that survives no matter how polite mainstream traditionalist leaders try to be today. Evangelical and fundamentalist preachers regularly show up in the news with contemptuous, even murderous anti-LGBT declarations.[29] These few sacred texts actually go further

in their rejectionist rhetoric than many traditionalist evangelicals want to go these days.

(2) The biblical texts focus on sexual acts and in one case sexual passions. This produces a continued narrow focus of traditionalists on same-sex acts to the exclusion of other dimensions of a complex human issue.[30] This might fairly be described as creating a legalistic, moralistic, and even casuistic rendering of the LGBT issue. It systematically blocks attention to the human beings who happen to be lesbian, gay, bisexual, or transgender; to relationships, not just acts; and to the mental and emotional health of LGBT people at all developmental stages.

(3) Because the biblical texts do not discuss what today is called sexual orientation and identity, traditionalists continue to struggle with these human realities. The reparative/ex-gay therapy temptation survives, attempting to grind same-sex sexual desires out of those who have them—despite clinical evidence of the ineffectiveness and harm of these efforts and including a notable abandonment by some of their most visible former practitioners.[31] Some traditionalists, as well, encourage LGBT people (and sometimes straight people) to reject the very concepts of gender identity or sexual orientation by refusing any identity other than Christian. Such efforts fail to take seriously the extent to which human beings are bearers of multiple identities, including gender identity and sexual orientation. They also disregard the part that psychosocial discovery of gender and sexuality, and formation of gender- and sexual identity, plays in human growth and development.

(4) In general, the fixed nature of the interpretive paradigm around the Big Six texts blocks engagement with any other data: the claims of contemporary research and clinicians, personal experiences of and with LGBT people, or alternative renderings of the biblical witness. Some conservative evangelicals are methodologically committed precisely to *not engaging* such other potential sources of knowledge.

Shaking the Consensus: A Youthful Movement of Dissent

This once-immovable posture has begun to totter. The most important factor is not external-cultural but internal-generational. It has come from a youthful movement of dissent in the evangelical world. This dissent increasingly takes institutional form among the young: in Facebook groups; gay–straight alliances; campus groups, often called ONE[School]; Christian college alumni; national groups like Level Ground and the Reformation Project; and resistance efforts such as Soulforce.[32]

In ascending order of challenge to their schools, these groups are demanding (a) safe space for LGBT students to gather for mutual support; (b) institutional acceptance and even sponsorship of such support groups; (c) permission and even sponsorship of public campus dialogue around LGBT issues;

(d) reconsideration of student life, admission, and hiring policies viewed as stigmatizing and discriminatory; and (e) an overturning of the traditionalist view in favor of either a silent or neutral institutional stance or full acceptance and complete equality for LGBT persons and their marital-covenantal relationships.

Where these dissenting movements are strongest, they place real pressure on administrations caught between pro-LGBT and anti-LGBT forces. The greatest pressure being placed on the traditionalist position and its institutional embodiments has come from these youthful dissenting voices, which have found more success in schools than in churches.[33] The more recent scholarship noted in this essay has responded to, rather than created, this movement of dissent, which—whether it uses this language or not—strikes me as genuinely a liberationist-solidarity movement from below.

My Own Normative Proposal

In *Changing Our Mind*, I begin by moving early into at least brief analysis of the exegesis, cultural backgrounds, and hermeneutical issues raised by each of the Big Six passages, even though I am less and less convinced that this is where the real issue truly lies. Still, a summary is in order.

Genesis 1–2 / Matt. 19 / Mark 10. I engage the claims that (a) these texts establish an eternal creation design rooted in God-given male/female genital/anatomical complementarity (sometimes also claims about the centrality of procreation for legitimate sexuality) and that (b) these texts forever rule out the moral legitimacy of same-sex relationships. I propose three biblically serious alternatives for reading Genesis.[34]

1. Christians earlier had to learn to read the creation accounts of Genesis 1–2 in intelligent conversation with scientific discoveries about the world (e.g., a heliocentric rather than earth-centered solar system, and an old earth versus a young earth). Perhaps the same principle applies to the issue of gender identity and sexual orientation. Not every person is clearly either male or female, not every person is heterosexual, therefore not every person's sexuality will be procreative—and this exceedingly well-documented diversity in the actual creation must be taken seriously in reading biblical creation texts that do not mention such diversity. This is a solvable faith/science problem. Scriptures about creation and sexuality need to be integrated with reasonably certain claims from science about gender- and sexual-orientation diversity, leading to the conclusion that just because creation accounts fail to mention this diversity, it does not mean that it does not exist or that such diversity is morally problematic.

Perhaps we will one day conclude that such sexual diversity has as little moral significance in itself as "handedness" diversity, which also was once seen as a problematic orientation in need of correction.

2. Christian theology does better looking forward to redemption in Jesus Christ rather than gazing back into the mist of an unreachable pristine creation. Numerous Christian ethical disasters based on creation or "orders of creation" claims can be identified—such as the supposedly divinely ordained subordination of women and subjugation of earth and her creatures.[35] Perhaps the LGBT issue is best understood in this light, with the same solution—looking forward to redemption, not back to creation—as long as we don't understand redemption as some kind of return to Eden. If "redemption" is understood to mean a return to Eden, a restoration of pristine original creation, looking forward to redemption helps little. But if redemption looks more like gathering up the good-yet-broken strands of human existence and moving forward into a kingdom of forgiveness, grace, and new beginnings, that's different.

3. Perhaps we should focus not just on Genesis 1–2 but also Genesis 3. The Pauline-Augustinian-Lutheran tradition takes Genesis 3 to be the account of the entry of sin into the world (see 1 Cor. 15). A thoroughgoing understanding of the pervasiveness of human sinfulness would include every human's sexuality, which should be seen as good-yet-fallen like every other aspect of human existence. One implication is that instead of straight people's sexual desires and acts being seen as innocent (especially if they are married), and gay people's sexual desires and acts being seen as sinful (under all circumstances), no one's sexual desires or acts would be viewed as entirely innocent. Everyone's sexuality is good-yet-fallen and needs to come under the discipline of covenant. This approach would eliminate straight Christians' sense of prideful superiority and might lead to greater acceptance of the idea that a rigorous covenantal-marital sexual-ethical norm can apply to all human beings, whom we now know come into the world with a range of sexual orientations, and also with sinful tendencies in relation to sex that need covenantal ordering.

Leviticus 18:22 / 20:13. There is an obvious problem in focusing on two verses from the Levitical holiness code, one of which carries the death penalty, when Christians apply almost none of the rest of it to our lives today. Moreover, biblical commentators express uncertainty and considerable difference of opinion about why exactly those two verses ban male (but not female) same-sex acts. Many of these possible reasons (male superiority as penetrator but not penetrated in sex, sex-for-procreation-only, the need to distinguish Israel from pagan neighbors, etc.) are not normatively compelling for Christians today.[36]

Genesis 19 / Judges 19. It is widely agreed by most commentators that these texts are about the attempted violent gang rape of strangers, and the Genesis text concerning not just visitors but angels. No biblical text mentions "homosexuality" among its many references to the sins of that legendarily evil city. These two texts are essentially irrelevant.

Romans 1 / 1 Corinthians 6 / 1 Timothy 1. Paul, the only New Testament writer who addresses same-sex issues, wrote in a context where such acts were often adulterous, debauched, and exploitative, easily viewed by any conservative moralist of his day as abusive and excessive.[37] This context had to affect what he said about same-sex acts in both 1 Corinthians and Romans, the latter perhaps in connection to the debauchery of the Roman court under Caligula and Nero, which included violently abusive same-sex acts and reprisals.[38] This is relevant hermeneutically for the church today when thinking about same-sex acts that are not adulterous, debauched, exploitative, or imperial-pagan but instead covenantal and marital. It also could help account for the profound harshness of the language Paul uses when speaking about same-sex acts. And it may speak to the best way to translate vice-list terms in 1 Corinthians 6:9 and 1 Timothy 1:10. We should translate them in a manner that links them to sexual predation, abuse, and exploitation.[39]

The supposedly ironclad reading of these Big Six texts to ban any and all same-sex relationships today turns out to be very much arguable, especially when ancient contexts, modern contexts, and their great differences are taken seriously.[40]

Real Lives Matter

There is also serious attention to real contemporary human beings. A young evangelical Christian discovers he is gay. Devout parents experience their fifteen-year-old daughter coming out as a lesbian. A transgender teenager shows up for youth group. Often LGBT evangelicals and then their families move from the traditionalist at least into the "conflicted" category through these experiences. Their "heart" tells them one thing (be who you are / love your child!) and their "head" tells them something different (all same-sex attraction is sinful).

The methodological question here—indeed, a theological question—is what to make of the extraordinary power of transformative encounters with oneself or a loved one as a sexual minority.[41] Is perspective-shifting sympathy with the suffering of one's child a tempting seduction from God's Truth or is it a path into God's Truth? Do we read ourselves and other people through the lens of sacred texts that we love or do we read texts through the lens of sacred people that we love? Or do we encounter both sacred people and sacred texts through the lens of Christ whom we love above all?[42]

Many grassroots evangelicals who have broken with the traditionalist posture emerge out of this conundrum. They have not figured out what to do with the Big Six passages. But now "the LGBT issue" has become the face of a beloved person. It's about loyalty and love for that person. Then perhaps they make a theological move: *I have to believe Jesus stands with my loved one, not with those who reject her, regardless of what it seems to say in Romans 1.* I will therefore love her "beyond my theology."[43] It may not be enough for a complete Christian ethic. But what if fierce parental love actually comes closer to the heart of Jesus and the meaning of Christian discipleship than simply quoting the Big Six passages? The emotional well-being of gay young people seems to depend on finding some family and friends who will make this kind of move.

LGBT Youth Suffering and Family Rejection

The Center for American Progress did a key policy report on LGBT homeless youth.[44] Homeless youth are defined as "unaccompanied young people between the ages of 12 and 24 for whom it is not possible to safely live with a relative or in another safe alternative living arrangement." Among these homeless youth are "runaways" and "throwaways." The center cites commonly reported estimates that there are between 2.4 million and 3.7 million homeless youth.

LGBT youth are vastly overrepresented among the homeless youth population. "Several state and local studies from across the United States have found shockingly disproportionate rates of homelessness among LGBT youth compared to non-LGBT youth." For example, 33 percent of homeless youth in New York City identify as LGBT. In Seattle it is 39 percent, in Los Angeles it is 25 percent, and in Chicago it is 22 percent.

The most common reasons that LGBT homeless youth cite for being out of their homes are family rejection and conflict. Much of this family rejection and conflict is religiously motivated. The data are clear that all too often when young people come out or are found to be LGBT, they are met with family rejection, especially from religiously conservative families whose faith leaves them unprepared to accept who their child has turned out to be. The indispensable Family Acceptance Project (FAP) has identified and researched dozens of different family responses to LGBT children and measured them to show the relationship between experiencing specific family-accepting and family-rejecting behaviors during adolescence and health and well-being as young adults. The higher the level of family rejection, the higher the likelihood of negative physical health, mental health, and behavioral problems.[45] The tragedy is that most devout religious parents are attempting to love and serve their children through the very behaviors that their children find emotionally devastating. They have no idea, at least at first, what their version of "religiously faithful parenting" is doing to their children. When it does become clear, sometimes the damage is impossible to reverse. And sometimes parents spend the rest of their lives grieving those damages.

FAP found a direct correlation between "highly rejecting" families and the following behaviors: LGBT youth are

- more than eight times as likely to have attempted suicide at least once,
- more than six times as likely to report high levels of depression,
- more than three times as likely to use illegal drugs, and
- more than three times as likely to be high-risk for HIV and STDs.

Looking at "the LGBT issue" from the perspective of struggling adolescents and their families, especially having seen numerous reruns of a disastrous Christian script leading to mental illness, family fractures, and even suicide, has revolutionized my entire perspective.

From the Big Six to the Bigger Six Thousand

With the faces of legions of exiled and wounded gay adolescents in mind, I have found my way from the Big Six to the Bigger Six Thousand. I have come to conclude that the most important theological and ethical themes in scripture point toward full acceptance rather than the wary distance or angry contempt that now characterizes evangelical responses to gay people so much of the time. Other evangelicals are beginning to make this move as well, believing that

1. *The Gospel is that God loves good-yet-fallen human beings* and has offered all of us needy sinners redemption in Christ Jesus. But a tragic misreading of scripture has blocked access to God's grace on the part of those considered unworthy of it, like the lepers of biblical times. This in turn has hurt the evangelistic witness of the Church in culture, with LGBT persons, and in our churches.

2. *The Church is a community of humble/grateful forgiven disciples of Jesus.* Christians are called to welcome as family all who believe in and seek to follow Jesus, and to live together in unity and shared commitment to the work of God's reign. A tragic misreading of scripture has tempted straight Christians to view themselves as superior to gay Christians (or to reject the idea that there could be gay Christians) and to exclude them from the Body of Christ (or to leave a church or denomination if perhaps gay people might actually be fully welcomed). It has created first- and second-class Christians and has damaged the unity of the Church.

3. *The great ethical imperatives of the Christian life* center on justice, deliverance, compassion, human dignity, and love. But a tragic misreading of scripture has produced a harvest of bitter fruit: injustice, oppression, mercilessness, degradation, and hatred or indifference. If, as Glen Stassen argues, you can know an ethical tradition by its historical fruits, these fruits are not appealing.[46] They are the opposite of what the Kingdom of God looks like, which is justice, peace, healing, deliverance, inclusion in community, and joy in God's presence.[47]

4. *It comes down to Jesus* and how those who claim his name understand the meaning of his incarnation, ministry, teaching, death, and resurrection. A tragic misreading of scripture, I believe, has actually taught traditionalists to deny the Jesus we meet in the Gospels, and to do so in the name of Jesus himself.[48] It has created an unchristlike body of Christian tradition that continues to deliver damage every day, all around the world.

Transformative encounters with LGBT people in recent years have led me (and others) to fresh encounters with the Gospel, the Church, Christian Ethics, and above all Jesus. I have moved into deep solidarity with LGBT people, with a special focus on evangelical young people. In making this move, I am not setting aside scripture. I am embracing its deepest and most central meaning.

Conclusion

Many evangelical Christians have thought the LGBT issue was a sexual ethics issue. They thought our job was to draw a moral boundary line between whose desired or actual sexual acts are morally legitimate and whose are illegitimate. Because we fixated on the sexual ethics issues, we tragically failed to notice our LGBT neighbors bleeding by the side of the road, mainly bleeding because of what we Christians had done to them while not even knowing we were doing it.

The fundamental "LGBT issue" is that a misreading or at least a misapplication of six texts in scripture taught many Christians a tradition of contempt toward sexual and gender minorities. That teaching of contempt has cost many lives, fractured many families, and wounded the mental health of millions. It has driven many away from God and church. The LGBT issue is a Gospel issue, a human dignity issue, a family wholeness issue, a church unity issue, an adolescent health issue, a justice and love issue, a solidarity-with-the-oppressed issue, and a reconciliation-in-Christ issue. It is not fundamentally a sexual ethics issue.

We have labeled as sinful or as rebellion against God a form of human diversity that has shown up in every society and every era. We have done so despite the overwhelming research evidence and urgent appeals for destigmatization by our culture's leading scientists, clinicians, and mental health experts. In doing so, traditionalist Christianity still trains many of its most devout adherents to disdain and reject a small but significant minority of the human population, including their own children, church members, and fellow believers, leaving a legacy of great harm. This obvious moral blind spot on our part has deeply discredited the moral witness of Christianity.

It is time to end the suffering of the church's own most oppressed group. It is time to reconcile evangelical Christianity with our sexual minorities.

Notes

1. I mainly deploy the acronym LGBT in this paper to refer to lesbian, gay, bisexual, and transgender persons while recognizing that there is not quite consensus on the best shorthand terminology: LGBTQIA+, etc. For brevity, I do not even attempt to address parallel conversations in Catholicism or other communities.

2. Global South evangelicals are not proving friendly to any rethinking of this issue. Sometimes they are aided by US anti-LGBT evangelicals. See Alex Seitz-Wald, "Evangelicals Are Winning the Gay Marriage Fight—in Africa and Russia," *National Journal*, January 23, 2014, http://www.nationaljournal.com/gay-washington/evangelicals-are-winning-the-gay-marriage-fight-in-africa-and-russia-20140123.

3. See the website of Evangelicals Concerned: http://ecinc.org/.

4. Mel White, *Stranger at the Gate: To Be Gay and Christian in America* (New York: Penguin, 1994).

5. Lewis B. Smedes, "Like the Wideness of the Sea?" *Soulforce*, August 13, 2004, http://abouthomosexuality.com/lewissmedes.pdf. This essay is sometimes referred to as "There's a Wideness in God's Mercy," other times "Like the Wideness of the Sea." These are of course references to two parts of one line of a classic Christian hymn.

6. David G. Myers, *Psychology*, 10th ed. (New York: Worth, 2013); and David G. Myers and Letha Dawson Scanzoni, *What God Has Joined Together: A Christian Case for Gay Marriage* (New York: HarperSanFrancisco, 2005).

7. Andrew Marin, *Love Is an Orientation: Elevating the Conversation with the Gay Community* (Downers Grove, IL: Intervarsity Press, 2009). He also founded the Marin Foundation to further this work: http://www.themarinfoundation.org/.

8. Wendy VanderWal-Gritter, *Generous Spaciousness: Responding to Gay Christians in the Church* (Grand Rapids, MI: Brazos, 2014).

9. Ken Wilson, *A Letter to My Congregation: An Evangelical Pastor's Path to Embracing People Who Are Gay, Lesbian, and Transgender into the Company of Jesus* (Canton, MI: Read the Spirit Books, 2014).

10. Wesley Hill, *Washed and Waiting: Reflections on Christian Faithfulness and Homosexuality* (Grand Rapids, MI: Zondervan, 2010); Justin Lee, *Torn: Rescuing the Gospel from the Gays vs. Christians Debate* (New York: Jericho Books, 2012); and Tim Otto, *Oriented to Faith* (Eugene, OR: Cascade, 2014).

11. Jennifer Knapp, *Facing the Music: My Story* (New York: Howard Books, 2014). Perhaps the most visible evangelical lesbian in good standing was, for a while, Wheaton College staffer Julie Rodgers. The legitimacy of her service at Wheaton even as a celibate lesbian was questioned in this piece published in December 2014: Julie Roys, "Wheaton's 'Gay Celibate

Christian,'" *World*, December 11, 2014, http://www.worldmag.com/2014/12/wheaton_s_gay_celibate_christian. Then, in July 2015, she abandoned both her Side B posture and her Wheaton post. See Julie Roys, "Why Julie Rodgers Is Right—and Tragically Wrong on Same-Sex Relationships," *Christian Post*, July 15, 2015 http://www.christianpost.com/news/why-julie-rodgers-is-right-and-tragically-wrong-on-same-sex-relationships-141552/.

12. I find little evangelical conversation on transgender issues to this point. The only source I have found is not an evangelical one: Justin Tanis, *Trans-Gendered: Theology, Ministry, and Communities of Faith* (Cleveland: Pilgrim Press, 2003).

13. James V. Brownson, *Bible, Gender, Sexuality: Reframing the Church's Debate on Same-Sex Relationships* (Grand Rapids, MI: Eerdmans, 2013).

14. Matthew Vines, *God and the Gay Christian: The Biblical Case in Support of Same-Sex Relationships* (New York: Convergent Books, 2014).

15. See "About the Reformation Project," http://www.reformationproject.org/about/, accessed June 11, 2015.

16. David P. Gushee, *Changing Our Mind: A Call from America's Leading Evangelical Ethics Scholar for Full Acceptance of LGBT Christians in the Church* (Canton, MI: Read the Spirit Books, 2014).

17. See Dennis Hollinger and David Gushee, "Evangelical Ethics: Profile of a Movement Coming of Age," *Annual of the Society of Christian Ethics* 20 (2000): 181–203. See also David P. Gushee and Isaac B. Sharp, eds. *Evangelical Ethics: A Reader* (Louisville, KY: Westminster John Knox Press, 2015).

18. For example, see the polls of the Public Religion Research Institute, www.publicreligion.org.

19. See Kelly Brown Douglas, *Sexuality and the Black Church* (Maryknoll, NY: Orbis Books, 1999); Delroy Constantine-Simms, ed., *The Greatest Taboo: Homosexuality in Black Communities* (Los Angeles: Alyson Books, 2000); Patricia Hill Collins, *Black Sexual Politics: African Americans, Gender, and the New Racism* (New York: Routledge, 2005); Yvette A. Flunder, *Where the Edge Gathers: Building a Community of Radical Inclusion* (Cleveland: Pilgrim Press, 2005); Horace L. Griffin, *Their Own Receive Them Not: African American Lesbians and Gays in Black Churches* (Eugene, OR: Wipf & Stock, 2006); G. Winston James and Lisa C. Moore, eds., *Spirited: Affirming the Soul and Black Gay/Lesbian Identity* (Washington, DC: RedBone Press, 2006); and Traci C. West, *Disruptive Christian Ethics: When Racism and Women's Lives Matter* (Louisville, KY: Westminster John Knox, 2006).

20. However, this too is changing. Mark Achtemeier offers a good example of a mainline evangelical changing his view on LGBT issues; see Achtemeier, *The Bible's Yes to Same-Sex Marriage: An Evangelical's Change of Heart* (Louisville, KY: Westminster John Knox Press, 2014). Similarly in the United Methodist Church one finds former Asbury professor Steve Harper. See his *For the Sake of the Bride: Restoring the Church to Her Intended Beauty* (Nashville: Abingdon, 2014). More often today mainline evangelicals vis-à-vis LGBT issues look like the Evangelical Covenant Order of Presbyterians, founded in 2012 by disaffected conservatives who left the PCUSA primarily over the LGBT issue.

21. See National Association of Evangelicals, "Statement of Faith," http://www.nae.net/about-us/statement-of-faith; Southern Baptist Convention, "Baptist Faith and Message," http://www.sbc.net/bfm2000/bfm2000.asp; and with more nuance, Fuller Seminary, "Statement of Faith," http://fuller.edu/About/Mission-and-Values/Statement-of-Faith/, accessed December 16, 2014.

22. Carefully analyzed and pungently critiqued by sociologist of religion Christian Smith, in *The Bible Made Impossible: Why Biblicism Is Not a Truly Evangelical Reading of Scripture* (Grand Rapids, MI: Brazos Press, 2011). Interestingly enough, Dr. Smith transited right out of evangelicalism to Catholicism not long after publishing this book. A popular new

book for evangelicals on the same problem is Peter Enns, *The Bible Tells Me So: Why Defending Scripture Has Made Us Unable to Read It* (New York: HarperOne, 2014).

23. Among the many who have challenged this populism/democratic perspicuity has been Stanley Hauerwas, *Unleashing the Scriptures: Freeing the Bible from Captivity to America* (Nashville: Abingdon, 1993). Not coincidentally, though Hauerwas is popular with evangelicals, his own affinity has turned Anglican. The sometimes chaotic and disastrous consequences of evangelical populist biblicism has driven many an evangelical toward Canterbury, Rome, Byzantium, and the Church Fathers.

24. See Molly Worthen, *Apostles of Reason: The Crisis of Authority in Modern Evangelicalism* (New York and London: Oxford University Press, 2014).

25. Christian Smith, among others, attributes this to an evangelical lineage going back to Scottish common-sense realism. *Bible Made Impossible*, chap. 3. I got the term from David L. Balch, ed., *Homosexuality, Science, and the 'Plain Sense' of Scripture* (Grand Rapids, MI: Eerdmans, 2000). A number of learned evangelicals, motivated in part by the weaknesses of evangelical biblicism, have been attracted to the broader Christian tradition, or Tradition, in recent decades. See D. H. Williams, *Evangelicals and Tradition: The Formative Influence of the Early Church* (Grand Rapids, MI: Baker, 2005).

26. James Brownson, for example, now a revisionist on LGBT issues, expresses dissatisfaction with the broader-theme move as a response to the Big Six passages, though he does suggest a close attention to the "underlying moral logic" governing texts; see Brownson, *Bible, Gender, Sexuality*, 15.

27. The Southern Baptist Convention makes a good case study. Compare the 1963 Baptist Faith and Message with the 2000 revision: http://www.sbc.net/bfm2000/bfmcomparison .asp, accessed December 16, 2014.

28. The extent of this hypercognitivism in conservative evangelicalism has become clearer to me in exchanges related to the LGBT issue. I am hearing from many LGBT young people describing their efforts to dialogue with family members or church leaders. In many such dialogues the only admissible evidence is biblical exegesis.

29. Two terrible recent stories involving conservative preachers expressing public desires for gay people to die or be killed come from Arizona: Tram Mai, "Tempe Pastor Calls for Killing Gays to End AIDS," *USA Today*, December 6, 2014, http://www.usatoday.com/ story/news/nation/2014/12/04/pastor-calls-for-killing-gays-to-end-aids/19929973/; and from New Zealand, Teuila Fuatai and John Weekes, "Pastor Tells Gay Christian to Commit Suicide," *New Zealand Herald*, December 8, 2014, http://www.nzherald.co.nz/nz/news/ article.cfm?c_id=1&objectid=11370806.

30. The Romans 1 passage, which mentions illicit lusts and degrading passions and links these to same-sex acts, also makes it difficult for evangelicals to maintain a clear distinction between lesbian and gay sexual orientation, on the one hand, and same-sex sexual acts, on the other—as some Christian thinkers and communities have tried to do in order to make space for LGBT people in the churches. If that distinction collapses, it becomes next to impossible for any evangelical who acknowledges LGBT sexual orientation to be seen as a Christian in completely good standing.

31. See this famous renunciation: Warren Throckmorton, "Alan Chambers: 99.9% Have Not Experienced a Change in Their Orientation," *Patheos*, January 9, 2012, http:// www.patheos.com/blogs/warrenthrockmorton/2012/01/09/alan-chambers-99-9-have-not-experienced-a-change-in-their-orientation/, accessed December 15, 2014.

32. A good example is OneGordon: http://www.onegordon.com; for Level Ground, begun out of Fuller Seminary, see http://onlevelground.org/; for Soulforce, see http://soulforce .com/, accessed December 11, 2014.

33. It appears that the power structures of evangelical churches more often push out LGBT Christians and their families, whereas students and alumni remain associated with evangelical colleges and have financial power in relation to them.

34. This section draws from Gushee, "Creation, Sexual Orientation, and God's Will," chap. 15 in *Changing Our Mind.*

35. See Dietrich Bonhoeffer, *Ethics: Dietrich Bonhoeffer Works*, vol. 6 (Minneapolis: Fortress Press, 2005), 388–408; see also Clifford J. Green, "Editor's Introduction to the English Edition," in ibid., 17–22. This idea was suggested to me by James M. Childs. See his "Eschatology, Anthropology, and Sexuality: Helmut Thielicke and the Orders of Creation," *Journal of the Society of Christian Ethics* 30, no. 1 (Spring–Summer 2010): 3–20.

36. Background sources for this paragraph can be found in Gushee, *Changing Our Mind*, chap. 12, "Leviticus, Abomination, and Jesus."

37. For fuller discussion, see Gushee, *Changing Our Mind*, ch. 14, "God Made Them Male and Female," informed especially by William Loader, *The New Testament on Sexuality* (Grand Rapids, MI: Eerdmans, 2012), chap. 6.

38. Brownson, *Bible, Gender, Sexuality*, 156–57.

39. Ibid., 274.

40. An increasingly massive literature related to sexuality in the ancient world is now available, sometimes with connections to ancient Jewish and Christian texts. Few can claim to have mastered it. A leader is Australian scholar William Loader, with his five-volume series, "Attitudes towards Sexuality in Judaism and Christianity in the Hellenistic Greco-Roman Era," published by Eerdmans. See also Finnish scholar Martti Nissinen, *Homoeroticism in the Biblical World: A Historical Perspective* (Minneapolis: Fortress, 1998); Kirl Ormand, *Controlling Desires: Sexuality in Ancient Greece and Rome* (London: Praeger, 2009); Bernadette Brooten, *Love between Women: Early Christian Responses to Female Homoeroticism* (Chicago: University of Chicago Press, 1996); Sarah Ruden, *Paul among the People: The Apostle Reinterpreted and Reimagined in His Own Time* (New York: Image Books, 2010); Dale B. Martin, *Sex and the Single Savior: Gender and Sexuality in Biblical Interpretation* (Louisville, KY: Westminster John Knox, 2006).

41. For fuller discussion, see Gushee, *Changing Our Mind*, chap. 17.

42. This is an issue much-discussed online by families of LGBT Christians. A small number of books are now out as well, including Carol Lynn Pearson, *No More Goodbyes: Circling the Wagons around Our Gay Loved Ones* (Walnut Creek, CA: Pivot Point Books, 2007); and Susan Cottrell, *"Mom, I'm Gay": Loving Your LGBTQ Child without Sacrificing Your Faith* (Austin, TX: FreedHearts, 2014).

43. Larry L. McSwain, *Loving beyond Your Theology: The Life and Ministry of Jimmy Raymond Allen* (Macon, GA: Mercer Press, 2010).

44. Andrew Cray, Katie Miller, and Laura E. Durso, "Seeking Shelter: The Experiences and Unmet Needs of LGBT Homeless Youth," *Center for American Progress*, http://cdn .americanprogress.org/wp-content/uploads/2013/09/LGBTHomelessYouth.pdf, accessed December 16, 2014. All citations in this section are from this report.

45. San Francisco State University, Family Acceptance Project, http://familyproject.sfsu.edu/. Some of the family rejecting behaviors documented and studied by FAP include hitting/ slapping/physical harming; verbal harassment and name-calling; exclusion from family activities; blocking access to LGBT friends, events, and resources; blaming the child when he or she experiences abuse or discrimination; pressuring the child to be more masculine or feminine; threatening God's punishment; making the child pray and attend religious services to change their LGBT identity; sending them for reparative therapy; declaring that the child brings shame to the family; and not talking about their LGBT identity or

making them keep it a secret from family members and others. Everyone needs to read this document from FAP: *Supportive Families, Healthy Children*, available in English, Spanish, and Chinese at http://familyproject.sfsu.edu/publications.

46. See Glen Harold Stassen, *A Thicker Jesus: Incarnational Discipleship in a Secular Age* (Louisville, KY: Westminster John Knox Press, 2012).

47. Our list in Glen H. Stassen and David P. Gushee, *Kingdom Ethics: Following Jesus in Contemporary Context* (Downers Grove, IL: Intervarsity Press, 2003).

48. In dialogue, a traditionalist on this issue cited Matthew 10:37 to me in relation to a father rejecting and shunning his gay son for his entire adult life: "Whoever loves son or daughter more than me is not worthy of me." Therefore: loving Jesus "more" means rejecting one's gay child in Jesus's name. I don't recognize that Jesus.

Natural Law Revisited: Wild Justice and Human Obligations for Other Animals

Celia Deane-Drummond

This essay lays out preliminary grounds for an alternative theological approach to animal ethics based on closer consideration of natural law theory and ethological reports of wild justice compared with dominant animal rights perspectives. It draws on Jean Porter's interpretation of scholastic natural law theory and on scientific narratives about the laws of nature to navigate the difficult territory between nature and reason in natural law. In Western societies, attempts to detach from our animal roots have fostered forms of legal provisions that treat animals as property rather than as living, social beings entangled with human societies.

Introduction

This essay considers the significance of reports of wild justice and political alliances in social species for an interpretation of natural law and legal obligations to animals. Animal rights offer the dominant philosophical alternative to the legal position of animals as human property.[1] Peter Singer's animal liberation approach differs insofar as it uses a utilitarian calculus based on creaturely interests and the capacity for sentience, but Catholics in particular are inclined to react either negatively because of Singer's accusation of speciesism, or more positively through attempts at accommodation.[2] A theoretical discussion of animal rights, plagiarizing as it does from equally theoretical modern notions of human/natural rights, is not a convincing starting point for delivering a framework for protection of other animals and their ethical treatment, however shrill its original advocates.[3] If animals are given "rights," then their moral worlds are automatically circumscribed within that of human moral advocacy. Particular humans may act as proxies for animals, rather as an adult might act

Celia Deane-Drummond, PhD, is director of the Center for Theology, Science and Human Flourishing and professor of theology in the Department of Theology at the University of Notre Dame, 130 Malloy Hall, Notre Dame, IN 46556; Celia.Deane-Drummond.1@nd.edu.

on behalf of a child. Rights understood as a particular demand arising from an individual subject does not make sense in the case of animals except by a kind of co-option by human advocates. Further, it seems likely that modern stress on autonomy and avoidance of suffering, which Charles Taylor characterizes as a particular feature of modern Western civilizations, becomes transposed onto animal worlds.[4] Animals thus enter our world according to our particular cultural sensitivities and are treated accordingly.[5] The door is still left open for a comparative human exceptionalism with little room for maneuver. So far there have been few attempts to search for alternatives, other than outright rejection, either from a philosophical or theological standpoint. This essay lays out the preliminary ground for an alternative by probing aspects of natural law and wild justice that so far have not received sufficient attention.

One of the first issues to address in charting what that possible alternative might look like is that the relationship between "nature" and "reason" in natural law is an edgy one. The argument of this essay builds in the following way. First: What are the ways in which natural law might be understood to reflect both internal capacities and external constraints? Both aspects also raise issues about the way natural law might cohere with or challenge secular accounts of evolutionary ethics. More explicitly, how is natural law in the moral sphere related to laws of nature in the scientific sphere, and is a scholastic account of natural law still defensible in the light of modern science? The third section of this essay tackles the more specific issue of justice and subjective and objective "natural rights." However, rather than extend natural (or human) rights to other animals by proxy, as in animal rights, I argue instead for an *ethological* starting point in critical engagement with *wild justice*. Instances of capabilities in animals cohere to some extent with scholastic natural law perspectives. But the latter fail to appreciate the level of sophistication in the complex social worlds of animals. Laws, operative in all social species, including humans, can be interpreted as controlling functions of highly complex self-organizing social systems. All these factors point to a rather different approach when one considers human obligations to other animals.

What Is the "Natural" in Natural Law?

One might think that if natural law is a *capacity*, then it could be lined up with standard neo-Darwinian versions of evolutionary ethics where moral capability is understood as a sophisticated cognitive skill learned in order for individuals to act successfully in complex social groups. According to this scenario, human moral reasoning develops within restraints set by particular cognitive functions. Something like this is implied in the scholastic understanding of the soul where the rational soul is inclusive of vegetative and animal souls.[6] It makes sense, then, for Aquinas to view natural law in a primary sense as that which reflects the flourishing of life, the sentient life of animals, and, finally, the rational life of humans.[7] Even if it is difficult to make a convincing case that such gradation in natural law mirrors in any accurate sense current evolutionary understanding, it is consistent with it at least at a superficial level. There is, however, an important difference worth noting. Moral capacities are *emergent* in evolutionary terms. There are reasons *why* such capacities appeared or, in other words, *why* it proved to be a selective advantage. For Aquinas, divine law provides the teleological orientation for natural law in a manner that would be alien for evolutionary ethics. According to an evolutionary perspective, moral judgments are part of a wider emergence of complex forms of cooperative behavior. Many species, including social insects, such as bees, ants, and so on, with far less intelligence than humans are clearly capable of intense cooperation. Rather, the point is that in complex societies there is an option to *opt out*, so regulating behavior is required for social flourishing.

However, if natural laws are not so much an individual moral compass but objective moral rules for human societies, then these rules are embedded in social structures. Restraints appear independent of individuals who, by their moral agency, have particular capacities to conform to or reject such rules. Accordingly, societal rules protect individuals from those who might otherwise refuse to cooperate. Standard evolutionary psychology narratives presuppose that all *external* regulatory devices emerge in order to restrain individual selfish behavior. Religion, rather than having its own ontology of revelation, is perhaps the crowning thesis of sociobiological emergent narratives. Although I am critical of such accounts, I mention them here to mark the boundaries of this discussion.

In the first case, natural law is operative through internal restraints, while in the second they are external, either as revealed (ontology of creation) or as emergent, evolutionary, or even socially constructed phenomena. Such judgments depend on particular beliefs about the origin of and authority of such external rules. Traditionally, Roman Catholic teaching leans toward an interpretation of natural laws as having an ontological basis in a doctrine of creation, thus linking natural law with divine fiat. Natural law understood in this way conflicts with dominant philosophical naturalism in secular ethics. Robert Audi believes naturalism approaches intellectual orthodoxy among philosophers in the West, so for him there are only some convincing versions of theologically orientated ethics.[8] Evolutionary ethics, which Audi does not consider, is realist with respect to the psychological roots of human action, but antirealist when considering the ontological or normative basis for moral systems, making moral claims neither true nor false.[9] Audi suggests that nonreductive ethical naturalism can anchor normative properties in the natural world without necessarily abandoning a theologically orientated ethics, so goodness and obligation still can be connected with natural properties without being reduced to them.[10]

But what would a nonreductive ethical naturalism really look like in practice? Jean Porter's work on natural law in *Nature as Reason* is particularly illuminating for this discussion. Porter defends a naturalistic ethic but still works within a theistic perspective in the context of contemporary philosophical and scientific reasoning.[11] She avoids imposing theological reasoning onto "recalcitrant material" while at the same time being "responsive to relevant scientific perspectives."[12] Finding creative ways through this labyrinth requires selectivity, but the revival of interest in natural law ranges far wider than theological or philosophical discourse, taking in lawyers, politicians, and activists. Porter's realist stance immediately creates common ground with most scientific practitioners, so knowledge is not *just* constructed but represents genuine knowledge of the way things are.

Few would go back to a rigid modernist understanding of natural law as a respectable alternative to traditional ecclesial authority.[13] Postfoundational philosophy in theology and science pioneered by the work of Wentzel van Huyssteen unsettles premature statements.[14] Porter is correct to claim that rejection of foundationalism need not equate with antirealism. Her retrieval of scholastic natural law shows that it is double edged. On the one hand, scholastics perceived the "natural" in natural law as being much wider culturally than contemporary meanings given to "nature," so natural law embraced preconventional grounds for moral norms, or reason as such, or even scripture.[15] On the other hand, they were also prepared to understand the "natural" in natural law to include the pre-rational as well as rational elements, and hence searched for intelligibility in the natural world, with a focus on the wisdom rather than the power of God expressed in that world.[16] For the scholastics, "human reason reflects the same intelligible structure of existence and action as are manifested in pre-rational animals, to which it brings understanding, and the possibilities of deliberate organized realization."[17] Albertus Magnus's sense of continuities between humans and other animals is striking.[18] For scholastics, therefore, such intelligibility does not mean that human beings are necessarily obliged to imitate other animals, or that continuities necessarily reflect biological kinship with them.[19] Their views are in one sense naturalistic but still resist presuppositions of evolutionary ethics.

Laws of Nature and Natural Laws

It is worth pausing on the theme of natural law through the lens of intelligibility since scientists commonly use laws of nature and sometimes even natural law to describe this feature of science. Physicist John Polkinghorne believes the term "law" is justified in science where there is evidence of an underlying ontological structure; some facets are "revealed" to the scientist rather than being an occasion of phenomenological adequacy.[20] But he also admits of slippage in the use of the term "law"; further, what he terms "natural law" can be indicative of probabilistic tendencies toward chaos, as in the second law of thermodynamics, rather than reflecting any underlying regularities in structure.[21] This goes back to Porter, namely, that realism does not necessarily mean fundamentalism. In the case of modern physics, for example, indeterminacy can be integral to intelligibility. For Polkinghorne, "natural law" provides a metaphysical foundation for scientific laws of nature. For Niels Gregersen, such laws only arose in the early modern period when "naturalistic explanation was propelled by theological assumptions."[22] God, as the giver of the laws of nature, is then uncovered by discovering laws of science.[23] Scientists in a post-Enlightenment context mean something different from scholastics when they speak of natural law; both search for intelligibility, though for different reasons.

Once biological sciences come into the picture, "law" as implying fixed regularity becomes problematic. Biologist Jeffrey Schloss's discussion is pertinent.[24] He offers four important observations. First, many generalizations used in biology are descriptive and contingent rather than law-like, in the sense of reflecting some kind of underlying structure.[25] Second, most generalizations in biology have important exceptions.[26] The law of natural selection seems like a tautology once it is couched in terms of survival of the fittest; "survival" means successful reproduction, as does "fittest," so what does survival of the fittest really mean? As Schloss states, "The Darwinian insight can be phrased simply as: The composition of a population will change in the direction of those entities that make more copies of themselves than others. But this could not possibly be false."[27] It seems, then, that a logical truth is being co-opted as a biological law, leading to considerable doubts about the validity of naming evolution by natural selection a law at all! Third, phylogenetic survival does not just depend on natural selection; it also includes many other factors, some of which Schloss mentions—neutral variation, genetic drift, and contingent cataclysms—though I would also want to add behavioral factors. And so many biologists today are realizing that framing evolutionary biology exclusively through natural selection will not suffice. Evolution is a complex interactive process between a number of different inheritance systems, genetics being only one of these.[28] If behavior is important in the overall trajectory of evolutionary processes, as it seems to be, then individual agency once more becomes significant. Rather than a natural selection of traits where internal characteristics survive against an external background, there is reciprocal interaction and niche construction, providing a much richer evolutionary account.

This raises a dilemma. If there are any law-like generalizations in biology, then they are only descriptive and inductive rather than being causal explanations. Such laws are not constructed out of thin air but are arrived at through generalizations from detailed observations. The tension between morphologists, who historically insisted on essential structure, and teleologists, who preferred to highlight function, still persists in evolutionary debates. Michael Denton and Craig Marshall claim, "Physical laws must have had a far greater role in the evolution of biological form than is generally assumed. And it will mean a return to the pre-Darwinian conception that underlying all the diversity of life is a finite set of natural forms that will recur over and over again anywhere in the cosmos where there is carbon-based life."[29] Functionalists, however, view any regularity as emerging from trade-offs between different possibilities according to the best function in a given set of conditions. Inasmuch as functionalist approaches imply directionality, it is better to name this "telonomy" rather than "teleology" since they eschew any notion of final causation.

Natural Rights and Justice

Natural law is complex in that within its scope there are not just internal and external facets but also, arguably, structural or functional dimensions, even though the topics of those structural or functional distinctions are inclusive of their cultural products. Scholastic natural law could be viewed as one more way to soften the post-Enlightenment divide between "natural" and "cultural" that has plagued biologists, social scientists, lawyers, and political scientists as well as theologians, philosophers, and humanities scholars. Natural right is structural in that it presupposes a principled basis of the good. It is functional in that it includes what it means for a society to function well in maintaining such individual human rights among its members.

Porter's analysis of justice and natural rights claims shows that, until comparatively recently, scholars assumed that Aquinas did not have a concept of subjective natural rights but rather of the right, or the object of the virtue of justice, *jus*, according to objective standards of equity and nonmaleficence.[30] Aquinas allows for subjective natural rights even if not as well developed as modern theory. More specifically, the scholastic jurists' conception of natural rights is reflected in their practices rather than specific theories, so they "regard at least some appeals to right as discretionary claims" either through an obligation or duty to act in a certain way or through immunity from coercion.[31]

Wild Justice

Wild justice is premised on the notion of fairness in social animals. The fact that something that looks like fairness is not evident in all animals should not concern us here; the point is that recognition of the presence of fairness across social species can impact on our sense of obligation to other animals. Ethologist

Marc Bekoff and philosopher Jessica Pierce have discussed social rules of animal societies in their book *Wild Justice*.[32] In standard economic tests chimpanzees did show clear differences compared with humans in what they deemed "fair" and were willing to accept *any* offer from a partner. However, that does not mean that they do not have any sense of fairness.[33]

Bekoff and Pierce define what they term a "justice cluster" as those observable behaviors found in social animals in relation to a sense of fairness, including "a desire for equity and a desire for and capacity to share reciprocally"; reactions to equity in expressions of "pleasure, gratitude and trust"; and reactions to inequity, including "retribution, indignation and forgiveness."[34] Many biologists prefer to call such fairness "inequity aversion" rather than the more anthropomorphic language of "wild justice."[35] The primary tool is cognitive ethology—animal behavior in their natural settings. Just as biologists are hesitant to use the term "freedom," preferring the generic "agency," likewise most biologists studying social animals hesitate to use the term "justice." Bekoff and Pierce are prepared to go further in using the term "wild justice" based on the following: (a) a keen sense of justice as fairness is universal in humans; (b) even very young prelinguistic babies have a strong sense of fairness; and (c) direct observation of animal behavior. While they press for evolutionary continuity, that can include divergence in what justice entails. It is significant, too, that just as cooperation has come into its own in contemporary evolutionary biology, fairness is also not simply an overlay that masks otherwise selfish tendencies.

Bekoff's close study of play behavior is particularly illuminating, for it provides an important bridge between a sense of fairness in individual animals and particular social rules that bears an analogy with aspects of natural rights and natural law. The rules of social play depend on fairness, cooperation, and trust. Accordingly, "during social play individuals can learn a sense of what's right and wrong—what's acceptable to others—the result of which is the development and maintenance of a social group (a game) that operates efficiently."[36] Animals also learn to take turns and set up "handicaps" in order to make play fair between different ages or sizes. The rules of engagement include ways of agreeing to play, how hard to bite, avoiding mating attempts, minimizing assertion of dominance, and what to do in the event of a mistake. Play teaches its participants social skills and cements social bonds. By definition, play cannot be unfair since if it was, it would no longer be play but something else, such as coercion. Of course, in social animals the tendency to play "unfair" is still present, but the point is that when play leans in this direction, such as biting too hard among dogs, or inappropriate sexual advances, there has to be admission of wrong by the offending party, and then either a resumption of play or a refusal by the one who has been offended during play to carry on. There is even some evidence that play stimulates brain development in young animals and the growth of larger brains.[37] Psychologist Gordon Burghardt finds evidence of play behavior one million years ago among placental mammals, birds, and even crustaceans.[38] Bekoff recognizes that play behavior is distinct in tolerating capability differences. If, by definition, play cannot be unfair, then it is different from other collective social activities such as caregiving or hunting. Bekoff believes that this makes play a form of wild justice, "a set of social rules and expectations that neutralize differences among individuals in an effort to maintain group harmony."[39]

Is it reasonable to call such hints in the animal world "justice"? I believe that it is as long as its meaning is clear, and I believe that wild justice in animal societies is not intended to be identical to or necessarily precede that in humans. Porter locates Aquinas's interpretation of justice primarily as a capacity of the will "away from its more spontaneous orientation toward the agents' own good, so as to create a standing disposition to regard and pursue the good of others."[40] One of the difficulties of any treatment of animal ethics, including animal rights approaches, is that adjudicating the intention of animals can only be approached with difficulty and indirectly. Yet even Aquinas argues that voluntarism of a partial sort is found in other animals, even if not full blown and not with the deliberative capacity of the will.[41] Now wild justice by definition cannot be premised on the kind of volitional decision making of humans. Fair play complicates even modest claims for such assertions in that the good of the agent matches the good of others; so it is good for all parties, including the most vulnerable.

Hence, while a sense of fairness is certainly present, wild justice seems to lack a reflective and deliberative concern for the other that is integral to human justice. Sarah Brosnan and her colleagues have assembled good scientific evidence for "second-order fairness" in chimpanzees in experimental contexts. Second-order fairness is a technical term that means that the participants, in this case chimpanzees, show sensitivity to the way another neighbor chimpanzee is being treated. That sensitivity is expressed by refusing to cooperate with the researcher in a given task where that chimpanzee neighbor does not receive the anticipated reward.[42] So those who received grapes (the preferred food) also reacted when their partners received a lower reward for doing the same task. This implies at least a second-order sense of fairness.

Aquinas's belief that nonrational creatures only move toward perfection through spontaneous natural inclinations is complicated by Bekoff's belief that play is *chosen*, even if humans choose more deliberately. So as humans can pursue perfection in a wrong way, other animals can pursue play in a wrong way also, and when they do, play is no longer play but something else. Mistakes are permissible in play if they are admitted to; for dogs this would be through a repetition of a play bow, showing genuine intent to carry on with play, but if "offenses" are repeated, then play ceases. Human persons are, through their tendency to sin, according to Aquinas's view, even less capable of self-sacrifice than they would be in their "natural" state.[43] Justice in human communities is both necessary in the light of human sin and capable of perfecting natural capacities of agents.

Natural Law and Positive Law

Natural laws, as currently inscribed in many modern forms and insofar as they might seem to take their bearings from natural inclinations, could be viewed as providing a more conservative basis for ethics compared with legal positivism rooted in conventions and human will. This differs from scholastic accounts, which resisted any sharp divide between natural and positive law.[44] At the same time, the moral obligation to respect positive law is not so much coerced as chosen if it is going to have moral weight. Ethical naturalists and evolutionary ethicists like Frans de Waal find continuities between human beings and primates not just in terms of inclinations to act in certain ways, to play fair, but also through particular social conventions or what could be termed chimpanzee "politics."[45] De Waal is cautious about making direct claims for animal morality while insisting that morality found in human societies builds on common social emotions in other species.[46] He is not so naïve as to assume the two are identical, or that the global perspectives in ethics, for example, are not unique to human societies. Unjust "politics" in animal communities does not make sense, nor does some sort of deliberative positive law. He puts particular emphasis in his work on the more cooperative and empathetic aspects of primate behavior, especially that in bonobos, and is prepared to claim that humans have something to learn morally given that he rejects other sources of moral authority such as religious belief.[47]

His concept of a tower of morality leading eventually to human moral systems presupposes an emergent morality and thus does not give sufficient credit to the specificity of other animal social lives. So comparing human reasoning power with that of even the most advanced social species is inevitably going to put humans in a position of supremacy. Social conventions in animal societies are more like coercion; other animals do have reasoning powers, but their cognitive powers are more limited and less deliberative; support for any social animals having a theory of mind is still contested; there are certainly no religious or goal-directed aspects of justice or morality, and so on ad infinitum. This comparative narrative does not take us all that far in terms of articulating what human obligations to other animals might be like. De Waal's view collapses back into a rather unconvincing evolutionary ethics. Agustin Fuentes, in a review of de Waal's most recent book, *The Bonobo and the Atheist*, captures this succinctly: de Waal fails to appreciate that "the human lineage is characterized by a distinctive capacity to alter and shape our niche, by language, symbol, and meanings derived from more than the materiality of our social and ecological surroundings. Human moral systems do not need religion to exist, but they do need humans. In the end, bonobos cannot tell us very much about being human at all."[48] But, like Fuentes, I suggest that they *can* tell us about being bonobos, and what fairness means in their world, separated as they are from humans by millions of years of evolutionary history.

A systems approach may help put our own human capacities for moral agency and those of other animal societies in a broader perspective. Donella Meadows pioneered this approach, which has been around for over a quarter of a century but is not yet widely appreciated. Systems theory uses computer modeling to envisage social and ecological systems and the relationships between them. A system is "a set of things—people, cells, molecules, or whatever—interconnected in such a way that they produce their own pattern of behavior over time."[49] Systems can change and, importantly, many include both human and nonhuman elements and may function in a way not intended by a single actor. Meadows claims: "The most stunning thing living systems and some social systems can do is to change themselves utterly by creating whole new structures and behaviors. In biological systems the power is called evolution. In human economics it is called technical advance or social revolution. In systems lingo it's called self-organization."[50]

And, importantly, it is the rules for self-organization that are responsible for the way that system changes. Rules are "high leverage points," so "power over rules is real power. . . . If you want to understand the deepest malfunctions of systems, pay attention to the rules and to who has power over them."[51] At the same time, self-organizing nonlinear feedback systems are unpredictable. Rather than trying to impose our will on a system, Meadows advises: "listen to what the system tells us, and discover how its properties and our values can work together to bring forth something much better than could ever be produced by our will alone."[52] Complex systems, including ecological systems, can be viewed as demonstrating characteristics such as resilience, hierarchy, and self-organization. Highly developed legal provision is deliberatively self-conscious rather than emergent in a way that regulatory devices in other animal communities are not, though impacts of positive law are also often unforeseen. Positive laws in such a perspective are regulating feedback devices operating in complex human systems, embedded in ecological systems, including those animal systems regulated by wild justice.

Hence, a systems approach tries to view the way the planetary system as a whole works as a network of highly complex systems in a way that is inclusive of human interactions with the planet rather than assuming, as most humanities scholars commonly do, that human social activity is separated from natural processes. Positive laws that contribute to social stability in an uncertain world therefore can be thought of as partially contributing to the resilience of a given social system by providing the kind of feedback that promotes societal peace rather than disunity. But systems thinking, in its emphasis on unpredictability, would remain cautious about naming given positive laws in terms of cause and predicted effect.

Should moral theologians be concerned that a systems approach points to another form of ethical naturalism? As long as suitably qualified, there are arguments that support the idea that a systems approach can give some useful insights about the unpredictability of human societies and a clearer recognition of entanglement between human, animal, and ecological systems.

Some Steps toward Human Obligations to Other Animals

This essay has presented an argument for closer attention to the social and moral lives of other animals, including wild justice, as a way of appreciating more deeply their worlds. Natural law, at least in its scholastic form, presupposes lines of continuity between other animals and humans and resists too sharp a separation of "nature" and "culture" while still retaining an emphasis on human reason and its eventual expression in positive laws. A systems approach, in its attempt to view social networks through systems logic, highlights the indeterminacy aspect of all complex systems and therefore qualifies human hubris. But, if wild justice is viewed as a regulating device, what might this suggest about human obligations to animals? The scholastic notion that intelligibility evident in natural law reflects the wisdom rather than the power of God is unfashionable when parsed as a crude version of natural theology. However, recognition of the proper regulatory function of animal societies in wild justice that are simultaneously interconnected with our own self-organizing systems should give us pause for thought. In other words, given the way human and animal communities are closely interlaced, it is inadequate to consider wild justice as cut off from human communities. Human action and interaction, including the laws generated in given human societies, dominate the life on the planet to such an extent that to name a specific conservation area "wild" or even a wild species "wild" is no longer fully convincing.

The difference between the scholastic approach to natural law and reductive naturalism is that instead of equating moral properties with natural ones, natural properties, at least inasmuch as they point toward a teleological approach, open up a liminal space for the appearance of divine wisdom. That is why Albertus Magnus was so fascinated with the details of the lives of other animals and spent much energy on their intricate observation. Are such renditions of theological ethics an endorsement of naturalism? No; since as naturalism can be nonreductive, it is still qualified by a recognition that not all that we find in the natural world can be placed in the category of the good, and that humans are often obliged to make choices between good acts, so discernment is necessary even in making decisions about obligations to other animals.

Charles Taylor contends that among the moral imperatives in modern culture is a demand for universal justice and beneficence. For him, moral sources operate in three domains: theistic, naturalistic (scientistic), and expressivist.[53] Yet a more integrative way forward takes account of scholastic natural law, which is still sensitive to what can be known about the world without succumbing to the pretense of evolutionary ethics. Theological ethics insists that "good" is an ideal worth aiming for, and the shape of what that might look like in terms of our obligations to other animals as a bare minimum needs to be informed by what we know about their lives.[54] To move toward what some of those legal obligations might look like in light of the above discussion, I will end with some practical suggestions about where priority needs to be given:

1. Legislation toward the protection of the social function of animal societies, including those living in national parks.

2. Legislation against those forms of animal husbandry that refuse to respect the social context of animal lives: factory farming, including battery-caged chickens, pigs, cattle, etc.

3. Tighter legislation of commercial and private zoos so owners are obliged to care for animals in social settings that resemble more closely their natural states.

4. A legislative ban on hunting animals for pleasure or for nonessential products such as fur or horn, and a limitation by license on those communities who hunt in order to meet their own survival needs.

5. Greater openness in labeling of consumer products that are reliant at different production stages on the cruel treatment of animals, including a denial of their social well-being—hence, the establishment of a Fair Treatment Index and not just a Fair Trade Index.[55]

6. Economic incentives built into legislation for those who change their practices, including, for example, tax breaks or other relevant economic measures.

7. Tighter international legislation to protect the movement of animals between nations.

8. Stronger international agreements on animal welfare, where there would be penalties (such as trade sanctions) for noncompliance.

Notes

I thank the editors of this journal and the anonymous reviewers for their helpful comments, and David Clairmont for prompting me to write on this topic.

1. A full discussion of the different alternatives within animal rights perspectives is outside the scope of this essay. I have summarized animal rights approaches elsewhere, for example, in Celia Deane-Drummond, *The Ethics of Nature* (Oxford: Wiley/Blackwell, 2004), 54–85. It should be noted that medievalists generally thought of animals as property rather than beings that had any rights.

2. For discussion, see Charles Camosy, *Peter Singer and Christian Ethics: Beyond Polarization* (Cambridge: Cambridge University Press, 2012).

3. Andrew Linzey has championed the notion of animal rights from a theological perspective in his *Animal Rights: A Christian Perspective* (London: SCM Press, 1976). His more recent work stresses animal suffering, although he still relies on a comparative case with children and still regards in a negative light the Thomistic-Aristotelian tradition. For a discussion of Catholic perspectives on animal ethics, see John Berkman, Charles Camosy, and Celia Deane-Drummond, eds., *Journal of Moral Theology* 3, no. 2 (2014), *Non-Human Animals*.

4. Charles Taylor, *Sources of the Self: The Making of the Modern Identity* (Cambridge: Harvard University Press, 1989), 12.

5. Martha Nussbaum, *Frontiers of Justice* (Cambridge, MA: Belknap/Harvard University Press, 2006).

6. Thomas Aquinas, *Summa Theologiae*, vol. 11, *Man*, trans. T. Suttor (London: Blackfriars, 1970), 1a Qu. 75.1.

7. Thomas Aquinas, *Summa Theologiae*, vol. 28, *Law and Political Theory*, trans. T. Gilby (London: Blackfriars, 1966), 1a2ae, Qu. 94.1.

8. Robert Audi, "Ethical Naturalism as a Challenge to Theological Ethics," *Journal of the Society of Christian Ethics* 34, no. 1 (2013): 21–39.

9. Ibid., 24.

10. Ibid., 32.

11. Jean Porter, *Nature as Reason: A Thomistic Theory of the Natural Law* (Grand Rapids, MI: Eerdmans, 2005), 55. See also Philippa Foot, *Natural Goodness* (Oxford: Clarendon, 2001); and Mary Midgley, *The Ethical Primate: Humans, Freedom and Morality* (London: Routledge, 2001).

12. Porter, *Nature as Reason*, 56. I press for an even bolder claim—that theology might actually bring insights that serve to *enrich* the scientific enterprise by posing new questions for its interrogation rather than just a respondent in the face of its authority. See Celia Deane-Drummond, *The Wisdom of the Liminal: Evolution and Other Animals in Human Becoming* (Grand Rapids, MI: Eerdmans, 2014).

13. Porter, *Nature as Reason*, 62.

14. Wentzel van Huyssteen, *Essays in Postfoundationalist Theology* (Grand Rapids, MI: Eerdmans, 1997).

15. Porter, *Nature as Reason*, 68.

16. Ibid., 69.

17. Ibid., 70.

18. Albertus Magnus, *On Animals: A Medieval Summa Zoologica*, vol. 1 and vol. 2, trans. Kenneth F. Kitchell and Irven Michael Resnick (Baltimore: John Hopkins University Press, 1999).

19. Porter, *Nature as Reason*, 71.

20. John Polkinghorne, "The Character of the Laws of Nature," in *Concepts of Law in the Sciences, Legal Studies, and Theology*, ed. Michael Welker and Gregor Etzelmüller (Tübingen: Mohr Siebeck, 2013), 12.

21. "It turns out that there are alternative interpretations of quantum theory available, each of the same empirical adequacy, which correspond either to the indeterministic view (Niels Bohr) or to the deterministic view (David Bohm). The choice between them can only be made on metascientific grounds, such as judgements of economy, elegance, and 'naturalness' (the absence of manifest contrivance)"; Polkinghorne, "The Character of the Laws of Nature," 16.

22. Niels Henrik Gregersen, "From Laws of Nature to Nature's Capacities: A Theological Thought Experiment," in *Concepts of Law in the Sciences, Legal Studies, and Theology*, ed. Michael Welker and Gregor Etzelmüller (Tübingen: Mohr Siebeck, 2013), 109.

23. Gregersen resists the idea of natural theology as providing proofs for the existence of God. He holds back, therefore, from giving such laws a strong theological warrant. So, "Offering a fitting meta-scientific interpretation does not imply that there could not be other reasonable truth candidates, for example, that the existence of the laws of nature is simply a brute fact (beyond which one should not speculate) or a result of a cosmic lottery in which we, as sentient beings, just happen to be the lucky winners." Hence, while Polkinghorne sides with Theism, Gregersen is also prepared to wager that Brute Fact Empiricism or Lady Luck Hypothesis (terms that he uses) are three rival metaphysical candidates for truth. Ibid., 110.

24. Jeffrey Schloss, "Laws of Life," in *Concepts of Law in the Sciences, Legal Studies, and Theology*, ed. Michael Welker and Gregor Etzelmüller, 61–82 (Tübingen: Mohr Siebeck, 2013).

25. An example of this might be the universal use of L-amino acids in protein synthesis.

26. The so-called cell law—that every cell comes from a cell—must have had an origin in noncellular life unless the emergence of life is denied.

27. Schloss, "Laws of Life," 65.

28. The others are epigenetics (which Schloss acknowledges), behavior, and symbolic inheritance. For further discussion, see Eva Jablonka and Marion Lamb, *Evolution in Four Dimensions: Genetic, Epigenetic, Behavioral and Symbolic Variation in the History of Life* (Cambridge, MA: MIT Press, 2005).

29. Michael Denton and Craig Marshall, "Laws of Form Revisited," *Nature* 410 (2001): 417.

30. The view that Aquinas did not have a concept of subjective natural rights is presupposed, for example, in Charles Taylor's account of natural law. Taylor, *Sources of the Self*, 11. He claims that subjective right is a central feature of the modern Western outlook with its stress on autonomy (12).

31. Jean Porter, "Justice, Equality and Natural Rights Claims," *Journal of Law and Religion*, forthcoming, 2015. I am grateful to Jean Porter for access to this article prior to publication.

32. Marc Bekoff and Jessica Peirce, *Wild Justice: The Moral Lives of Animals* (Chicago: University of Chicago Press, 2009).

33. Raisins were used instead of money for chimpanzees. Keith Jensen's initial conclusion that primates do not have *any* sense of fairness was subsequently challenged. See K. Jensen, J. Call, and M. Tomasello, "Chimpanzees Are Rational Maximizers in an Ultimatum Game," *Science* 318 (2007): 107–9.

34. Bekoff and Pierce, *Wild Justice*, 113.

35. Alexandra Horowitz and Marc Bekoff, "Naturalizing Anthropomorphism: Behavioral Prompts to Our Humanising of Animals," *Anthrozoos* 20 (2007): 23–35.

36. Bekoff and Pierce, *Wild Justice*, 116.

37. Ibid., 118–19.

38. Gordon M. Burghardt, *The Genesis of Animal Play: Testing the Limits* (Cambridge: MA: MIT Press, 2005).

39. Bekoff and Pierce, *Wild Justice*, 121.

40. Porter, *Nature as Reason*, 207. See also Jean Porter, "Moral Passions: A Thomistic Interpretation of Moral Emotions in Nonhuman and Human Animals," *Journal of Moral Theology* 3 (2014): 93–103.

41. Thomas Aquinas, *Summa Theologiae*, vol. 17, *Psychology of Human Acts*, trans. T. Gilby (London: Blackfriars, 1970), 1a2ae Qu. 6.2. For further discussion, see Deane-Drummond, *Wisdom of the Liminal*, 88–120.

42. Sarah Brosnan, Catherine Talbot, Megan Ahlgren, Susan P. Lambeth, and Steven J. Schapiro, "Mechanisms Underlying Responses to Inequitable Outcomes in Chimpanzees," *Animal Behavior* 79 (2010): 1229–37.

43. See Celia Deane-Drummond, "The Birth of Morality and the Fall of Adam through an Evolutionary Inter-Species Lens," *Theology Today* 17, no. 2 (July 2015): 182–93.

44. Porter "Justice, Equality."

45. Frans de Waal, *Chimpanzee Politics: Power and Sex among the Apes* (Baltimore: Johns Hopkins University Press, 2007); and Frans de Waal, *The Bonobo and the Atheist: In Search of Humanism among the Primates* (New York: Norton, 2013).

46. For example, De Waal, *Bonobo*, 228

47. Ibid., 23. He does so on the basis that the origins of morality are "bottom up" rather than "top down," though he is more reserved than the new atheists in criticizing religion. De Waal's caricature of religion as nonrational buys into the naturalism/religion divide; see Jürgen Habermas, *Between Naturalism and Religion* (Cambridge: Polity Press, 2008).

48. Agustin Fuentes, "Book Review: The Bonobo and the Atheist: In Search of Humanism among the Apes," *American Journal of Physical Anthropology* 154, no. 2 (June 2014): 315.

49. Donella Meadows, *Thinking in Systems: A Primer* (White River Junction, VT: Chelsea Green Publishing, 2007), 2.

50. Ibid., 159.

51. Ibid., 158.

52. Ibid., 169–70.

53. Taylor, *Sources of the Self*, 495.

54. Taylor denounces the affirmation of "ordinary life" as the main locus of the good life since he believes it leads to reductive forms of naturalism and utilitarianism, ignoring ancient distinctions between the ordinary life and the good life of contemplation. Ibid., 23–24.

55. A Fair Treatment Index has not yet been developed, and the author is not aware that the term has been used elsewhere. The suggestion is that the index, once agreed upon through an analogous political process to fair trade, would permit easy consumer evaluation of products that are deliberately committed to animal welfare according to specific recognized standards. The Fair Treatment label would therefore indicate more than simply "organic" on food or other products that use parts of animal bodies.

The Legal Suppression of Scientific Data and the Christian Virtue of *Parrhesia*

Paul Scherz

Powerful interest groups have responded to evidence of environmental or health risks by manufacturing doubt, partially through attacks on scientists. The current legal standard for the admissibility of scientific evidence in court enables such strategies for generating doubt. In the face of attacks on their reputations and careers, researchers working on public interest science need the courage to speak the truth despite risk, which Michel Foucault described as the virtue of *parrhesia*. *Parrhesia* is also a Christian virtue shown in the willingness to witness to truth in the face of risk because of one's confidence in God. This essay argues that Christianity possesses resources to form individuals in *parrhesia* in ways that support the dedication to scientific truth.

TODAY OPEN DISCUSSION OF SCIENTIFIC RESEARCH ON ISSUES of the common good, like climate change, toxic chemicals, pharmaceutical side effects, and environmental justice, is under attack. Political and corporate interests have discovered that the best way to block regulatory action is to generate doubt about research that argues for such regulation, a strategy exemplified by the tobacco industry's response to evidence of cigarettes' tie to lung cancer. As part of a strategy to discredit science, corporate actors have attacked individual scientists, threatening careers and reputations through legal and extralegal means. Because courts are central to regulation on these issues, this essay focuses on the role of three Supreme Court decisions that introduced the Daubert standard for limiting what scientific evidence is admissible in court. Drawing on scholars of science and law, I discuss how these rulings shifted the rules of the game in favor of corporations by encouraging the exclusion of scientific evidence. The Daubert standard increases the incentives for corporations to discredit individual scientists and keep experimental results from the scientific literature. Such maneuvers have grave impacts on public health,

Paul Scherz, PhD, is an assistant professor of moral theology in the School of Theology and Religious Studies at The Catholic University of America, 620 Michigan Ave., NE, Washington, DC 20064; scherz@cua.edu.

making it imperative for scientific, environmental, and social ethics to address these attacks on scientists.

The constructive portion of this essay describes the virtue necessary for the scientist to perform and publicize research on behalf of the common good in the face of risk, the virtue of *parrhesia*, of truth-telling. In his last lecture series at the College de France, Michel Foucault defined an ethic for contemporary intellectuals modeled on how ancient philosophy prepared the philosopher to confront rulers over injustice. In his lectures, he noted the conceptual links and divergences between philosophical *parrhesia* and Christian *parrhesia*. The truthful, trusting relationship between God and the Christian formed in baptism serves to undergird the Christian's public witness of both the gospel and justice. I argue that Christian practices that shape one to witness to revealed truth can support the scientific dedication to speaking the truth, especially in public interest research. *Parrhesia* is an emblematic virtue of the contemporary scientist who is a Christian, a virtue in which faith in God and commitment to scientific truth combine to enable scientific research to serve the common good.

The Example of Tyrone Hayes

The case of the response of the agrochemical corporation Syngenta to the Berkeley scientist Tyrone Hayes's findings on its pesticide atrazine shows the dangers that threaten scientists performing public interest research.[1] Internal Syngenta documents brought to light in a lawsuit over contaminated drinking water show that, after Hayes identified potential dangers of atrazine, Syngenta's public relations team attempted to discredit Hayes and his research. To this end they performed a psychological evaluation. They coached or paid seemingly neutral third parties, such as professors, op-ed writers, and think tanks, to present their case in the media. When Hayes was considered for a job at Duke, a Syngenta vice president contacted one of the deans. Syngenta sent representatives to his talks to ask hostile questions. It even considered investigating Hayes's wife, and Hayes alleges that a Syngenta agent made veiled threats against his family.[2] The attacks took a toll on Hayes, in terms of both his psychological well-being and his career, but he continued to publicize his findings.

Hayes did not engage in this dispute out of hostility to agribusiness. His initial studies on atrazine arose through a research contract with Syngenta. Once his data seemed to show that atrazine disrupted frog sexual development, Syngenta researchers began to attack his findings and delay funding for further studies necessary for publication. Hayes repeated the studies on his own and published them independently because of his commitment to truth. "Science is a principle and a process of seeking truth. Truth cannot be purchased and, thus, truth cannot be altered by money. Professorship is not a career, but rather a life's pursuit."[3] It is this commitment to speaking the truth that Hellenistic philosophers denoted as *parrhesia*. *Parrhesia* was not a minor virtue because, as discussed below, it was tied to the form of the philosophical life, which was devoted to living the truth and, as with science, pursuing the truth. Moreover, as with Hayes, *parrhesia* involved speaking the truth in the face of risk.[4] Structural conditions have made truth-speaking in public interest science increasingly risky.

Agnotology

Syngenta's response to Hayes reflects a common corporate strategy. Its goal was not to disprove Hayes's findings and replace them with a more accurate account, an aim that would be perfectly legitimate given disputes in the scientific literature over the effects of atrazine. Instead Syngenta sought to create doubt about his results by discrediting him personally. Robert Proctor coined the term "agnotology" to name the study of such active production of ignorance by social actors through the generation of doubt about scientific results.[5]

The paradigmatic case of the production of doubt is that of the tobacco industry, which even created a handbook for their strategy.[6] In 1953, facing evidence that cigarettes caused cancer, tobacco industry executives met with the public relations firm Hill and Knowlton.[7] This firm concluded that, while it would be impossible for the industry to disprove the mounting evidence of cigarettes' harm, the industry could create an atmosphere of doubt in the public mind that would hamper legal and regulatory action. Because of the centrality of this strategy to its continued survival, one industry executive wrote that "doubt is our product."[8] How does one generate doubt? Positively, industries can create alternative centers of scientific research, such as the Tobacco Industry Research Committee in 1954, which became the Council for Tobacco Research in 1964.[9] These centers used grants to amplify the voices of sympathetic scientists and those pointing to other causes of lung cancer. Negatively, this funding cultivated a group of friendly researchers who would criticize negative research and researchers as part of an aggressive campaign to disseminate the message of doubt. Since no research is perfect, such analyses merely needed to show that a study is not absolutely conclusive and that other questions can be raised. These tactics created the appearance of scientific uncertainty on the question of whether cigarettes cause lung cancer, a conclusion that was untrue but that stymied regulatory action. Companies also engaged friendly think tanks and grassroots organizations to publicize this seeming doubt. In response to research on secondhand smoke's ties to cancer, the tobacco company Philip Morris joined with other companies to form The Advancement of Sound

Science Coalition in 1993, a seeming grassroots organization that opposed the use of environmental research in government regulation.[10]

These tactics undermine the public consensus necessary for costly regulation. Instead of science presenting facts for politicians to analyze in light of their values, it appears that science just generates confusion. As we shall see, such strategies also undermine lawsuits seeking damages for disease and disability. In general, these maneuvers can only delay regulation because, in the long run, research becomes too strong to ignore. State governments have targeted smoking through bans in enclosed workplaces starting in 1995, increased taxation, and a legal settlement in 1998.[11] But in the delay before such action—delays that often last decades—industries reap billions of dollars of profit, lives are lost, the environment is degraded, and the common good suffers.

Law, Science, and the Daubert Standard

Given the difficulties of establishing regulations and the lack of premarket or postmarket testing of chemicals in the United States, the legal system is central to environmental and product safety. Lawsuits remove products from the market both by threatening compensatory and punitive damage awards and by bringing problems to the attention of regulators. They also serve commutative justice by providing funds for medical treatments or toxic cleanup. With the growing attention to environmental threats in the 1970s and 1980s came an explosion of liability lawsuits, so-called toxic torts, whose large settlements could bankrupt whole firms, as seen in the asbestos industry.[12]

To confront this threat, industry-funded think tanks mounted an attack on the research used to show that chemicals and products caused the specific injuries claimed in the lawsuits. The science used by plaintiffs was tarred as "junk science," a category that, according to these advocates, stood apart from the sound science of the regular scientific community. Junk science is supposedly produced by experts to serve the needs of plaintiffs' attorneys and is thus compromised by conflicts of interest.[13] These arguments are not entirely wrong. Many questionable experts were used in trials, and some companies paid settlements for products that were safe. Even well-done public interest science is noticeably distinct from general scientific research. Alvin Weinberg called such public interest science "trans-science" since it can give important insights and guidance but not the finality claimed by other fields because well-controlled experiments that would prove a connection between chemicals and cancer in humans, for example, are unethical.[14] This observation does not disqualify this science as bad science; it merely means that our methods have limited ability to attain certainty in these areas. Yet we have no other option than to depend on such research to guide policy.

Scientific testimony has generated similar debates since it was first introduced in court.[15] Expert scientific testimony is based on constantly developing theories and methods, leading to greater disagreement among experts than is otherwise the case. As far back as the nineteenth century, distinguished scientists on opposite sides of patent and insurance cases presented contradictory evidence, undermining the public's faith in science. The judge's power to exclude testimony is one way to minimize conflicting scientific evidence, but this solution requires criteria for determining whether testimony is truly scientific. The crisis of toxic torts and the junk science campaign increased the drive to find adequate grounds for excluding expert testimony.

The Supreme Court addressed this issue in *Daubert v. Merrell Dow Pharmaceuticals, Inc.* in 1993, a case regarding two children with birth defects alleged to have resulted from their mothers' use of Bendectin to treat morning sickness. Many scholars of law and science have concluded that this decision, along with its specification in *General Electric Co. v. Joiner* in 1997 and *Kumho Tire Co. v. Carmichael* in 1999, instituted a new exclusionary ethos in the judiciary, a tendency to prevent plaintiffs' scientific evidence from court.[16] First, in *Daubert*, the Court intensified the federal judge's gatekeeping function to ensure the validity of scientific evidence. The problem with this aspect of the decision was recognized in Chief Justice William Rehnquist's dissent: "I do not think [the Federal Rules of Evidence] imposes on [judges] either the obligation or the authority to become amateur scientists."[17]

Second, the court made the legal model for analyzing scientific evidence much more stringent than the models used in science or regulatory hearings. In *General Electric v. Joiner*, the Court suggested that the judge should evaluate each paper, study, and piece of evidence independently rather than take a weight of the evidence approach. Thus, the judge asks whether *this* study, on its own, proves the point at issue, rather than looking at the ensemble of evidence presented. Dissenting in *Joiner*, Justice John Paul Stevens questioned the rejection of the weight of the evidence approach, which he notes is how scientific evidence is analyzed in regulatory decisions and in science itself.[18] Making each study stand alone puts a heavy burden of proof on a study. This way of analyzing studies tends to sweep most of them away because, as philosophers of science have argued for a century, it is methodologically inaccurate to think that any one study contains a crucial experiment.

This consideration leads to the third problem, the four criteria that the court suggested a judge use to determine whether evidence represented scientific knowledge or not: (1) Can the evidence be tested? (2) What are the method's error rate and standards of reliability? (3) Are the methods generally accepted? (4) Is the research peer reviewed and published? Debates over the role of falsification in science suggest the problems of the first criterion, but it is the last one that is most concerning, especially as it was emphasized by Appeals Court Justice

Alex Kozinski on remand.[19] The problem is that, because of the difficulties of trans-science and because showing that a chemical is toxic is unlikely to advance one's career, many researchers avoid this field. There is little independent research into these public interest areas, so the company that produces a particular chemical generates almost all the published research on it. By rejecting research produced by plaintiffs' experts on account of its interested nature, courts have inadvertently ceded the field to just as interested research produced by companies. Moreover, since plaintiffs can use internal research found through discovery, this situation creates disincentives for companies to perform research on the potential dangers of their products.[20]

Beyond internal research—and here is where the Daubert standard is central to agnotology—emphasizing publication encourages companies to prevent negative evaluations of their intellectual property from entering the scientific literature.[21] It is this fact that encourages threats to the career of the individual scientist. If a hostile article is about to appear, journal editors may be contacted, and an online campaign against it may be coordinated. Because they are largely rhetorical maneuvers to prepare the way for a call for retraction, these attacks will consist of very particular attacks on methods. Such attacks will not suggest how different methods might provide a similar result, and they might even be attacks on generally accepted methodologies. This is an odd way to do science. Generally, if you disagree with a paper's conclusions, you perform the experiments that will show that they are incorrect. These are generally not good faith criticisms to aid the search for scientific knowledge but are targeted attempts to prevent papers from providing support for possible litigation or regulation.

If researchers with whom a company has a contractual relation produce threatening results, a number of legal means help the company prevent publication. The contracts of employees and external researchers contain nondisclosure clauses that prevent the publication of negative data.[22] External researchers who use a corporate product are saddled with material transfer agreements that can require company approval before publication.[23] While researchers are not without free will when they enter these arrangements, the contemporary context of research in many fields makes it impossible to do without such funding and materials. If a hostile scientist is not contractually connected to a company, he can be threatened with a libel lawsuit for criticizing a product.[24] It is not necessary for a scientist to lose the lawsuit to silence him because the mere threat of a lawsuit silences many. Defending oneself against libel or breach of contract can be bankrupting, and universities frequently will not support the defense. Even if one perseveres in the suit, years of research will be lost, and one's reputation will be damaged.

If legal means are unavailable, then companies can use extralegal means to attack a hostile scientist to prevent her from providing future expert testimony. Given their sponsorship of academic departments and buildings, corporations can apply pressure on university and college officials. More troublingly, industry-backed scientists can accuse hostile scientists of scientific misconduct, leading to investigations and ethics hearings.[25] Even the taint of such an investigation could end many careers. Finally, industry actors may engage in a pattern of harassment against antagonistic scientists, as happened to Hayes. These attacks discredit specific researchers and their work, thus preparing the way for the exclusion of evidence by courts and regulators. Individual scientists rarely have the resources or strength to withstand such assaults. Thus, doubt is produced.

Parrhesia

How can Christian ethics aid scientists who are faced with such great risks as they seek to serve the common good by professing unwelcome truths? Michel Foucault, who initially may seem like an unlikely source, is helpful in this regard because he recognized the importance of the scientific expert for combating problematic structures of power.[26] Many people misinterpret Foucault as arguing that knowledge is reducible to power, making science a mask of power. He actually argued that even though knowledge and power are always interrelated domains, neither is reducible to the other: "I am absolutely not saying that games of truth are just concealed power relations. . . . My problem . . . is in understanding how truth games are set up and how they are connected with power relations."[27] For example, the practice of science depends on institutions like universities, hospitals, and the government to provide resources for research; science engages problems that are of public concern, like pollution, and may have been produced by deployments of power; and science itself contains structures of hierarchy and authority. Structures of power also depend on science to describe contemporary problems such as climate change and to recommend possible solutions. It is because these systems of knowledge and structures of power are interconnected that Foucault sees intellectuals embedded in the apparatus of power as agents for social change. By deploying a different sort of knowledge, intellectuals can shift the system of power, such as when the introduction of ecological science opened other avenues of regulation from the ones available when industrial chemistry was the primary form of science advice to government. His analyses emphasize the importance of scientific research on issues of public concern for structural change.

Foucault, though advocating resistance to power, does not argue for blind acts of opposition. In his later work, he argued that individuals aiming to resist power should reflectively develop an ethos, what we might describe in the terms of moral theology as virtue, which, for the intellectual, took the form of the ancient virtue of *parrhesia*, the speaking of risky truth.[28] For Foucault and the

Stoics, the ethics of truth goes beyond the duty to abstain from lying, although this vision of ethics does not reject norms. For them, ethics denotes not so much the following of norms as how one shapes one's subjectivity in relation to norms. Ethics is a specific relationship one has with oneself and the norms that one embraces.[29] For the Stoics, especially the Roman Stoics such as Seneca, Epictetus, and Marcus Aurelius, this relationship took the form of attempting to embody the Stoic philosophical system in one's character. The Stoics, according to Foucault, attempted to transform a logos into an ethos through the practices of the care of the self.[30] They used meditative and ascetic practices to make their philosophical doctrines ready at hand to meet the difficulties of daily life. Thus, continuous meditation on Providence allows one to face misfortune with the belief that a greater good will come of it. The embodied knowledge that truth is a greater good than wealth, reputation, or life allows one to face persecution, exile, and death rather than betray one's convictions. These operations on the self tie one to the truth and drive one to speak openly for truth. *Parrhesia* is this relation to the self shaped by devotion to truth that leads to speaking the truth.

This analysis is grounded in Foucault and the Stoics; as such it differs from Aristotelian or Thomistic conceptions of virtue on many points, and, although a thorough discussion of the differences between these systems is beyond the scope of this essay, it is useful to indicate the most distinctive features of Stoicism. Fundamentally, Stoic psychology is monistic, lacking separate affective faculties and describing affective responses as judgments.[31] Stoicism retains the Socratic emphasis on knowledge to which Aristotle objected. Therefore, individual virtues are not as distinct as in an Aristotelian system because they are interrelated within the possession of a coherent system of knowledge. *Parrhesia* cuts across many of the virtues: connections between justice and truth, courage and martyrdom; the timeliness of prudence; charity's relations of spiritual guidance and friendship with God. It integrates political, social, and interpersonal structures. It is not that one cannot make these kinds of connections in an Aristotelian or Thomistic analysis (for example, Thomas Aquinas sees martyrdom as an act of courageous adherence to truth, and truth itself is a virtue connected to justice), but the analysis is more complicated and takes a different form.[32]

Given Stoic emphases on dignity, equality, and mercy, their truth-speaking frequently addressed kings and tyrants in an attempt to remedy injustice or implore mercy for the unfortunate. This speech was not merely an agonistic speaking of truth to power but was mixed with an appeal to the moral nature of the ruler and elements of spiritual guidance.[33] In the democratic polis, *parrhesia* took the form of Socrates's attempts to correct the ignorance of Athenian citizens, while in tyrannies, empires, and kingdoms, it is exemplified in Plato's confrontation with Dionysius of Syracuse, Aristotle's teaching of Alexander the Great, or Seneca's advice to Nero. As these examples show, speaking moral truth to the powerful is risky. Socrates and Seneca were forced to commit suicide, Plato was sold into slavery, and many Stoic philosophers were exiled as part of the Republican opposition to the Roman Empire. Truth-speaking is only *parrhesia* if it entails such risk: risk to life, reputation, prosperity, or even just the risk of severing a relationship.[34]

A final condition that Foucault puts on this courage of truth is that the truth spoken must not just be an objective, impersonal truth; it must be a truth that the one speaking has made his own. This subjective dedication to truth is demonstrated by one's entire life lived in devotion to truth. It is this last condition that raises questions for how well *parrhesia* fits the ethics of science. It is clear that the scientific life involves a dedication to truth. For the issues discussed here (e.g., chemical toxicity, environmental justice, and climate change), scientists are attempting to remedy injustice. Further, the dangers of lawsuits, fraud investigations, denied career opportunities, and personal harassment show that this sort of truth-speaking is risky. Yet an objection could be that scientific truth is general objective knowledge, not the kind of subjectively held truth at the heart of *parrhesia*. After all, science is precisely the method by which our society tries to attain objective truth through ideals such as reproducibility, falsifiability, and methods and conceptual frameworks developed by the scientific community. For such an objector, the solution to these problems might be found through a better description of scientific knowledge.

The promotion of objective knowledge over time is an accurate description of science's functions in general. Yet such a description is less helpful when one is in the midst of scientific controversies bearing upon the common good. Beyond the problem of finding criteria that consistently demarcate science from nonscience, a controversy is precisely the point where accepted methodologies are challenged and new ones created, where new communities of researchers come into being and old ones are superseded. Court cases provide a spur for the development of science by introducing new pressing problems to the scientific research agenda, new problems that require new tools for understanding reality.[35] General philosophical accounts of what is scientific knowledge or who is an expert can distort understandings of science and invalidate new but rigorous methods or concepts emerging at the moment of controversy. Corporate proponents of "sound science" use such philosophy to invalidate environmental science.

The chemist and philosopher of science Michael Polanyi has a different concept of the practice of science. For him, all scientific knowledge is personal knowledge in two ways. First, researchers are formed through an apprenticeship into a community of research under the authority of a mentor who shapes how they see the world and how they interact with the world in daily practice. Second, science involves a personal commitment to reality.[36] It is this commitment that allows the scientist to break free from established scientific paradigms to introduce a new understanding of reality, ensuring that a paradigm does not just become an instance of group-think. And it is this commitment that Foucault sees as underlying the speaking of truth. This conception of scientific knowledge as ethically engaged by the subject can help the scientist in the midst of an agnotological conflict.

Christian *Parrhesia*

Parrhesia is not merely a secular virtue; Hellenistic Judaism and early Christianity embraced this virtue as well.[37] The Stoic or Polanyi's commitment to truth is similar to the Christian faith that ties the believer to the Logos who creates the world. For both the Christian and the Stoic, Reason is revealed in Creation, and thus one must be committed to the truth of this Creation. Yet *parrhesia* is fundamentally modified in Christianity because this truth takes the form of a personal God who became Incarnate to redeem humanity from sin.

Made in the image of God and called to imitate Christ, Christians should embrace *parrhesia* because God Himself is a *parrhesiast*. In Proverbs, Wisdom calls forth on the street corner with *parrhesia* (Prv 1:20–21). Psalm 94:1 uses *parrhesia* in a request for God to act to enforce justice, translating a Hebrew term meaning "shines forth" that is used for theophanies in other passages (Dt 33:2, Ps 49:1–3). Jesus is a *parrhesiast* in the gospel of John, defending himself to Annas by saying, "I have spoken openly to the world; I have always taught in synagogues and in the temple, where all the Jews come together. I have said nothing in secret" (Jn 18:20).[38] Human truth-speaking can reflect divine self-revelation and the communication of the Logos.

For Christianity, the most important context for *parrhesia* is one's relationship with God. Building on philosophical links between *parrhesia*, friendship, and spiritual guidance, the friendship gained with God through Christ's sacrifice gives Christians the confidence to call to Him in prayer (1 Jn 5:14). In the Letter to the Hebrews, this confidence flows from Jesus's sacrifice on the Cross (4:14–16, 10:19). To give this virtue its full Trinitarian foundation, the Christian gains this virtue through the gift of the Holy Spirit in response to prayer. In the face of persecution in Jerusalem, the apostles prayed: "'Lord, look at their threats, and grant to your servants to speak your word with all boldness. . . .' When they had prayed the place in which they were gathered together was shaken; and they were all filled with the Holy Spirit and spoke the word of God with boldness" (Acts 4:29–31). The basic form of Christian truth-speaking is confidence in prayer to God, a confidence gained by our filiation to God through Christ's sacrificial death and bestowed by the Holy Spirit in response to prayer.

This gift from God requires a human response in the Christian life. In the Old Testament and Philo, bold speech toward God is the privilege of the righteous who complain and plead with God.[39] A tie to ethics exists in the New Testament as well: "Beloved if our hearts do not condemn us, we have boldness before God; and we receive from him whatever we ask, because we obey his commandments and do what pleases him" (1 Jn 3:21–22). In a different way, perseverance in martyrdom both expresses *parrhesia* and gains one friendship with God, allowing the saints intercessory powers, and later authors associated this *parrhesia* with ascetic or contemplative exercises.[40] It is thus closely tied to moral action and formation.

This *parrhesia* does not merely remain within one's relationship with God, but this confidence and trust undergirds the speaking of truth to others. As the quote from the Acts of the Apostles shows, the most basic form of Christian truth-speaking is the proclamation of the gospel, as do descriptions of Paul as *parrhesiast*. Martyrs were seen as *parrhesiasts* par excellence in Maccabees and early Christian writings on martyrdom, showing that witness to truth leads to risk in the Christian context as well. The Christian must also speak truth on more general ethical issues. In late antiquity, bishops came to act as *parrhesiasts* on behalf of their community in regard to the justice of the ruler's actions. Peter Brown has shown that bishops took up and modified the forms of *parrhesia* used by pagan philosophers. For example, in his confrontation with Emperor Theodosius over the massacre at Thessalonica, Saint Ambrose deliberately styled himself as a philosopher and spiritual guide, addressing the imperial anger with the healing of Christian penance.[41] Thus, *parrhesia* was a central ethical concept in Scripture and the early church.

Christian *Parrhesia* and Science

This analysis suggests the resonances and distinctions between philosophical, scientific, and Christian *parrhesia*. In each, devotion to truth is both a personal moral imperative as well as a goad to serve justice, strengthening the individual to speak truth in the face of threats from the powerful. Yet one might still prefer a secular to a Christian *parrhesia* to address the risks of science. Such an ethic was sought by those, like Foucault and Pierre Hadot, who called attention to the care of the self. Christian ethicists should not oppose such a secular ethic of truth since all devotion to truth is at least a first step toward the Logos who is Truth, but there are obstacles to such a secular ethics of truth. Despite its practical failings, Christianity, like other religions, has three resources that can aid scientific truth-speaking: a moral vision of the world to provide a broader context for truth-speaking, another community devoted to truth that can serve as a counterweight to problems in the scientific community, and conscious spiritual practices that help one acquire the virtue of truth-speaking.

To take the first point, for Stoicism and Christianity, truth-speaking is tied to a larger vision of the world since everyone is meant to form himself as a subject of philosophical or revealed truth. The scholar might exemplify truth-speaking in a special way, but every person is meant to develop this quality to some extent. For contemporary scientists without a broader moral vision, *parrhesia* would be another of what Alasdair MacIntyre calls moral fragments: ideals and norms dissociated from older intellectual systems.[42] Thus, Max Weber sees the scholar as choosing science and its associated *parrhesia* as a vocation against other possible choices, and Foucault's ethics is purely formal.[43] These would be purely subjective choices of an ethical stance, meaning that science could just as well be only a career in which truth is sacrificed for other goods and desires. This position is not possible for Christianity.

Second, classically, moral formation is dependent on others, on training in a Stoic school, and on advice from spiritual guides. Christians develop their form of life through teaching and ongoing guidance from the church. The scientist who is a Christian must adapt this guidance for the life of science since Christian doctrine will not specifically advise her on how to act in the lab. The church only guides her in a general way of being in the world. The scientific community also serves as a community of moral formation, as Polanyi has argued, but it may be failing in that duty today in regard to the temptations of money because the scientific life has become structured around the need to obtain grants and patents to fund research as well as the monetary rewards that can be gained from research. The biotech start-up promises great wealth to those researchers who can commodify their knowledge, and pharmaceutical corporations can richly reward biologists who consult for them. As Sheldon Krimsky and his collaborators have shown, it was precisely the most influential figures and mentors of science who moved most rapidly into relations with industry.[44] With the most important figures embracing the tie between science and money, it is hard for the community to support resistance in the name of truth. There are still some in the scientific community who support those under attack, but most avoid these battles either because they fear that their reputations will be put at risk through legal action or because they have embraced doubt as well. The scientific community alone is no longer strong enough to form the scientist to speak truth on these issues.

Finally, forming oneself to speak the truth requires *askesis*. By this I do not primarily mean renunciation, although that can be an important part of formation. The tattered cloak of the ancient philosopher spoke in favor of his truthfulness, as did the ascetic life of the monk. In science, too, Steven Shapin argues that the poor pay of the scholar was viewed by society as ensuring his truthfulness.[45] Such asceticism prevented the temptations of money from skewing statements of scientific truth, but it is no longer the norm for major scientists who receive rich personal monetary rewards through patents, consulting fees, and the sale of stock from biotechnology companies.

More than renunciation, encouraging *askesis* points toward spiritual exercises by which one forms one's self and prepares oneself to meet the problems of the day. Thus, Stoics meditated on philosophical propositions and performed the *praemeditatio malorum* by which they imaginatively placed themselves in the worst possible outcome of a situation and used that imaginative encounter to prepare themselves to bear anything rather than betray the truth.[46] Early Christian writers saw ties between monastic ascetic exercises or mystical contemplative exercises and growth in this virtue.[47] Today Christian private devotional practices along with the liturgical practices of the community focus one on carrying one's Cross and one's need to imitate Christ even to the point of suffering for faith. Most importantly, Christians can confidently pray to receive this virtue. Such practices strengthen one to face misfortune through preparations before a trial. As Foucault argued, contemporary pursuits of knowledge, including science and philosophy, lack these ascetic practices of the care of the self.[48]

Christianity thus provides many elements to support scientists' development of *parrhesia:* a broader moral vision of the life of truth within which to place scientific truth-speaking, a community that is devoted to truth and encourages the individual to aim at truth that can counteract some of the possible corrupting effects of monetary rewards on scientific research, and daily practices that shape one in devotion to truth and prepare one for the dangers that such devotion may entail. Yet this argument must be qualified on four points. First, despite impediments to developing *parrhesia* in contemporary science, the many biologists who withstand legal threats and attacks on their character show that this devotion to truth is not absent among secular scientists. There are still many mentors and colleagues who train and support biologists in truth-speaking. Moreover, people can find resources and communities for moral formation outside of science and religion. For example, the leftist political views of J. B. S. Haldane and others helped inspire their scientific opposition to negative eugenics.[49] Richard Lewontin and Richard Levins compare Stephen Jay Gould to Haldane, arguing that his formation in political radicalism supported his opposition to the genetic determinism of sociobiology.[50] Although Christianity provides helpful resources for scientists, many acquire scientific *parrhesia* without it.

Second, just professing Christianity is not sufficient for a person to acquire *parrhesia.* Just because one is a Christian does not mean that one will have this virtue. Many Christians separate their commitment to religious truth from their commitment to truth in other areas of their life, in science just as much as in business. Too often Christians fail in the commitment to truth altogether. Forming this virtue requires ethical work and *askesis.* The argument here is merely that Christian ethical formation can actually help in scientific truth-speaking, especially if it focuses on *parrhesia* as a virtue that exemplifies a life lived in devotion to all truth, including the truths of faith, justice, and society.

Tied to this last point, integrating the Christian and scientific life within a general commitment to truth will frequently require challenging prevailing views in each sphere. Thus, the scientist who is a Christian will have to stand against unethical practices or problematic visions of the person prevalent in science, just as Haldane and Gould challenged negative eugenics and the genetic determinism of sociobiology. Similarly, the Christian researcher may have to promote the best understanding of reality provided by contemporary science against the opposition of religious authorities and other believers, as in the case of Galileo, evolution, or climate change. Commitment to truth entails risk in all areas of life.

Finally, a focus on the virtue of truth-telling could be considered too individualist. Recent discussion of religious action in politics has focused on social movements and community organizations.[51] Yet social movements need scientific evidence to succeed, and much of the work of undermining social movements occurs by attacking individual scientists and their research in court. For movements to succeed, the individual scientist must be formed in such a way as to fight for justice.

Attention to structural issues is also critical, but it is important not to set personal commitment and structural justice in opposition to each other. Structural change is necessary: more toxicity testing should be done by regulators, science should be less dependent on private funding, conflicts of interest should be disclosed, and judges should engage Federal Rule of Evidence 706, which allows them to appoint independent experts to advise the court and would change the incentives of businesses for attacking scientists and creating doubt.

Even so, Foucault's thought reminds us that there are dangers in even the best structures of power, and the Christian doctrine of sin suggests that a perfect model of power awaits the *eschaton*. Greater government involvement in regulation can lead to its own forms of corruption.[52] Court-appointed expert testimony can be stymied by the difficulty of finding experts without financial ties to industry.[53] Alterations to the Daubert standard might provide resources to social movements that would undermine public health. Both Foucaultian and Christian ethics teach that the first point of resistance to dangerous deployments of power is the conversion of individual subjectivity. If scientists are not encouraged in their devotion to truth, structural changes will not be effective.

Conclusion

The Daubert standard for the exclusion of expert testimony is a central element of a general strategy for producing doubt. This doubt undermines regulation, public support of change, and legal rectification of injustice. Because of the

Daubert standard, this strategy encourages corporations to attack scientists and their research before they come anywhere near a courtroom, suppressing publications, ruining careers, and creating generalized conflicts of interests. These problems are important for Christian ethics because such research is crucial for social movements on important issues such as environmental justice or climate change.

While structural and legal changes, including changes to the Daubert standard, are necessary to confront this problem, the success of such changes depends on scientists' dedication to truth and willingness to speak the truth. This virtue of *parrhesia* is even more necessary for the individual scientist who is attacked under the current agnotological regime because it supports the courage to speak the truth in the face of threats to a career. Yet the scientific community alone may not have the resources necessary to form scientists in this virtue. Thus, Christian moral formation can serve as an essential support to the scientific enterprise as long as the scientist who is a Christian realizes that her research must also serve the common good.

Notes

I would like to thank Gerald McKenny, Gretchen Reydams-Schils, Jean Porter, China Scherz, Todd Whitmore, and William Mattison for their comments on earlier versions of this essay.

1. Rachel Aviv, "A Valuable Reputation," *New Yorker*, February 10, 2014, http://www.newyorker.com/magazine/2014/02/10/a-valuable-reputation; and Dashka Slater, "The Frog of War," *Mother Jones*, February 2012, http://www.motherjones.com/environment/2011/11/tyrone-hayes-atrazine-syngenta-feud-frog-endangered. Syngenta documents were reported on at Clare Howard, "Pest Control: Syngenta's Secret Campaign to Discredit Atrazine's Critics," *100 Reporters*, June 17, 2013, http://100r.org/2013/06/pest-control-syngentas-secret-campaign-to-discredit-atrazines-critics/.

2. Hayes responded with emails to Syngenta officials containing disparaging rap lyrics. Syngenta complained to the University of California, Berkeley, but an investigation found no ethics violation. See Howard, "Pest Control"; and Slater, "Frog of War."

3. Aviv, "A Valuable Reputation."

4. These cases are distinct from whistleblowing because of their tie to the vocation of science. Whereas whistleblowing reveals unethical practices within an organization, these conflicts concern different interpretations of reality, and the researchers frequently have no involvement with the corporation. Many people attacking environmental research believe it is false. See Naomi Oreskes and Erik Conway, *Merchants of Doubt* (New York: Bloomsbury Press, 2010).

5. Robert Proctor and Londa Schiebinger, *Agnotology* (Stanford, CA: Stanford University Press, 2008).

6. Oreskes and Conway, *Merchants of Doubt*, 144.

7. This account of the tobacco strategy draws on ibid., 10–35, 136–68.

8. Brown & Williamson, "Smoking and Health Proposal" (1969), Legacy Tobacco Documents Library, University of California, San Francisco, accessed March 13, 2015, http://legacy.library.ucsf.edu/tid/rgy93f00.

9. Robert Proctor, *Golden Holocaust* (Berkeley: University of California Press, 2012), chap. 16.

10. For details, see Oreskes and Conway, *Merchants of Doubt*, 150–52.

11. California enacted the first workplace smoking ban with AB 13 in 1995. The 1998 Master Settlement Agreement between tobacco companies and forty-six attorneys general can be found at the Public Health Law Center website, accessed March 13, 2015, http://publichealthlawcenter.org/topics/tobacco-control/tobacco-control-litigation/master-settlement-agreement.

12. For the tie between toxic torts and concerns about expert testimony, see Tal Golan, "Revisiting the History of Scientific Expert Testimony," *Brooklyn Law Review* 73 (2008): 933. For a sympathetic discussion of asbestos manufacturers, see Peter Huber, *Galileo's Revenge* (New York: Basic Books, 1993), 148–91.

13. Gary Edmond, "Supersizing Daubert: Science for Litigation and Its Implications for Legal Practice and Scientific Research," *Villanova Law Review* 52 (2007): 857; and Huber, *Galileo's Revenge.*

14. Alvin M. Weinberg, "Science and Trans-Science," *Minerva* 10 (1972): 209–22.

15. Golan, "Revisiting the History of Scientific Expert Testimony."

16. Margaret Berger, "Upsetting the Balance between Adverse Interests: The Impact of the Supreme Court's Trilogy on Expert Testimony in Toxic Tort Litigation," *Law and Contemporary Problems* 64 (2001): 289–326; Edmond, "Supersizing Daubert"; Golan, "Revisiting the History of Scientific Expert Testimony"; and Sheila Jasanoff, "Representation and Re-Presentation in Litigation Science," *Environmental Health Perspectives* 116 (2008): 123–29.

17. *Daubert v. Merrell Dow Pharmaceuticals, Inc.*, 509 U.S. 579 (1993).

18. *General Electric Co. v. Joiner,* 522 U.S. 136 (1997).

19. *Daubert v. Merrell Dow* 43 F.3d 1311 (9th Cir. 1995).

20. Edmond, "Supersizing Daubert," 905.

21. Ibid.; and Thomas O. McGarity and Wendy E. Wagner, *Bending Science* (Cambridge: Harvard University Press, 2008).

22. McGarity and Wagner, *Bending Science*, 109–15.

23. Philip Mirowski, *Science-Mart* (Cambridge: Harvard University Press, 2011), 139–93.

24. McGarity and Wagner, *Bending Science*, 168–77.

25. For example, lead paint industry experts launched an ethics investigation into the researcher who demonstrated connections between lead exposure and decreased cognitive ability. He was found innocent after much stress and research disruption. See Herbert Needleman, "Salem Comes to the National Institutes of Health: Notes from Inside the Crucible of Scientific Integrity," *Pediatrics* 90 (1992): 977–81.

26. Michel Foucault, "Truth and Power," in *Power*, ed. James Faubion, 126–33 (New York: New Press, 2001).

27. By "game" Foucault means "a set of procedures that lead to a result, which, on the basis of its principles and rules of procedure, may be considered valid or invalid." Michel Foucault, "The Ethics of the Concern for Self as a Practice of Freedom," in *Ethics, Subjectivity, and Truth*, ed. Paul Rabinow (New York: New Press, 1998), 296–97.

28. He explores this concept of *parrhesia* as an ethos in two lecture series he devoted to it; see Michel Foucault, *The Government of Self and Others*, trans. Graham Burchell (New York: Palgrave Macmillan, 2010); and Michel Foucault, *The Courage of Truth*, trans. Graham Burchell (New York: Palgrave Macmillan, 2011).

29. Michel Foucault, *The Use of Pleasure* (New York: Vintage Books, 1985), 6.

30. Michel Foucault, *The Hermeneutics of the Subject*, trans. Burchell (New York: Palgrave Macmillan, 2005), 327.

31. For thorough explorations of the distinctions between Aristotle and the Stoics on which this analysis is based, see Julia Annas, *The Morality of Happiness* (New York: Oxford University Press, 1993), 364–438; Christopher Gill, *The Structured Self in Hellenistic and Roman Thought* (New York: Oxford University Press, 2006), 4–45, 75–99, 207–90; Margaret Graver, *Stoicism and Emotion* (Chicago: University of Chicago Press, 2007); Martha Nussbaum, *The Therapy of Desire* (Princeton, NJ: Princeton University Press, 1996), 48–101, 316–401; and John Sellars, *The Art of Living* (Burlington, VT: Ashgate, 2003), 33–85.

32. Thomas Aquinas, *Summa Theologica* (New York: Benziger Bros., 1947), II-II 109.3, 124.2.

33. Foucault, *The Government of Self and Others*, 192–96.

34. Ibid., 56.

35. Jasanoff, "Representation and Re-Presentation in Litigation Science"; Edmond, "Super-sizing Daubert"; and Gary Edmond and David Mercer, "Litigation Life: Law-Science Knowledge Construction in (Bendectin) Mass Toxic Tort Litigation," *Social Studies of Science* 30 (2000): 265–316.

36. Michael Polanyi, *Personal Knowledge* (Chicago: University of Chicago Press, 1962), 5.

37. This discussion of Christian *parrhesia* draws on Foucault, *The Courage of Truth*, 326–38; Heinrich Schlier, "Παρρησία, Παρρησιάζομαι," ed. Gerhard Kittel and Gerhard Friedrich, *Theological Dictionary of the New Testament* (Ann Arbor, MI: Eerdmans, 1967); G. J. M. Bartelink, "Quelques observations sur parrēsia dans la littérature paléo-chrétienne," in *Graecitas et Latinitas Christianorum Primaeva. Supplementa; Fasiculus 3* (Nijmegen: Dekker & Van de Vegt, 1970), 7–57; Peter Brown, *Power and Persuasion in Late Antiquity: Towards a Christian Empire* (Madison: University of Wisconsin Press, 1992); and Stanley Marrow, "*Parrhesia* and the New Testament," *Catholic Biblical Quarterly* 44 (1982): 431–46. For alternative uses of *parrhesia* in Christian ethics, see Craig Hovey, *Bearing True Witness* (Grand Rapids, MI: Eerdmans, 2011); and Rachel Muers, "The Ethics of Stats," *Journal of Religious Ethics* 42 (2014): 1–21.

38. Scriptural quotations are from Harold Attridge, ed., *The HarperCollins Study Bible* (New Revised Standard Version) (New York: HarperCollins, 2006).

39. Schlier, "Παρρησία, Παρρησιάζομαι," 876 78; and Bartelink, Quelques observations, 10–11.

40. Bartelink, "Quelques observations," 25–29.

41. Brown, *Power and Persuasion in Late Antiquity*, 113–14.

42. Alasdair MacIntyre, *After Virtue*, 2nd ed. (Notre Dame, IN: University of Notre Dame Press, 1984), 6–36.

43. Max Weber, "Science as a Vocation," in *From Max Weber*, ed. H. H. Gerth and C. Wright Mills, 129–59 (New York: Oxford University Press, 1958).

44. Sheldon Krimsky, James G. Ennis, and Robert Weissman, "Academic–Corporate Ties in Biotechnology: A Quantitative Study," *Science, Technology, & Human Values* 16 (1991): 275–87.

45. Steven Shapin, *The Scientific Life* (Chicago: University of Chicago Press, 2008), 45.

46. Foucault, *The Hermeneutics of the Subject*, 471.

47. Bartelink, "Quelques observations," 26–29.

48. Foucault, *The Hermeneutics of the Subject*, 14–18.

49. Daniel Kevles, *In the Name of Eugenics* (Cambridge: Harvard University Press, 1995), 122–28.

50. Richard Lewontin and Richard Levins, "Stephen Jay Gould—What Does It Mean to Be a Radical?" in *Stephen Jay Gould: Reflections on His View of Life*, ed. Patricia Kelley and Robert Ross (New York: Oxford University Press, 2009), 199.

51. E.g. Jeffrey Stout, *Blessed Are the Organized* (Princeton, NJ: Princeton University Press, 2010); and Willis Jenkins, *The Future of Ethics* (Washington, DC: Georgetown University Press, 2013).

52. See, for example, the corruption in the military and Atomic Energy Commission's control of radioactive waste during the Cold War documented in Kristin Shrader-Frechette, *Taking Action, Saving Lives* (New York: Oxford University Press, 2007), 39–42.

53. Such problems occurred in litigation on silicone gel breast implants. See Sheila Jasanoff, "Science and the Statistical Victim: Modernizing Knowledge in Breast Implant Litigation," *Social Studies of Science* 32 (2002): 37–69.

Book Reviews

REVIEW OF

The Scandal of White Complicity in US Hyper-Incarceration: A Nonviolent Spirituality of White Resistance

Alex Mikulich, Laurie Cassidy, and Margaret Pfeil

NEW YORK: PALGRAVE MACMILLAN, 2013. 203 PP. $90.00

As a white American Catholic ethicist, I often envy my Protestant counterparts' legacy of acknowledging and fighting racism. Catholic moral theology lacks Protestantism's bodies of literature, activism, and bold ecclesial statements addressing racism in the United States. (For more on this, see Bryan Massingale's *Racial Justice and the Catholic Church*.) *The Scandal of White Complicity in US Hyper-Incarceration* demonstrates how Catholicism might approach American racism using several elements of Catholic theology.

The book opens with series editor Mary Jo Iozzo's introduction to the Content and Context in Theological Ethics series, of which this is the fifth book. A personal and reflective foreword by Sr. Helen Prejean follows. Then the book's argument begins with a description of the United States' practice of mass incarceration and brief discussions of what is meant by "whiteness" and "complicity." This book employs a phenomenological understanding of race and of whiteness, taking whiteness as habitus. The literature about this approach to race and to identity is enormous, but familiarity with that literature is not necessary to follow this book's presentation, argument, or use of the idea.

Each of the book's three authors has written a two-chapter section. Alex Mikulich's explanation of white habitus speaks on levels of social thought and of the individual's experience. Laurie Cassidy's section looks at the culture of hyperincarceration and the development of the "dangerous black man" myth, and Margaret Pfeil's section on spirituality works from the beatitudes, John of the Cross, and a wide array of other sources to describe a political spirituality of resistance for white Christians.

This book would be most useful to masters-level graduate students in theological ethics or anyone preparing to begin teaching in areas of ethics related to racism or criminal justice (particularly in Catholic institutional settings). Rather than drawing exclusively on Catholic social teaching to talk about white participation in racism, these authors more satisfyingly put many Catholic traditions into action. For example, the book demonstrates careful use of the concepts of complicity, responsibility, participation, and intention; it considers specific actions while maintaining focus on systems' structures; and it uses a wide range of Catholic thinkers, including Metz, Copeland, Soelle, Gutiérrez, Carmelite Sr. Constance FitzGerald, Lonergan, Day, and John of the Cross.

This book assumes and asserts that racism still exists, that whiteness exists and aims to make itself invisible, and that racism is kept alive through social structures that flow from white habitus. However, the book does not assume the reader's agreement with any of these. Instead, the book first makes the case that these things are true and then takes next steps toward responsive practices of resistance. Rhetorically tinged homiletic shortcuts are not used to bolster this argument. For example, in similar works, the question of moral culpability for racist social structures is sometimes managed only with a discussion of how such structures distribute benefits and harms unequally. In this book, that argument is not used alone but in tandem with a careful look at the intention of one's participation in such structures.

Minor problems exist. The book would have benefited from one more round of editing to eliminate minor punctuation and writing problems, and the Catholic moral concept of "scandal" receives little systematic attention despite its presence in the title. Otherwise, the book demonstrates well what Catholic moral theology could do if applied to American white racism. Here's hoping that this is just the beginning of more such scholarship.

Nancy M. Rourke
Canisius College

REVIEW OF

Shopping for Meaningful Lives: The Religious Motive of Consumerism

Bruce P. Rittenhouse

EUGENE, OR: CASCADE, 2013. 211 PP. $ 33.00

Are there any theories of consumerism that characterize people's lives on a global scale? What motivates them to choose a consumerist lifestyle? If possible, how can we overcome this lifestyle that entails destructive consequences? In this new book, *Shopping for Meaningful Lives*, Bruce Rittenhouse answers these questions by critically appropriating Paul Tillich's theological insights. He first diagnoses consumerism as "not only a pattern of behavior that characterizes an individual life, but a way in which an individual organizes his or her particular life to seek to give it meaning" (3). It is thus more insidious than the mere acquisition of goods and services in ever-increasing amounts because humans are not meant to be mere consuming animals.

In attempting to deconstruct consumerism, Rittenhouse first points out that it has been poorly understood despite its seeming ubiquity. He launches his own investigation to look for possible theories of consumerism, which he then evaluates according to a consistent set of empirical criteria. In chapter 3 he enumerates five main types that describe Western consumerism: "1, greed, i.e., consumers' intemperate materialistic hedonism; 2, status signaling, i.e., consumers' desire to communicate superior social status; 3, manipulation of consumer by the producers of economic goods through marketing and advertising; 4, imaginative hedonism, i.e., consumers' seeking emotional pleasure through the imaginative identities; 5, parental concern, i.e., parents' desire to maximize their children's well-being" (47). According to Rittenhouse, these five theories of the motivations for consumerism provide anecdotal support to demonstrate their practical relevance, but they "fall short of demonstrating their theories' empirical possibility, let alone their empirical superiority over the rival theories" (95).

Rittenhouse's alternative theory is then developed in chapter 5, after he provides empirical evidence (including economic charts and analyses) for his own critique in chapter 4. His years of experience as a professional economist aptly qualify him to develop his social-scientific argumentation. Rittenhouse's constructive proposal is hinged upon his critical insight that consumerism's motivation may best be understood as religious. By religious, he means that it "answers a question posed by the nature of human existence" (132). Consumerism is now newly understood both as existential and as religious matter, and here Rittenhouse critically appropriates Tillich's ontotheological categories and concepts, such as the three pairs of ontological elements in the self-world structure of being (individuation and participation, dynamics and form, and freedom and destiny). Since consumerism's motivation is existential and religious, Rittenhouse attempts to resolve the moral and religious failings of consumerism by demonstrating the "correlation between the existential question of meaning and the answer of existential Christian faith" (133).

Rittenhouse concludes his book by calling for existential conversion through the means of grace—that is, "the means of conversion to existential Christian faith and of ongoing conversion within ambiguous existential Christian faith" (175). The strength of this book lies in his discovery that consumerism is a spurious form of religious life that only destroys those who are intoxicated by its lifestyle. Given that consumerism has taken root everywhere affected by ever rising globalization, Rittenhouse's existential investigation and theological remedy are definitely a welcome voice in the field of Christian ethics. His expertise in social-scientific study and empirical analysis is also a rare strength in this important pursuit. This book is well suited for upper-level college students as well as seminarians and theological school students. It is also a wonderful text for adult Bible study groups in churches and religious communities.

Ilsup Ahn
North Park University

■

REVIEW OF
A Political Theology of Climate Change
Michael S. Northcott

GRAND RAPIDS, MI: EERDMANS, 2013. 335 PP. $30.00

Restored to Earth: Christianity, Environmental Ethics, and Ecological Restoration
Gretel Van Wieren

WASHINGTON, DC: GEORGETOWN UNIVERSITY PRESS, 2013. 208 PP. $29.95

These two excellent books, *A Political Theology of Climate Change* by Michael S. Northcott and *Restored to Earth* by Gretel Van Wieren, offer distinct directions for Christian environmental ethics: Northcott develops a rigorous analysis of climate change as a failure of enlightenment rationality and politics, while Van Wieren argues that those who care about the earth can connect with it through the practice of ecological restoration. Northcott theologically defines a complex global problem; Van Wieren theologically engages a community-based solution. Each book advances Christian environmental ethics in important ways; considered together, they have much to teach about the content and methods of the field.

Northcott's *A Political Theology of Climate Change* argues that climate change is a "cosmopolitical crisis" and that Christians should embrace a more ecological and theological politics in response. Theologians and ethicists have long argued that environmental degradation has cosmological roots: The belief that human beings are separate from nature makes global-scale degradation and pollution acceptable. Northcott adds a nuanced political analysis, noting that modern politics is based on a denial "that the weather is political, or that politics influences the climate" (46). Enlightenment thinkers who laid the groundwork for contemporary political structures insisted that storms and floods were not divine responses to human behavior, so modern nation-states are premised on an ideological separation from nature. Climate change reveals the failure of such thinking, so the facts of climate change pose an inherently political challenge.

Thus, failures to act on climate change are political failures. Mainstream politics cannot consider that economic growth is unsustainable because it is premised on ignorance about nature. Nations cannot collaborate to solve the problem because they have no common moral agreement "about the ends and goals of human life" (245). Any response to climate change that simply extends the enlightenment project—by ascribing "rights" to the natural world, or by trusting existing secular political structures—is doomed to failure. Instead, climate change calls for a different cosmology and a different politics.

Northcott argues that both can be found in the Christian tradition. Natural law thinking respects the relationship between human beings and external moral standards "set into the structure of the cosmos," demanding careful accounting for the atmospheric consequences of human action (246). Virtue ethics teaches the ideal of politics as a "community of friendship and love," nurturing practices of participation in the good life, lived with less consumption and less destructive energy (200).

Northcott hopes that small-scale communities inspired by Christian cosmology and Christian politics will transition away from destructive practices and thereby demonstrate a new way of life to the world. His book concludes by reasserting that because climate change is a political problem, it is fundamentally a theological problem, calling human communities to "re-create the historic and customary connections between nature and culture, land and life, love for neighbour and nature which are central to the Jewish and Christian messianism of empire-challenging love" (316).

In contrast to Northcott's focus on political and philosophical failures, Gretel Van Wieren's *Restored to Earth* seeks a "more positive, solution-oriented" approach to Christian ethics (viii). The book is about reconnecting humans with the natural world through ecological restoration, "the science and art of repairing ecosystems that have been damaged by human activities" (2), and it argues that restoration models moral life by creating physical, intellectual, emotional, communal, and spiritual connections with the natural world.

Van Wieren begins with an interdisciplinary definition of ecological restoration and argues that views on the practice depend upon varied definitions of nature. She then moves to a nuanced account of restoration ecology as a spiritual practice (chapter 3) of community formation (chapter 4). Evocatively recounting a controlled prairie burn in Illinois on Maundy Thursday, Van Wieren argues that ecological restoration is spiritual and ritualistic, a practice in which participants seek "wholeness in the midst of brokenness" (96). Furthermore, she argues, restoration moves from spiritual reflection to communal action, becoming public and participatory, thereby empowering diverse human communities to engage constructively with the nonhuman world (114).

Chapter 5 argues that restoration should be understood as sacramental healing: "There is still room, restoration work reminds us, to learn how to live more harmoniously, more beautifully, more meaningfully with land" (166). The final chapter then argues that the narrative of restoring nature offers a new story for human society. Ecological restoration presents a "theoretical, methodological basis for better understanding the human relationship to nature and for generating a restorative environmental ethic" (185). Among the most interesting themes of this new ethic is one of atonement, the idea that restoration answers people's "guilt for ecological sins" with the positive step of working to undo past damage (177).

One way Van Wieren summarizes her argument is to rewrite Aldo Leopold's famous saying that "to live with an ecological education is to live alone in a world of wounds." Emphasizing the communal and religious power of restoration, Van Wieren asserts: "To live with an ecological restorationist's education is to choose to live with a group of people in a world of wounds in an attempt to heal them within and without—and, in the process, experience just how forgiving, how gracious land, humanity, and God can really be" (179).

These books raise important questions for one another. Van Wieren's careful attention to diverse expressions of religious impulses raises this for Northcott: What lessons do Christian theological analysis offer to people of other faiths or of no faith who share political contexts with Christians, or to Christians who seek to enact his proposals in diverse and secular societies? Meanwhile, Northcott's trenchant political analysis poses an equally important question to Van Wieren: Is it possible to develop a grand, new story restoring the human relationship to the earth without a careful examination of and wrenching break from the cosmological mistakes and sociopolitical institutions that presently exacerbate environmental degradation?

Bringing these books into conversation reveals some key methodological choices facing Christian environmental ethics: Van Wieren begins from local communities and focuses on community restoration, only moving to a global ethic at the end of her book; Northcott focuses on a global problem and its intellectual roots, only focusing on concrete communities at the end of his book. Should Christian environmental ethicists begin from the local or the global?

Northcott develops his radical ethic in dialogue with thinkers like Bruno Latour, Alasdair McIntyre, and William Blake; Van Wieren takes a pragmatic approach while learning ethics from restorationists in the field, such as the Benedictine Sisters at Holy Wisdom Monastery who work their land, and a group of artists in Pennsylvania restoring a creek polluted by acid mine draining. Should Christian environmental ethicists focus primarily on prophetic revolution or pragmatic reform, on academic discourse or concrete communities?

Van Wieren's book is about a practice of healing; Northcott's book is about a profound problem. Is it more important to cultivate hope by highlighting positive steps toward a solution, or to name and analyze the problems facing humanity?

By answering these methodological questions in such distinct ways, Northcott and Van Wieren advance the field and demonstrate that there are many directions for it to move forward. Christian environmental ethics is better for having both of these books. Because they are so methodologically clear and consistent and their arguments so sophisticated, both would be useful texts for teaching, though Van Wieren's is likely more accessible for the undergraduate level. Any scholar or advanced student of the subject should read both.

Kevin J. O'Brien
Pacific Lutheran University

■

REVIEW OF

US War-Culture, Sacrifice and Salvation

Kelly Denton-Borhaug

OAKVILLE, CT: EQUINOX, 2011. 279 PP. $34.95

In *US War-Culture, Sacrifice and Salvation*, Kelly Denton-Borhaug uses cultural and linguistic analysis in order to understand the place of war in American culture and discourse. She begins by noting that war culture is so deeply embedded in America's ethos that its citizens are generally unaware of the extent to which the United States has been militarized, with both weapons and ideology. With sobering detail, Denton-Borhaug documents how the military has penetrated and shaped institutions ranging from colleges to industry. She explains how militarization is exemplified in the consumer and civilian culture through video games and the rise of a surveillance state. By way of this analysis, the author makes the case that Dwight Eisenhower's fear concerning the influence of the military-industrial complex has fully been realized in modern America.

Denton-Borhaug then addresses what she considers to be the ideological fountainhead for America's militarism: the Christian doctrine of substitutionary atonement. In short, as Christianity teaches that an innocent man had to sacrifice himself to save humanity, so also American war-culture ideology teaches that soldiers, citizens, and the country must sacrifice on the battlefield in order to achieve national or political salvation. Denton-Borhaug suggests that politicians and others draw on the notion of the necessity of sacrifice as a way to convince people to support militarized conflict and to endure the inevitable hardships that result. By analyzing US political rhetoric between 2001 and 2003, Denton-Borhaug makes a compelling case that the Bush administration used sacrificial images of victims and abusers to set up a simple black-and-white ethical paradigm to justify the war in Afghanistan and Iraq.

From there Denton-Borhaug turns to feminist theological and linguistic analysis to deconstruct the language of sacrifice in political discourse. She argues that when sacrifice in war is seen as a necessity, the brunt of its effects is often borne by the weakest groups in society. The sacrifice motif also sets up a problematic model of active masculine protectors and passive women in need of protection, which leaders often exploit to convince the public to "trust them."

If Denton-Borhaug simply asked Christian leaders to guard against the use of Christian theology to justify national or political war-making interests, I doubt few would object to her case. In fact, I commend her for drawing attention to these critical issues and arguing for tactics that encourage peacemaking. Unfortunately, Denton-Borhaug argues that the solution to the political use of sacrificial theology is to jettison it, or at least to marginalize its use in Christian teaching. She proposes that we replace it with a theology of work, a cure that may be even worse than the disease she diagnoses and that is, moreover, not logically required to achieve the peacemaking she promotes. In this regard Denton-Borhaug could have been more transparent about her own presuppositions. For example, she clearly leans toward non-violence, leaving readers to wonder whether genocide, nuclear buildup, and state-sponsored terrorism are the only justifications for war (222). Moreover, I am not completely convinced that America's use of sacrificial language is an unvarnished harm. I suspect that at least some of the United States' use of sacrificial language stems from a desire to avoid language that glorifies war. Would America be better off if we used militaristic terms like "Death to Afghanistan" that emphasize domination, rather than the suffering associated with "sacrifice"?

Despite these weaknesses, Denton-Borhaug's book is a valuable antidote for Christians who have grown too comfortable with America's military-industrial complex and ideological war-culture machine. We would do well to take seriously her exhortation to work to remove the roots of war in our effort to create a world of peace.

Stephen M. Vantassel
King's Evangelical Divinity School

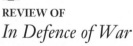

REVIEW OF
In Defence of War
Nigel Biggar
OXFORD: OXFORD UNIVERSITY PRESS, 2013. 371 PP. $55.00

Nigel Biggar's recent work, *In Defence of War*, is, from the first page, a provocative work. Theological defense of military intervention has fallen on hard times in recent decades, though historically the tradition of Christian ethics tilts decidedly in this direction. Over seven chapters, Biggar offers not a comprehensive analysis of just war but in many ways a theological apologia and retrieval of some of its more salient aspects.

Biggar opens his book by taking on the most well-known proponents of Christian pacifism (Stanley Hauerwas, John Howard Yoder, and Richard Hays), finding their collective work wanting on empirical and moral grounds, naming the "Anabaptist distinctive" as "theologically incoherent and morally hypocritical" (60). In the next chapter Biggar begins to unpack his realist account for Christian participation in war, exploring the role of love in combat, arguing that a form of "forgiving retribution" is intrinsic to a Christian account of forgiveness (71). This ethic, central to the moral deliberations of the just war tradition, is a scriptural ethic routinely ignored by pacifists.

Throughout the work, Biggar defends against pacifisms of various types, both theological and philosophical. Chapter 5, for example, attends to the philosophical work of David Rodin, a contemporary critic of the just war theory; criticisms against both philosophical and theological pacifism likewise undergird his chapters on double effect and interventionism. While Biggar gives a good deal of attention to philosophical and political pacifism, his Christian pacifist target seems to be quite narrow. The opening chapter, "Against Christian Pacifism," focuses on the work of Hauerwas, Hays, and Yoder with the implicit assumption that, having dealt with them, Christian pacifism as such can be shown to be untenable. The reduction of the polyphony of Christian pacifism, however, to this recent Anabaptist-influenced work was not entirely persuasive.

Later chapters take up various and often undiscussed aspects of the just war tradition, including the principle of double effect, proportionality, and the relation between the just war tradition and international positive law. In each of these chapters Biggar offers a theological account of war that is rich and multidisciplinary, with analysis that is not strictly analytical but deeply historical. Throughout the book, this reviewer was reminded of Michael Walzer's classic *Just and Unjust Wars*, as Biggar peppers his comments with military history and firsthand accounts by soldiers in wars both modern and ancient. As the work unfolds, various case studies such as Kosovo and Iraq ground his discussions, avoiding much of the abstract argumentation that pervades so much literature on war ethics.

In the end the virtues of Biggar's volume lie not with a defeat of pacifism as an alternative approach to Christian ethics but with his careful descriptions and robust assessment of the contours of a Christian realist account of participation in war. Biggar rightly directs us to view just war not as a pragmatic concession but as a complicated facet of the moral life. The chapters on double effect, legal positivism, and especially his defense of the Iraq war as justifiable, are particularly worth the read and should be carefully debated. Biggar has done the discipline a great service by pushing ethicists beyond sloppy tropes and into the deeper waters of careful analysis of what a Christian account of war might look like.

Myles Werntz
Palm Beach Atlantic University

REVIEW OF

Offering Hospitality: Questioning Christian Approaches to War

Caron E. Gentry

NOTRE DAME, IN: UNIVERSITY OF NOTRE DAME PRESS, 2013. 200 PP. $20.00

Caron E. Gentry provides a constructive proposal for transforming *jus ad bellum*'s last-resort criterion through the reconceptualization of hospitality as "an essential practice" (2) in international relations, one that helps *jus ad bellum* "operate proactively instead of coercively and reactively" (35) by seeking to protect "without interest the good and the bad of humanity and humans" (3). Gentry is particularly concerned with marginalized peoples who inhabit failed states, whose realities are willfully ignored through the "abstraction" and "hegemonic masculinity" in international relations, as well as in the dominant voices in political theology (Reinhold Niebuhr, Stanley Hauerwas, and Jean Bethke Elshtain) that support an "uncritical complicity with power . . . unable to deal with vulnerable populations outside of the West" (27). Understood in Christian terms as a practice of "agape," or "self-giving love," Gentry demonstrates how hospitality may be a plausible alternative to the paradigmatic approach to power in international relations, suggesting that acting without self-interest is a path to greater and more sustainable security (62).

Gentry engages an impressive array of sources to structure her argument. For her critique of international relations discourse, she turns to feminist analyses of state sovereignty to demonstrate how a masculinized understanding of power abstracts the realities of war experienced by human populations (18). Drawing on a "human security" perspective (35), Gentry suggests that the prevention of violent conflict requires a proactive practice—using tools such as the Failed State Index—that attends to the realities of vulnerable populations within states before they erupt into violent conflict (34). Her emphasis on vulnerability and the mutual need for the other reveals Emmanuel Levinas as the primary influence on Gentry's approach. Refracted through this vision, she opts for a practice of hospitality that moves beyond the realist, pacifist, and just war traditions to cultivate a "proactive last resort" that would extend care to the needs of the vulnerable beyond one's own borders (136).

Strengthening *jus ad bellum*'s last-resort criterion through a reconceived, proactive practice of hospitality is Gentry's most compelling contribution, one that is particularly insightful for practitioners and theorists of the just war tradition. Yet readers may get the sense that Gentry wants to push her contribution beyond the limits of political theology to shape the normative practices of international affairs; this is where Gentry's persuasive force begins to wane. Specifically, Gentry obscures the genuine differences between an ecclesial practice of agape, embedded in a particular understanding of the nature of God, and the international affairs of a state, embedded in a game of realpolitik, where invulnerability is the rule. In order for Gentry to stake a claim in such a context, she needs to develop a more grounded account of how states could accept vulnerability as a normative practice in order to act without self-interest.

Certainly, interdependence and mutual vulnerability are the right place to start. However, this kind of change does not simply concern the dominant patterns of international relations but also involves a change in shared conceptions about basic human nature. As such, her wider contribution may be less about a comprehensive framework and more about a potentially transformational question for theorists in international relations, political philosophy, and Christian ethics alike: What will it require for populations within states to recognize their own vulnerability and dependency, to see the well-being of "the other," including the enemy, as essential to their own security? After Gentry, any answer to this question must move beyond patterns of hegemony and abstraction, toward proactive engagement with the realities of vulnerable populations.

Andrew C. Wright
Fuller Theological Seminary

■

REVIEW OF

Bonhoeffer the Assassin? Challenging the Myth, Recovering His Call to Peacemaking

Mark Thiessen Nation, Anthony G. Siegrist, and Daniel P. Umbel

GRAND RAPIDS, MI: BAKER ACADEMIC, 2013. 272 PP. $29.99

In their new book *Bonhoeffer the Assassin?*, Mark Thiessen Nation, Anthony G. Siegrist, and Daniel P. Umbel painstakingly reread primary texts in order to challenge the widely held belief that Dietrich Bonhoeffer participated in an attempt to assassinate Adolf Hitler. Their alternative to the usual narrative of Bonhoeffer's life holds that early in his career, long before the crisis of the Confessing Church and the rise of Nazism, Bonhoeffer made a commitment to

Christian pacifism that endured even through the war years and his resistance to Hitler.

To argue for this alternative telling, the authors analyze Bonhoeffer's three main "ethical" texts: the early "Barcelona lectures," *Discipleship*, and finally *Ethics*. On their telling, while the early ethics lectures were theologically deficient, by the time that Bonhoeffer wrote *Discipleship* he had developed "integration," which was "the primary theological catalyst for the ethical transition from Barcelona to *Discipleship*" (129). *Discipleship* is, they conclude, the pinnacle of Bonhoeffer's thought, and anything that comes after it, including *Ethics*, cannot in any fundamental way differ from it.

Alongside this diachronic analysis of Bonhoeffer's main ethics texts, the authors emphasize two letters that Bonhoeffer wrote in 1935 and 1936. In the first, Bonhoeffer asserts that, because of his theology, he is "sometimes perceived as fanatical" (223). The second he wrote describing his "conversion experience" in 1930, in relation to the Sermon on the Mount and "Christian pacifism." Read singly, these letters are interesting examples of Bonhoeffer's thought and life of faith. As the authors present the argument, though, the letters comprise a unified narrative and function as an interpretive lens by which the primary texts should be understood. They think that the "fanaticism" of the first letter refers to the faith brought about in the conversion experience described in the second. The "fanaticism" letter is important because in it he asserts that, "if he were to become more 'reasonable,' he would have to 'chuck [his] entire theology'" (223).

Because Bonhoeffer wrote that he would have to "chuck" his theology if he made it more "reasonable," the authors think that the theology that emerged from the conversion experience has a foundational role in his later works. Whatever Bonhoeffer wrote in *Ethics*, then, simply cannot disagree with the "fanaticism" that "is most fully articulated in . . . *Discipleship*" (223). Because of the importance of the "Christian pacifism" of the conversion and *Discipleship*, it is thus impossible—or at least highly unlikely—that Bonhoeffer participated in the assassination attempts.

Bonhoeffer scholars and nonspecialists alike will find this text provocative and interesting. The conclusions, though, are finally unconvincing. For the authors, the "conversion experience" is the central key to understanding Bonhoeffer, and it is clear that they understand "Christian pacifism" to be of primary importance in the conversion, but they never tell us to what variety of Christian pacifism Bonhoeffer converted. It is very likely that Bonhoeffer's Christian pacifism was different in kind than the Christian pacifism that the authors seem to endorse. That anachronistic reading alone renders the conclusions of the text suspect.

Apart from simple historical questions, the methodology the authors use to construct their hermeneutical lens is also problematic. It is difficult to submit

Bonhoeffer's entire corpus to two earlier letters that he wrote a full year apart. While readers may understand and agree that Bonhoeffer was not, in reality, an assassin (the minor claim), it will be hard to convince readers of the impassibility of his "Christian pacifism" (the major claim).

Dallas J. Gingles
Southern Methodist University

■

REVIEW OF

An American Scholar Recalls Karl Barth's Golden Years as a Teacher (1958–1964)

Raymond Kemp Anderson

LEWISTON, NY: EDWIN MELLEN PRESS, 2013. 438 PP. $159.95

The Westminster Handbook to Karl Barth

Edited by Richard E. Burnett

LOUISVILLE, KY: WESTMINSTER JOHN KNOX PRESS, 2013. 242 PP. $35.00

On April 2, 1966, Karl Barth received a letter from Peter Vogelsanger, informing him that Emil Brunner—the recipient of Barth's thunderous "Nein!" on the subject of natural theology in 1934—was on his deathbed. Two days later, Barth responded and asked Vogelsanger to tell Brunner that "the time when I thought I should say No to him is long since past, and we all live only by the fact that a great and merciful God speaks his gracious Yes to all of us." The irenic, compassionate, and affirming tone of this letter is typical of the "mature" Barth, whom Raymond Anderson studied under from 1958 to 1964 as a ThD student at the University of Basel. This period of doctoral study is the subject of Anderson's interesting and eminently readable new book. Anderson enjoyably weaves together several different genres in his reflections on his experience with Barth, smoothly transitioning back and forth between personal memoir, constructive theological argument, and thoughtful interpretation of Barth's life and writings.

Structurally, the book offers a series of recollections and reflections gathered loosely around common themes rather than a tightly knit argument pursued rigorously from beginning to end. In other words, the work is a series of sketches from the artist's notebook, as opposed to one intricate and detailed portrait focusing on a single subject.

In the first five chapters of the book, Anderson sketches a picture of the elderly Karl Barth who served as his "*doktorvater*," drawing material from his student notes and personal memories of the years he spent with Barth in Basel. While Anderson finds continuity between the earlier and later writings of Barth, he suggests that the older Barth began to increasingly unfold the "fuller, grace-centered and human-shaped positive implications" of the earlier writings (viii). In Anderson's experience, Barth's early appeal to "Let God be God!" had in those later years "mellowed to an even deeper appeal to let God be himself, *human as well*, in the most unexpected ways" (11). This mellowing extended beyond Barth's writing to his personality and demeanor as a teacher and theologian. The Barth whom Anderson knew was humble, understated, and compassionate, a sympathetic listener and a generous interpreter—in short, an "un-dogmatic" dogmatician (139).

In the sixth chapter, Anderson shifts gears and reproduces extensive transcriptions of his own notes from several of Barth's biweekly English-language colloquia on the topics of natural theology, the Old Testament promise, Paul Tillich, and existentialism. Anderson suggests that these notes are particularly valuable because in them one witnesses Barth explaining the bare essentials of his thinking in clear and simple English terms. This is true for large portions of the transcriptions. However, it must be said that there are also portions of these transcriptions that suffer from the lack of clarity that one might expect to find in student notes of discussions conducted in a language with which Barth was not completely comfortable. Nevertheless, these transcriptions provide previously unpublished primary source material from Barth that is worth examining.

From chapter 7 until the end of the book, Anderson takes up the task of "sketching key insights and special teachings from the mature Barth that in the years since Barth's death have shown themselves to carry special significance for our American college classroom, church school, and pulpit" (205). These include, but are not limited to, Barth's attitude toward America, his emphasis on the priority of grace, his theology of nature (*not* his natural theology), and his positions on theories of religion, satisfaction theories of the atonement, election, universalism, and even the possibility of extraterrestrial life. This section also includes practical advice to church leaders on liturgy, preaching, the celebration of the sacraments, and prayer. Finally, Anderson includes a chapter in which he speculates on what Barth might have had to say to the pressing political and ethical issues of the twenty-first century, were he alive today, singling out the American criminal "justice" system for particularly harsh critique.

Throughout the book, Anderson's style is accessible and his tone is conversational. He does not get bogged down citing an endless list of obscure secondary sources but instead refreshingly and unapologetically offers his own constructive perspective. This is a genuinely readable book on Karl Barth—making it an increasingly rare bird for which Anderson's audience ought to give thanks. Perhaps the greatest strength of Anderson's book is the attention he pays to the relationship between Barth and the United States. This extends beyond simply noting Barth's penchant for Civil War novels or recounting his occasional criticisms of Billy Graham to a serious reckoning with the fact that Barth saw a deep resonance between the situation of the German church in Nazi Germany and that of large parts of the American church as it facilitated and encouraged the development of a heinous mixture of racism and the doctrine of American exceptionalism. Anderson's work invites further analysis of Barth's reception in the United States and of the significance of his work for contemporary theology in the United States.

For integrating so much constructive theological and ethical reflection into an enjoyable portrait of Karl Barth in the early 1960s, Anderson is to be commended. Opponents and critics of Barth would do well to heed Anderson's nuanced explanations of Barth's positions, while proponents and followers of Barth would do well to take heed of Anderson's description of Barth's character and demeanor as a theologian—lest in their zeal to push forward their teacher's work, they betray the spirit in which he meant for that work to be done.

Speaking of Barth's proponents and followers, *The Westminster Handbook to Karl Barth* offers the fruits of the labor of the "largest team of Barth scholars that has ever been gathered to interpret Barth's theology" (xiv). True to its genre, it offers short articles arranged in alphabetical order on key themes, figures, and concepts from Barth's life and writings. These entries serve as "concise and accurate" entry points into Barth's life and thought (xiii). In his introduction to the work, Richard Burnett acknowledges that such a project has its limitations and dangers—foremost among which is the temptation for students to use the handbook as a replacement for engaging with Barth's actual writings—but nevertheless makes a compelling case that this volume can serve as an effective tool for teaching and research when used properly. After exploring the *Handbook*, I wholeheartedly agree. The entries clearly articulate the moving parts of each of the different basic aspects of Barth's thought and direct the reader to the relevant passages in Barth's own work—thus encouraging further study rather than attempting to serve as a replacement for the real thing. This volume clearly deserves its place on the growing shelf of resources dedicated to helping contemporary audiences learn from and about Karl Barth. While these two books could not be more different in terms of genre—one a work of autobiographical reflection, the other a work of encyclopedic description—both offer new resources and tools that will allow a broad audience to gain access to the thought of Karl Barth. For that I am deeply grateful.

Matthew R. Jantzen
Duke Divinity School

■

REVIEW OF

Revolutionary Christianity: The 1966 South American Lectures

John Howard Yoder. Edited by Paul Martens, Mark Thiessen Nation, Matthew Porter, and Myles Werntz

EUGENE, OR: CASCADE BOOKS, 2011. 193 PP. $18.00

John Howard Yoder: Spiritual Writings

John Howard Yoder. Selected with an Introduction by Paul Martens and Jenny Howell. Modern Spiritual Masters Series

MARYKNOLL, NY: ORBIS, 2011. 172 PP. $20.00

For more than sixteen years after his death in late 1997, John Howard Yoder has provoked, challenged, and inspired a new generation of theologians, ethicists, and pastors—including the editors of these two volumes—many of whom never met Yoder nor heard him speak. Now, just as this new generation prepares to preserve and enlarge his legacy, a series of revelations detailing Yoder's repugnant behavior against women and against administrators of the Anabaptist Mennonite Biblical Seminary (AMBS) in Elkhart, Indiana, compromises that legacy. It has been widely known that in 1992, after some initial resistance, Yoder submitted to a disciplining process initiated by his home congregation for inappropriate advances to women and that he had been reconciled and reunited in worship shortly before his death.[1] The new allegations, which have become broadly public only since 2013, are considerably more serious and include coercive—indeed, "violent"—advances toward a number of women over three decades, including many students and others in subordinate positions. Further, Yoder abused the power of his reputation by intimidating the president and other administrators of AMBS, compelling them to keep the matter quiet as he slipped away to a more prestigious appointment at Notre Dame in 1984.[2] According to some witnesses, this inappropriate behavior continued at Notre Dame.

[1] See Stanley Hauerwas, *Hannah's Child: A Theologian's Memoir* (Grand Rapids, MI: Eerdmans, 2010), 242–47.

[2] The most extensive narrative to date of these events is found in David Cramer, Jenny Howell, Paul Martens, and Jonathan Tran, "Scandalizing John Howard Yoder," *The Other Journal: An Intersection of Theology and Culture*, July 7, 2014, (www.theotherjournal.com). Extensive footnotes point to additional resources. A condensed version of this article without footnotes can be found in "Theology and Misconduct: The Case of John Howard Yoder," *The Christian Century* 131, no. 17 (2014). Note that Martens is the lead editor of both volumes under review, while Howell is coeditor of *Spiritual Writings*.

These revelations have complicated the process of writing even a simple review.[3] Were Yoder an astrophysicist with groundbreaking discoveries regarding dark matter, we would be disappointed with his behavior, but we would not challenge on those grounds the veracity of his discovery. With Christian ethics, the issue is more complicated, especially for someone of Yoder's stature whose persona suggested that he was committed to and embodied, however imperfectly, what he proclaimed. Reading these volumes a second time has brought several jarring moments. For example, in both volumes, Yoder defines in almost identical language the temptation of "egocentric altruism":

> The real temptation of good people like us is not the crude, the crass, and the carnal as those traits are defined in Puritanism. The real refined temptation, with which Jesus himself was tried, was that of egocentric altruism, of being oneself the incarnation of a good and righteous cause for which others are to suffer, of stating our self-justification in the form of a duty to others. (*Revolutionary Christianity*, 83; *Essential Writings*, 144)

Consider also the following statement on religious liberty, which is certainly prescient in view of the current conflicts being played out in the courts: "Religious liberty is not only a necessary limitation upon the power of the state; it also marks a voluntary renunciation by the church of any capacity to coerce" (*Revolutionary Christianity*, 11). At the very least, then, perhaps we should read Yoder's misdeeds as a warning: even we may be tempted by the crude and the carnal as well as by egocentric altruism; when threatened, even we may resort to coercion.

The fourteen lectures in *Revolutionary Christianity*, published here for the first time, are organized into three sections—"The Believers Church," "Peace," and "Church in a Revolutionary World"—roughly the order of presentation to predominantly Mennonite and Anabaptist groups in Montevideo and Buenos Aires in May–June 1966. Written and delivered when Yoder was only thirty-eight and not yet a full-time faculty member, it is remarkable how fully they anticipate his later work. Clearly he mined them for later writings. The four lectures titled "The Believers Church" may be the best theological introduction available to the Anabaptist/Mennonite tradition. Yoder's description of the church as a community of forgiveness, discernment, grace; of the mandate to share; and of a morality of participation and community is surely ironic in view of his behavior and his initial resistance to the process of "binding and loosing."

The collections on "Peace" and "Church in a Revolutionary World" introduce a host of themes prominent in Yoder's later work: the church as a community of discipleship; Jesus as model for Christians, especially in the renunciation

[3] The original review of these two volumes was submitted May 1, 2014, just weeks before this reviewer became aware of the additional charges made against Yoder. I am grateful to the book review editor for her excellent suggestions for rewriting this review.

of violence; love of neighbor and of enemy; the Constantinian model of church and state as a corruption of the New Testament understanding of the Christian community. Just two years before Medellín (1968) and only five before Gutiér-rez's *A Theology of Liberation* (1971), Yoder seems relatively uninformed about the extent of social unrest among the indigenous peoples of South America. (There is also a jarring statement in *Revolutionary Christianity* lumping Islam together with Marxism, secular humanism, and fascism as "not nature or culture religions but bastard faiths, all of them indirectly the progeny of Christianity's infidelity, of the spiritual miscegenation involved in trying to make a culture-religion out of faith in Jesus Christ" [114–15]. But then most of us studying theology in the 1960s had limited acquaintance with Islam.)

Spiritual Writings, which the title page of the book calls *Essential Writings*, is divided into four sections, each with a short introduction by the editors: "The Meaning of Jesus," "The Mandate of the Church," "A Cosmic Vision," and "Practices and Practical Considerations." Each section consists of a com-pendium of relatively brief selections from across Yoder's corpus. This format works well for Yoder, who was not a systematic theologian but one who wrote primarily for specific audiences and situations and who resisted requests that he write a "Systematic Introduction" to his thought. The selections are expertly chosen by Martens and Howell and provide a fine introduction to Yoder as theologian and ethicist.

Several themes at odds with popular visions of Christianity stand out to this reviewer as worthy of further reflection and application. First, "Justification by Faith," as promulgated by Martin Luther and John Calvin and widely accepted by Protestant and Evangelical Christians in North America, simply expunges guilt and the bad feelings that result from recognizing oneself as sinner. Yoder, on the other hand, insists that justification by faith, as understood by Paul, founds a new reality, the new community of Jews and Gentiles. Second, Yoder offers a penetrating analysis and critique of the Reformation's views on secular vocations. Yoder agrees with Luther and Calvin that secular vocations should be recognized and honored by Christians; but he rejects their conclusion that the moral criteria governing a particular vocation ought to be established solely by the guild itself, with no Christian witness. What should be the Christian witness to the moral vision guiding many corporate institutions?

Most significant, in my view, is Yoder's invitation to reconsider the way we read history, especially the history of the Church (e.g., 94–97). More specifi-cally, one should not assume that what happened had to happen exactly that way. Thus, we should not assume that the split between Jews and Christians in the first or second centuries was inevitable. Yoder's exegesis of the Gospels and of Paul in *The Politics of Jesus* (1971) is supported by recent scholarship, in-cluding the claim that neither Jesus nor Paul understood the nascent Christian movement as a necessary departure from the tradition of Judaism. A recent book by New Testament scholar Mary C. Boys, *Redeeming Our Sacred Story: The Death of Jesus and Relations between Jews and Christians* (Paulist, 2013), supports Yoder's basic claims and then builds an even stronger case that crucifixion was a "show killing" orchestrated by Rome to terrorize the populace, and that Jesus's crucifixion had little or no direct Jewish involvement. Hence the question: How can this reading of the apostolic era move us beyond merely lamenting the Jewish–Christian schism to restoring connections between Jews and Christians?

In a recent essay Marilynne Robinson observed that "the tragic mystery of human nature has by no means played itself out, and that wisdom, which is almost always another name for humility, lies in accepting one's own inevitable share in human fallibility." Yoder's legacy to the discipline of Christian ethics remains an open question. Those of us who have engaged and celebrated his written work cannot turn a blind eye to the failures of his embodied life. Accepting our share in human fallibility means, at the very least, that we can never again read Yoder's work without keeping those he persecuted at the forefront of our minds.

John C. Shelley
Furman University

REVIEW OF

Shaping Public Theology: Selections from the Writings of Max L. Stackhouse

Edited by Scott R. Paeth, E. Harold Breitenberg Jr., and Hak Joon Lee

GRAND RAPIDS, MI: EERDMANS, 2014. 392 PP. $40.00

Shaping Public Theology is the second major collection of essays focused on the work of Max Stackhouse to appear since his retirement from Princeton Theological Seminary, where he served as the Rimmer and Ruth de Vries Professor of Reformed Theology and Public Life. The first, *Public Theology for a Global Society*, was a Festschrift composed of short pieces by his former students and colleagues, edited by Deirdre King Hainsworth and Scott R. Paeth. *Shaping Public Theology*, which is also edited by Paeth along with E. Harold Breitenberg Jr. and Hak Joon Lee, is a helpfully representative compilation of Stackhouse's own writing across the span of his long and prolific career. As such, it demonstrates both the generous aspirations and the significant limitations of "public theology" as Stackhouse envisioned it, as a theologically informed discourse that should be equally accessible to Christians, people of other faiths, and people of no faith or religious background.

The first of the book's three sections, "Interpreting the Tradition of Public Theology," places Stackhouse in conversation with other figures in Christian theology and ethics, both past and present. These essays locate him firmly within the strand of Christian thought inhabited by Ernst Troeltsch, Walter Rauschenbusch, and Paul Tillich, and they also reflect his significant and ongoing disagreements with some of his contemporaries, including Alasdair MacIntyre and Stanley Hauerwas. The second section, "Developing a Method for Public Theology," provides a useful summary of Stackhouse's distinctive theological method, defining public theology and its relationship to individuals, communities, institutions, and states. The third and final section, "Constructing a Global Public Theology," turns to one of the major focal points of Stackhouse's work, examining the role of public theology in the context of globalization. The text concludes with a brief summary contributed by the editors, a response from Stackhouse describing both how his thought has changed over the years and the gaps that he perceives in his work, and a comprehensive bibliography.

As a collection, *Shaping Public Theology* provides the reader with a broad overview of the predominant themes in Stackhouse's work. The essays demonstrate his abiding concern for an apologetic and universal framework for Christian ethics as well as his emphasis on the covenantal basis for that framework. Stackhouse's affinity for both the Reformed tradition and the ideals of the Social Gospel movement are also evident throughout the text. In addition many of the essays reflect his ongoing engagement with the theme of "the global" and with globalization not only as a locus of critique but also as the vehicle for "the prospect of a world-comprehending culture, with a new recognition of certain common moral standards" (162).

Whether these ideas are theologically helpful, however, is a matter of long-standing disagreement that will not be resolved in the limited space of this review. By treating the covenant between the Triune God and Israel as merely one instance of a "universal moral law," and by moving from that particular to the universal through the doctrine of the Trinity, Stackhouse participates in a significant—and significantly problematic—strain of thought within the Christian imaginary (67). While he may reject the particularity espoused by George Lindbeck, Hauerwas, et al., he remains grounded within his own particularity with its own decidedly fraught history: that of the modern, progressive, Western civilizing project. As a work of moral theology, this text does have significant limitations. However, as a document of the history of Christian ethics of the twentieth century, *Shaping Public Theology* is a useful addition to the literature, both for research and for teaching purposes.

Kara N. Slade
Duke University

■

REVIEW OF

Approaching the End: Eschatological Reflections on Church, Politics, and Life

Stanley Hauerwas

GRAND RAPIDS, MI: EERDMANS, 2013. 251 PP. $24.00

Without Apology: Sermons for Christ's Church

Stanley Hauerwas

NEW YORK: SEABURY BOOKS, 2013. 169 PP. $18.00

Stanley Hauerwas is prolific. By my count, there are forty-six books to his name, including these two from 2013. And yet in the preface to *Without Apology*, he writes, "I am often asked, 'How many books have you written?' My truthful answer must be, 'I have no idea.' . . . I could count them, but I have no interest in doing so" (ix). Hauerwas's reluctance to number his career in books shows his preference for smaller units of measurement ("how some reader may find this sermon, or that sentence or chapter . . . helpful"), but it also reflects his view that he is not the sole author of his works. To his credit, he mentions two influential women—his wife, Paula Gilbert, an experienced clergywoman, and his assistant, Carole Baker, who gives the sermons a "work-over" after they are written (ix).

Those who know Hauerwas know what to expect from these volumes: thoughtful arguments that unflinchingly assert the centrality of Christ and of the Church; a heavy dose of pacifism; major appearances from John Howard Yoder and Karl Barth (as well as multiple cameos from fascinating authors who are now on my to-read list); and accessible, open prose outlining clear, thought-provoking arguments. The two books reviewed here are quite different from one another: *Without Apology* is a book of sermons; *Approaching the End* is a book of essays loosely organized around a theme of eschatology. But both contain the hallmarks of "classic Hauerwas"—his signature mix of virtue ethics, communitarian interests, and narrative sensibilities.

Without Apology contains recent sermons, primarily in Episcopal churches. Drawing on lectionary readings, Hauerwas brings his own theological interpretation and creates fairly short, satisfying sermons, which he readily describes (in Paula Gilbert's words) as "tight" (87). This collection also includes four sermons on the topic of priesthood and some other writings of note: the already-classic "An Open Letter to Christians Beginning College" (good for use with Christian undergraduates) and "Sexing the Ministry" (food for thought for seminarian and clergy alike). *Without Apology* manifests several major themes, but the biggest of these connects with the title: Hauerwas is "unapologetic" about his Christian faith and doesn't engage in theology of the "apologetic" style. His emphasis, rather, is on being truthfully present with one another in the church community.

Approaching the End promises eschatological reflections and delivers on the promise. Although he is writing about eschatology, Hauerwas strongly maintains that he is not reaching his own "end" and disavows any contention that *Approaching the End* is a kind of "swan song" (xiv). He addresses politics and war in several chapters. In "The End of Sacrifice: An Apocalyptic Politics," he makes the case that if Christians believe Jesus's sacrifice was "the end of all sacrifices," then we should not "continue to participate in the sacrifice of war" (36). Similar themes emerge in "War and Peace," later in the volume. In "Church Matters: On Faith and Politics," Hauerwas writes, "One of the challenges Christians confront is how the politics we helped create has made it difficult to sustain the material practices constitutive of an ecclesial culture to produce Christians" (68). He welcomes the "end" of churches and denominations as we know them because "it means that the church is finally free to be a politics" (86).

Hauerwas also discusses the future of churches and denominations. "The End of Protestantism" reiterates that "if the church is to be faithful . . . then we must recover what it means for the church to be an alternative politics" (92). This chapter's emphasis on Methodism and his appraisal of Methodists as "free church Catholics" (94) is of note. In "Which Church? What Unity?" Hauerwas discusses the ecumenical movement, prompted by George Lindbeck's challenge to do so (98). Hauerwas's response includes some personal reflection on his own involvement with churches and denominations, a foregrounding of Yoder's work on the topic, and the use of Anglicanism as a case study for Yoder's views.

Some chapters serve as updates of his previous work. In "Habit Matters: The Bodily Character of the Virtues," Hauerwas updates some of his arguments from *Character and the Christian Life*, including an insightful examination of Aquinas's work on habits and virtues. In "*Suffering Presence:* Twenty-Five Years Later," Hauerwas reprises his arguments about biomedical ethics, including reflection on Wendell Berry's "Health Is Membership." Other chapters in this book also address medical ethics in classic Hauerwas fashion—"Doing Nothing Gallantly," "Cloning the Human Body," and "Disability: An Attempt to Think With."

Though their audiences differ, these two books share many themes. I wish to emphasize two: truth and martyrdom. "Bearing Reality," in *Approaching the End*, is Hauerwas's presidential speech to the SCE, which has already been published in this journal. His final exhortation to the SCE reads, "let us be a society whose members strive to tell one another the truth about the difficulties of reality" (157). This emphasis on truth manifests throughout both books. In *Without Apology,* one of his stronger sermons, "Because It Is True," discusses truth-claims in Christianity and their fulfillment in Jesus—"Because he is the truth, we can speak the truth" (126).

Hauerwas's interest in truth-telling extends to his treatment of martyrdom. "Witness," (from *Approaching the End*) written with Charles Pinches, offers a deep and compelling account of what it means to be a Christian witness. They write, "Christian witnesses are . . . like people who have witnessed a horrible accident that cannot be forgotten; it lives with them daily, shaping the contours of their lives henceforth" (45). They offer an especially interesting examination of Paul as a witness, and as one who exhorts others to witness. They make a case for the connection between witness and martyrdom. Later, Hauerwas uncritically extols martyrdom—"The martyr wields a power that defeats the murderer because the martyr can be remembered by a community more enduring than the state" (70). Hauerwas also praises martyrdom in his sermons entitled "Glory" and "Saints."

While Hauerwas's views on martyrdom are moving, they also invite the feminist critiques to which he is often subject. Despite a deep appreciation for Hauerwas's embodied, relational theology that valorizes the disabled and promotes nonviolence, feminists still wonder: does his version of "the Christian story" include voices of women and other oppressed people? In an age when the word "martyr" conjures images of either pathologically self-effacing women or radically violent Muslim extremists, why does Hauerwas not make space for a fuller exploration of martyrdom's checkered role in Christian ethics and Christian history? How do we ethically evaluate martyrdom that goes too far (as in religiously motivated acts of violence, of which Christianity is far from innocent) or martyrdom that becomes a tool of oppression (as with women and others who bear inappropriately degrading or abusive conditions in the name of virtue and goodness)? Similar arguments could be made about his treatment of themes such as truth (whose truth?), virtue (whose definition?), and church community (who is included? Whose voices are heard?). Hauerwas insightfully critiques Christian warmongering throughout history but seems curiously blind to these other elements of the tradition that are equally unfaithful to the gospel.

Hauerwas has produced forty-six books'-worth of inspiring, thoughtful prose. These most recent books show an incredibly fertile mind and wide range of conversation partners. Nevertheless, his critics still wonder how and whether he can acknowledge and learn from subaltern views of Christianity, its narratives, and its community.

Laura M. Hartman
University of Wisconsin–Oshkosh

REVIEW OF

The Politics of Practical Reason: Why Theological Ethics Must Change Your Life

Mark Ryan

EUGENE, OR: CASCADE BOOKS, 2011. 229 PP. $20.80

If the spirited debate between Stanley Hauerwas and Jeffrey Stout remains front-page news in theological ethics, then Mark Ryan's subtle and penetrating *The Politics of Practical Reason* will help keep it there. Ryan argues that practical reason is the hinge of ethical thinking and that it is "political" in the sense of shaping the community or polis. Given this hinge, the pressing question is of course, "Whose practical reason?" To answer this, Ryan probes major contemporary ethicists from Charles Taylor to Alasdair MacIntyre, but the book always circles back to Hauerwas and Stout. Their debate is ultimately decided by proxy, through a mediating philosopher whose work on practical reason Ryan sees both as the gold standard and as the indispensable background for understanding Hauerwas. Expecting this to be MacIntyre, the reader may be surprised—and perhaps even convinced—that the philosopher who best explains and possibly vindicates Hauerwas is in fact Elizabeth Anscombe, Ludwig Wittgenstein's protégé, close friend, and translator.

The book opens with Anscombe's *Intention* (1957), which Donald Davidson called "the most important treatment of action since Aristotle." In it, Anscombe argued that intention presupposes desire and is declared in public language within a context of social practices presupposed for agency to be intelligible. The implication is that we form intentions as members of a community with a particular form of life sustained by social practices. With human desire as its motivating nisus, Ryan insists that intention "is part of the very form of practical reasoning, then, to be political" (144).

Having retrieved Anscombe's model of practical reason, Ryan examines the field of contemporary ethics to see who measures up. Charles Taylor fails to place agents in a particular community, locating us instead in that bloated abstraction called "modernity." Ryan therefore concludes that Taylor's is an "ethics for anybody," which leaves the self finally disembodied (94–98). Stout fares little better due to his refrain that Hauerwas went astray when he abandoned justice talk. Ryan counters that Stout's sort of justice *should* be abandoned; lacking a substantive vision of the good and a teleology of freedom, Stout's justice is reckoned a blind guide who cannot see or say why the polis should pursue one end and not another. Hauerwas, on the other hand, specifies a particular polis within which practical reason can intelligibly function: the church. It has a substantive vision of the good (i.e., the peaceable kingdom) located in a scriptural narrative displayed by social practices requiring formation in the virtues (119–21). Ryan therefore endorses Hauerwas's politics of practical reason, indebted to MacIntyre and made possible by Anscombe.

I see one lacuna in this otherwise excellent book. Ryan seemingly advocates a pragmatic model of practical reason that is wholly internal to the polis rather than grounded in "truths of human nature as such" (101). This makes Anscombe an uneasy ally. Her "Modern Moral Philosophy" famously proposed a retrieval of virtue that required an overhauled "account of human nature . . . and above all of human flourishing" (41). This move opened the door for ethical naturalism, perhaps even natural law—both of which Anscombe and the later MacIntyre endorse. But these look suspiciously like what Ryan calls an "ethics for anybody." So in the end are Anscombe and MacIntyre turncoats, or do Hauerwas and Ryan not follow them far enough? This crucial question remains unanswered.

Despite this wrinkle, Ryan's book is the best intervention in the Hauerwas–Stout debate that we now have. It throws light on Hauerwas, challenges Stout, shows why Anscombe matters, and gives practical reason its generous due. Philosophically deft and charitable in tone, it deserves to be read and studied as a major contribution to the field.

David Elliot
University of Notre Dame

REVIEW OF

The Development of Moral Theology: Five Strands

Charles E. Curran

WASHINGTON, DC: GEORGETOWN UNIVERSITY PRESS, 2013. 306 PP. $29.95

At least two entwined questions dominate Charles Curran's *The Development of Moral Theology:* first, what differentiates Catholic moral theology from other approaches to Christian ethics, and second, how we should understand, evaluate, and appropriate that tradition in light of its own pluralism and that of the broader society? Curran engages both of these concerns by critically tracing five historical strands that have shaped moral theology: sin, reconciliation, and the manuals of moral theology; Thomas Aquinas and the Thomistic tradition; natural law; the papal teaching office; and the Second Vatican Council.

The bulk of Curran's discussion consists of chapter-length treatments of each of these strands. This approach lends analytical clarity to a tradition with a varied, complex history, and provides the foundation for his later synthetic, evaluative discussion. The first chapter is characteristic of the manner in which subsequent chapters proceed: Curran begins with biblical treatments of the rupturing effects of sin before moving on to the emergence of formalized approaches to dealing with sin via penitential processes and, later, the manuals of moral theology. Incorporated into this historical discussion are evaluative and prescriptive claims. For example, in contrast to the dynamic and rich biblical understanding of the nature of sin, Curran suggests that the manuals of moral theology both possess an insufficiently full understanding of the reality of sin and conversion and distort the meaning of sin by focusing on the objective act alone (24).

The second through fourth chapters proceed in similar fashion, with critical readings of the varied history of each strand that underscore the internal pluralism of Catholic moral theology. Thus, chapter 2 shows that, while there is but one Thomas Aquinas, there are numerous Thomisms, and chapter 3 denies the presence of a unified, coherent theory of natural law, closing by arguing that this lack of coherence is synchronically discernible in contrasts between recent papal social and sexual teachings.

Following a similar treatment of the papal teaching office in chapter 4, Curran discusses the significance of Vatican II in chapter 5 before offering a broad evaluation of his historical surveys in the conclusion. There he calls for Church hierarchy to be more forthright in its recognition of the tradition's internal diversity, more open to dissent and disagreement, and receptive to the power of the Holy Spirit as the primary force enabling the Church as a people to live hopefully as mediating God's presence in the world.

There is much to be learned from Curran's impressive knowledge of his tradition. This is a text that will be especially valuable to graduate students and scholars and teachers of Christian ethics; the chapters on Aquinas and the Thomistic tradition, natural law, and Vatican II will have a particularly wide appeal. Nevertheless, I fear the book is less than the sum of its very informative parts. The lack of an initial chapter establishing the meaning and significance of Curran's study or of a conceptual framework to guide the reader in navigating deep and what are sure to many to be unfamiliar historical waters may leave some readers disoriented. Such a chapter would have been helpful in establishing a broader context for the study and identifying themes that arise repeatedly in the course of the discussion, for example: the nature of authority and dissent, the relationship between philosophy and theology, the relationship between truth and historical consciousness, and the nature of tradition as "living," to name a few. As it is, such themes emerge only gradually for the reader, rendering engagement with the text as a whole a less rewarding experience than it might otherwise be.

Christopher Libby
Missouri Valley College